Bor

British Science Fiction Paperbacks and Magazines
1949-1956

An Annotated Bibliography and Guide

by
Philip Harbottle
& Stephen Holland

Edited by Daryl F. Mallett and Michael Burgess

R . R E G I N A L D
The Borgo Press
San Bernardino, California □ MCMXCIV

THE BORGO PRESS

Publishers Since 1975

Post Office Box 2845

San Bernardino, CA 92406

United States of America

* * * * * * * *

Copyright © 1994 by Philip Harbottle and Stephen Holland

Library of Congress Cataloging-in-Publication Data

Harbottle, Philip.
British science fiction paperbacks and magazines, 1949-1956 : an annotated bibliography and guide / by Philip Harbottle & Stephen Holland ; edited by Daryl F. Mallett and Michael Burgess.
p. cm. — (Borgo literary guides, ISSN 0891-9623 ; no. 7)
Includes index.
ISBN 0-89370-821-6 (cloth). — ISBN 0-89370-921-2 (pbk.)
1. Science fiction, English—Bibliography. 2. English fiction—20th century—Bibliography. 3. Paperbacks—Great Britain—Bibliography. 4. Science fiction—Stories, plots, etc. 5. Great Britain—Imprints. I. Holland,
Stephen, 1962- . II. Title. III. Series.
Z2014.S33H37 1994
016.823'0876'08—dc19

87-752
CIP

FIRST EDITION

CONTENTS

DEDICATION

To all of those 1950s' authors,
editors, and artists (many, alas,
now dead) whose thoughts and works
influenced a generation and shaped
our childhood dreams—

this book is affectionately dedicated

ACKNOWLEDGMENTS

This book could not have been completed without the help of a great number of individuals. The authors, therefore, wish to thank the many writers, friends, and correspondents who have furnished information and confirmation of many of the literary and biographical facts presented in this volume. All of the information has been verified by reference to actual books and magazines in our personal collections. Very few published reference books on the period have been consulted, for the lamentable, yet excellent reason that very few exist! However, the following books have proven a valuable source of confirmation, and we hereby acknowledge their use and recommend them to anyone interested in researching further.

Ashley, Mike. *History of the Science Fiction Magazine*. London: New English Library, 1977, 1978.
_____. *Fantasy Readers' Guide to the John Spencer Publications*. Wallsend, England: Cosmos Literary Agency, 1979
Harbottle, Philip. *The Multi-Man: A Bio-bibliographical Study of John Russell Fearn*. Wallsend, England: Philip Harbottle, 1968.
Reginald, Robert. *Science Fiction and Fantasy Literature*. Detroit: Gale Research Co., 1979 (Supplement, 1992).
Strauss, Erwin S. *Index to the SF Magazines, 1951-1965*. Cambridge, Massachusetts: MITSF Press, 1965.
Tuck, Donald H. *The Handbook of Science Fiction and Fantasy*. Hobart, Tasmania: Privately published, 1958.

And to the following people, and anyone else we may have inadvertently omitted:

Sydney J. Bounds, John Brunner, Kenneth Bulmer, Jonathan Burke, A. Vincent Clarke, John Clute, Gerald Evans, R. Lionel Fanthorpe, John Russell Fearn, Ralph L. Finn, Stephen Frances, Dave Giarcardi, Peter Hawkins, George Hay, Leslie J. Johnson, Norman Lazenby, Ken Slater, Brian Stableford, Brian Teviotdale, E. C. Tubb, David Ward, Gerry Webb, and Lisle Willis.

HOW TO USE THIS BOOK

The first section of this book contains a complete listing of all original paperback SF books published in Great Britain between January 1949 and February 1956. The books are alphabetically listed by author name, and cross-referenced to pseudonyms. Biographical data is given where known, and each book entry includes: a reference number for use within this volume, title of the work, author's real name (where appropriate), city of publication, publisher, date of publication, number of pages, release price, and interior and cover artists (where known). Also included is a plot *précis* of each book, and occasional critical comments whereby the best and the worst stories can be identified by the discerning reader who does not want to wade through the whole lot to pick up the occasional gem.

While we have been unable to identify the real names of all of the authors, the following groups of books are probably by the same unknown writers:

Author #1: The same writer who penned *Spawn of Space* under the pseudonym FRANZ HARKON also did two ASTRON DEL MARTIA works, *Interstellar Espionage* and *Space Pirates*, identifiable by both the style of the books and the use of the same continuing characters.

Author #2: The same person appears to have written *Solar Gravita*, by BERL CAMERON; *Overlord New York*, by LEE ELLIOTT; *Tri-Planet*, by VON KELLAR; and *Dwellers in Space*, by VAN REED.

Author #3: FRANK LEDERMAN and ALVIN WESTWOOD are possibly the same author.

Author #4: RICK CONROY and LEE STANTON are probably the same author, whose real name is unknown.

Author #5: The following Gannet Press novels appear to have a common author: *Space Flight 139*, by BENGO MISTRAL, *Trouble Planet*, by MARK STEEL, and *Worlds Away!*, by CRAGG BEEMISH.

Author #6: The same author appears to be responsible for two futuristic medical thrillers: *The Seeing Knife*, by CRAWLEY FENTON, and *Time Drug*, by MILES CASSON.

The second section of this book comprises reprint paperbacks published during the same period, listed by publisher and date of publication. The original source and first book edition is given, along with page count, price, and cover artist (where known).

The third chapter is a listing of all magazines published in Britain during the same period, giving the date of each issue, volume number, size, page count, and cover artist (where known). The first column is an identifying code to each issue for use in conjunction with the magazine index in the fourth section.

The fourth section of the book is a complete index to all the magazine stories and articles. Also included are stories which appeared in two anthologies listed in section one and "filler" short stories which cropped up in original novels.

Finally, there is a complete title index in two parts, the first covering books, the second short stories.

INTRODUCTION

Modern day science fiction historians have, with few exceptions, drawn a murky veil over the British SF paperback novels published in the early 1950s. The impression they give is that none of these novels is worth reading, and one direct result of this has been that very few of these books have been reprinted in their country of origin. Why should this be, when new editions of contemporary American SF of the same period (and even earlier) appear from British publishers regularly?

Some of the answers to this question have been dealt with in our companion volume, *Vultures of the Void: A History of British Science Fiction Publishing, 1946-1956* (Borgo Press, 1992). We endeavored to show how wartime paper rationing gave rise to new opportunist publishers with no literary background. The stigma they created persists to the present day. Even though SF is now thoroughly respectable, there seems to be a fear amongst publishers and critics that to seek to revive any of the British novels of the 1950s would be to invite disaster, and which might somehow plunge SF back into the dark ages.

However, continental European publishers have not suffered from the same delusion, and so scores of these books have appeared in foreign translations—and do so to this day, particularly in Italy. And increasingly, these paperbacks are becoming appreciated by another section of society—the private collector.

In America, collecting paperbacks is big business, serviced by specialist dealers and semiprofessional magazines with titles like *Paperback Parade* and *Books Are Everything*. The annual Collectible Paperback Expo in New York attracts dealers from all over the country, while the smaller Paperback Collector's Convention in Los Angeles continues to swell in size. Collectors can take their pick of thousands of books, original cover artwork, pulp magazines, and more, and maybe get to meet some of their favorite authors for signings or just a chat.

Much the same thing, as yet on a smaller scale, is happening in Britain. 1991 saw the first Paperback Bookfair in London, backed by the leading British enthusiasts' magazine, *Paperback, Pulp, and Comic Collector*. Articles appearing in these journals are written by knowledgeable and genuine enthusiasts, and have been creating a rising demand for vintage paperbacks in general, and 1950s British SF publications in particular. Collectors know a good thing when they see it, and are backing their enthusiasm with hard currency. Put in contact with each other through the above-mentioned magazines, collectors on both sides of the Atlantic are busily engaged in buying, selling, or swapping these ephemeral publications.

Much of this upsurge in collector interest stems from appreciation of cover art. Compared to the deadly-dull striped billboards of Penguin Books and other more "literary" publishers, these vintage books must have leaped from the shelves into the eyes of the potential buyer. Nowadays, the sheer skill and panache of 1950s paperback cover paintings is being increasingly recognized. The SF artwork of such artists as Ron Turner, Gordon Davies, John Richards, James McConnell, and Reginald Heade, has made these books a prime collecting target. We make no apology, therefore, in departing from the usual presentation in bibliographies which limits information to the contents. In this book, we have identified and listed all of the interior and cover artists on whom we were able to find information.

Prices for fine copies of these books are escalating steadily, because most of the best surviving copies are locked away in private collections. Prices also vary according to scarcity of certain titles (some of which were recalled and destroyed), and some collectors are interested in only one or two authors; John Russell Fearn and E. C. Tubb are among the most heavily collected. A fan wanting just a few titles to complete his or her set of an author or artist might be prepared to pay in excess of $100 for a single title, whereas the average price would be considerably less.

We hope this book will be welcomed and used as a collector's guide. Dealers will rub their hands as they receive frantic letters and phone calls from collectors who discover they were unaware of pseudonymous titles by their favorite authors. Notwithstanding, such was not our main intention in compiling this book. Our purpose, simply stated, is to tell the stories of these largely unsung authors, editors, and artists, and to pay deserved tribute to them...where tribute is due. We do not hesitate to expose and castigate rubbish whenever and wherever we find it—and there is plenty of rubbish to be found in the mushroom jungle, along with some fascinating and collectible gems.

All of the research here presented has been achieved by our having read and personally examined *every* book and magazine referred to. The experience has been both wearisome and rewarding in equal measure. We have endeavored to be as complete and accurate as humanly possible, but there is much yet to be discovered. We have shone a spotlight into dark corners. What we have found may not please some members of the *literati*, but it is surely worthy of further study and reappraisal. We feel that our lifetime of research has entitled us to express our opinions in this book, along with the arrays of bibliographical detail. We have tried to be objective rather than subjective (not always successfully, we will admit!). It is our hope that this book will be a useful tool for other researchers and critics, and will find a niche in reference libraries. Here is the face of early 1950s British science fiction, warts and all. We await the verdicts of later researchers and critics with interest!

—Philip Harbottle & Stephen Holland
Wallsend, Tyne and Wear, England
4 March 1993 and 19 June 1994

A.

ORIGINAL SCIENCE FICTION PAPERBACKS
1946-1956

DRAX AMPER (Pseudonym)

A1.   *Far Beyond the Blue: A Science Fiction Thriller.* London: Gannet Press,
November 1953, 128 p., 1/6d. Cover by Ray Theobald.

This torturous story involves "Captain Nick Berry of the Space Patrol," a
sexually-repressed Boy Scout-type, much given to talking to himself and
uttering such fatuous ejaculations as "by dying Mars!" Other characters include the "snowy-haired" Professor Melket, "one of Britain's brainiest scientific research workers, besides being the father of a remarkably pretty
daughter," one Candy, whose "wide-set blue eyes" and "full warm lips"
combine to give an effect of "luscious beauty." The alien villains include a
"half-beast, half-man" and his "hornet woman" mistress, Selena du Mars.
Written with appalling "gangsterese," this ghastly book contains scenes of
miscegenatic rape and sleazy eroticism juxtaposed with juvenile space
opera. The reader has been warned!

MARVIN ASHTON—see: Dennis Talbot Hughes

RAY BARRY—see: Dennis Talbot Hughes

CRAGG BEEMISH (Pseudonym)

NOTE: The pseudonymous author may also have written *Space Flight 139*, by
BENGO MISTRAL, and *Trouble Planet*, by MARK STEEL.

A2.   *Worlds Away!* London: Gannet Press, November 1953, 128 p., 1/6d.
Cover by Ray Theobald.

The maiden flight of the world's first rocket ship, *Discoverer*, is buzzed by
alien blobs of energy. The engines are blanked out, and the ship is caught
in a magnetic flux generated by the aliens, a life form indigenous to the
sun. After some routine adventure, the ship returns to Earth, and the survivors find they have aged fifty years. A peculiar, confusing, but oddly
appealing story. The damnably bad cover is mercifully unrelated to the
story.

BRYAN BERRY, 1930-1955

Born in 1930, Bryan Berry made his first fiction sale while still in school at the age of sixteen, and wrote with increasing success for ten years for a wide variety of periodicals. He worked as a publisher's advertising copy writer, was a staff writer for an agency, and sub-editor for an international literary monthly. He also wrote educational film scripts, and was a comics illustrator. He began freelance writing in 1952. Interested in SF from the age of eleven, he attained the distinction of having three stories published in the January 1953 issue of *Planet Stories*, all under his own name. His promising career was cut short by his untimely death at the age of 25, by his own hand.

A3.   *Aftermath.* London: Hamilton & Co. ("Authentic" #24), August 1952, 109 p., 1/6d. Cover by Gordon C. Davies.

A well-written, readable story, ingeniously combining three stock plots: The *R.U.R.* plot, the pugnacious-superman plot, and the rampant-anti-science-religious-mob plot. The story neatly encapsulates most of the conventional SF elements concerning mutants, which were popular at the time of publication. It was reprinted as *Mission to Marakee* in the American magazine, *Science-Adventure Books* (Spring 1953).

A4.   *And the Stars Remain.* London: Hamilton & Co. ("Panther" no #), June 1952, 112 p., 1/6d. Cover by Gordon C. Davies.

An atmospheric interplanetary tale of the ancient Martians and their gift to humanity, which leads to Man's first starship. The ship is launched in glory, then lost, except for one fragment that drifts, years later, into the solar system. On it are marks, as if some giant hand had crushed the vessel. It is the hand of the Planners, who watch over the Galaxy to prevent immature races from contaminating others, firmly but apologetically swatting down Man's starship as Man might kill a fly.

A5.   *Born in Captivity.* London: Hamilton & Co. ("Panther" no #), November 1952, 192 p., 2/-. Cover by George Ratcliffe.

"We are in the world of 2018. So much can be accomplished merely by pressing a button that the sole ambition of Man is to invent a machine that will press it for him. The creation of synthetic beings, or 'androids,' together with a terrifying 'war to end all wars' forms the climax of this gripping story." Reprinted as *World Held Captive* in *Science-Adventure Books* (Spring 1954).

A6.   *Dread Visitor.* London: Hamilton & Co. ("Panther" #28), November 1952, 127 p., 1/6d. Cover by Gordon C. Davies.

A very ambitious early Berry novel telling of a van Vogtian monstrous alien, in the form of an eternal energy field, which returns to a futuristic Earth recovering from Atomic War. Plague belts and radioactive areas abound, and apart from humanity, there is a race of mutated apes, the

Lemurs, whom the alien enslaves. It is eventually defeated by the rediscovery of an ancient Atlantean weapon.

A7. *From What Far Star?* London: Hamilton & Co. ("Panther" #40), February 1953, 143 p., 1/6d. Cover by Gordon C. Davies.

"When Harry Sellars, a Security Officer, first became suspicious of one of the physicists working on the Spaceship Development Centre, he did not imagine that he would end up helping to win Earth's greatest battle. At first, when he saw a man walk through a solid wall, he thought that he was going mad. But his later investigations proved his sanity quite conclusively. Something had walked through the wall alright—but certainly not a man."

A8. *Return to Earth.* London: Hamilton & Co., November 1951, 110 p., 1/6d. Cover uncredited.

An intriguing story of Mankind in the future. Following atomic war on Earth, Man has established a colony on Venus. The colonists have grown to forget their savage ancestry with the passage of centuries. Then, Mike Woolf pays a clandestine visit to the ancient First Library, and recovers the forbidden old books...leading eventually to Man's return to his home planet and the overthrow of the mutant race that has developed.

A9. *The Venom-Seekers.* London: Hamilton & Co. ("Panther" #57), May 1953, 160 p., 1/6d. Cover by George Ratcliffe.

"Johnny Lamont isn't the sort of man you should trust too far, whoever you are. He's crooked, he's tough, and he's done a good bit of wandering around the planets. But when he took on the job of piloting a spaceship out into the heart of an alien planetary system for a girl who was searching for her brother, he took on the toughest assignment of his life. For the missing man had gone back in time to the planet's prehistoric past to search for a weapon, the possession of which could mean life or death to Earth." Imaginative story, but marred by pseudo-Chandler style.

as ROLF GARNER

A10. *The Immortals.* London: Hamilton & Co. ("Panther" #78), September 1953, 159 p., 1/6d. RESURGENT DUST #2. Cover by John Richards.

This book describes the rediscovery of science on Venus by Mankind's descendants, and their emergence from the dark ages of superstition following the Atomic War on Earth, an event paralleled centuries before by the native Venusian race. The Venusian Lords of Gryllaar seek to resurrect their ancient weapons of destruction, but their plans are thwarted by a young man, Kennet, one of the few true Earthmen remaining after the disintegration of the Terrestrial colony. Kennet ousts the Gryllaar Lords and, by marrying the young heir to the High Seat of the Land, himself becomes the Lord of Gryllaar. Under his rule, scientific experimentation is revived with benign motives. Encountering the Immortals, hidden survivors of the ancient

Venusians, Kennet and his wife, Syla, are given the secret of immortality in exchange for their promise to restore a new Golden Age.

A11.   *The Indestructible.* London: Hamilton & Co. ("Panther" #104), February 1954, 159 p., 1/6d. RESURGENT DUST #3. Cover by John Richards.

"The first spaceship since the legendary Golden Age was being built on Venus. And its first voyage took Lord Kennet of Gryllaar back to Earth—the planet from which his ancestors had come centuries before to colonize Venus. The voyage was made in spite of mysterious warnings that spoke in the minds of the spaceship's crew—and the voices said that the trip was suicidal! And when Earth was reached, the crew of eight men from Venus knew that these had been no idle warnings—for they landed in a trap from which escape seemed impossible. Only Lord Kennet could see a possibility of overcoming this peril, but his plan was fantastic, and not even his own crewmen could be told the secret of the Indestructible."

A12.   *Resurgent Dust.* London: Hamilton & Co. ("Panther" #68), July 1953, 160 p., 1/6d. RESURGENT DUST #1. Cover by John Richards.

Mankind settles on Venus after the destruction of life on Earth. "Could Science reclaim their Golden Age—or was Evil their inheritance?" Realistic depiction of the human colonization of Venus, if one accepts the impossibility of the Venusian locale. Typical Berry quality, though not quite his usual style. The trilogy gives evidence of the promising ability of Berry, sadly terminated by his early suicide.

WILLIAM (Henry Fleming) BIRD, 1896-1971

William Henry Fleming Bird was born March 3, 1896 at Thornton Heath Croydon, Surrey, the son of Frederick Edward John Bird (a Congregational minister) and Caroline Sandison. Bird was educated at Whitford Emmanuel College, Cambridge, where he received a B.A. in Science (1920), and at Goldsmith's School of Art. Early jobs included periods as Assistant Inspector of Taxes, a builder's draughtsman, and an architectural assistant.

During the First World War, he was a member of the Royal Field Artillery, and was taken prisoner by the Germans in 1918. After the war, he worked as an art school teacher and lecturer in sculpture (1928-58). Some of his own artwork was exhibited at the Royal Academy. He married Louise Smith on July 23, 1932, and died at Benfleet, Essex on July 26, 1971, aged 75.

Bird was also a writer, mostly of articles. He penned several children's books published by Hutchinson, Jonathan Cape, and Brookhampton, his first juvenile being entitled *Chimpy*. His first professional sale was "Critical Age," to *Futuristic Science Stories* #12 (1953). He later wrote under several pseudonyms, including HENRY FLEMING, JOHN EAGLE, and JOHN TOUCAN. He penned five early science fiction novels for Curtis Warren under the bylines listed below.

as ADRIAN BLAIR

A13.   *Cosmic Conquest.* London: Curtis Warren, June 1953, 160 p., 1/6d. Cover by Gordon C. Davies.

After the nuclear cataclysm of the 23rd Century, a race of mutants who do not require sleep was created. At first, their unremitting toil is of great help in rebuilding civilization, but as their numbers increase, they are perceived as a threat to Mankind. A great persecution of the mutants begins, and a small band of them escape to found a civilization on a new world. Now their descendants, sworn to avenge the wrongs done to their forefathers, return to Earth. The SF gimmicks are handled with surprising panache.

as LEE ELLIOTT, *house pseud.*

A14. *The Third Mutant.* London: Curtis Warren, October 1952, 160 p., 1/6d. Cover by Gordon C. Davies.

"The distant planet Trone, with her artificial satellite 'sun,' went behind an electronic curtain after an internal revolution and the rise of Karen, leader of the revolutionaries, as dictator. Now, the curtain has been temporarily raised to admit a trade delegation from Earth. Karen wishes to exchange, for machine-tools, his surplus agricultural produce, which the rest of the system, all highly mechanized planets, so badly need. But, given industrial plants, will Karen build other 'suns,' launching them into space on orbits calculated to scorch the worlds of the Solar Commonwealth into submission to his authority?" Agent Max Hansen is sent to Trone to save the third mutant, an agent with the secret of the "suns".

as RAND LE PAGE, *house pseud.*

A15. *War of Argos.* London: Curtis Warren, May 1952, 127 p., 1/6d. Cover by Gordon C. Davies.

For three centuries the planet Argos has been under the control of Earth, but now there is an uprising led by the telepathic Tran. Earth is losing ground as many high officials reveal themselves to be Tran spies. Colonel Othran of the Psychological Service, after a daring raid on an enemy ship, plans to have a ciliation grafted onto his brain to make him telepathic. He infiltrates the controlling panel of Argos and learns of a second invasion fleet about to land on Earth. He returns to Earth, but only after the Argan master has implanted the "death wish..." A somewhat plodding but fairly interesting study of a telepathic society.

as PAUL LORRAINE, *house pseud.*

A16. *Two Worlds.* London: Curtis Warren, October 1952, 128 p., 1/6d. Cover by Ray Theobald.

"The governments of Earth, Venus, and the twin planets known as the Ganadei, wish to put the atomic-fuel bearing atmosphere of Moon IV, a satellite of Ortos, out Jupiter way, under interplanetary control. The powerful Arions, however, wish to annex the Moon for themselves. To weaken the alliance ranged against them, the Arions secretly introduce a plague to the Ganadei, which are subsequently sealed off as infested planets by a superior Medical Command." Essentially a war story, decked out in interplanetary garb and SF jargon, the impact of which is blunted because the author has invented several new planets, the location of which is fairly hazy ("out Jupiter way"), but which appear to be in our solar system...utterly destroying all credibility.

as KRIS LUNA, *house pseud.*

A17.   *Operation Orbit.* London: Curtis Warren, November 1953, 159 p., 1/6d. Cover by Gordon C. Davies.

"Stalemate had occured on Earth between the Earthmen and the invading forces from Planet Hedra. Unable to fight in Earth's cold and temperate zones, the Hedrans have fallen back on India and there, with the aid of forced labor battalions, they prepare a monstrous scheme which, if successful, will give them final victory and power on Earth. Western Intelligence Agent Z.90 brings about his transfer from an Indian internment camp to a forced labor camp and, learning the Hedran plans, prepares a scheme which, using the Hedran idea, will bring about their death and defeat." Probably Bird's best SF novel, telling how mankind overcomes alien overlords.

ADRIAN BLAIR—see: William Bird

HUGO BLAYN—see: John Russell Fearn

S(ydney) J(ames) BOUNDS, 1920-

Sydney James Bounds was born in Brighton on November 4, 1920, and educated at Brighton Intermediate School. He worked as an electrical fitter before moving to Kingston-on-Thames to study electrical engineering at the local Technical College. During World War II he was an electrician and instrument repairman for the Royal Air Force Ground Crew. At this time, he began writing, and sold a story (never published) to Gerald Swan. He appeared in amateur magazines and his first professional story appeared in *Outlands* in 1946. After the war, he was a subway station attendant until 1951, when he became a full-time writer. Finding that SF alone could not support him, he turned to other fields, and has written westerns, gangster novels, crime (including three SEXTON BLAKE novels), war novels, confessions and juvenile stories. During brief slumps in writing, he was worked as a storeman, packer, machine operator, civil servant, and hospital porter. His best early novel was a murder mystery set in the publishing offices of a Chicago pulp magazine empire. It includes numerous in-jokes on science fiction and detective magazine publishing. The book was issued under a house name with title altered (without the author's knowledge) by John Spencer & Co., as *The Big Frame* by J. K. BAXTER (Crime Series No. 8, 1959), and had been highly regarded among crime collectors before the knowledge of the author's true identity was recently revealed. Bounds's later output was concentrated in the macabre field, but he has published many SF stories in most of the better SF magazines, plus four novels, including *The Moon Raiders* (1955), *The World Wreckers* (1956), *The Robot Brains* (1958) all in hardcover, and the novel listed below. Later SF novels have seen publication only in Italian translation. His short story "The Circus" was adapted for U.S. television by George Romero.

A18. *Dimension of Horror.* London: Hamilton & Co. ("Panther" #70), August 1953, 160 p., 1/6d. Cover by John Richards.

"Alexander Black's orders when he left Earth for Venus were: 'Prevent war from breaking out between the two planets!' But hatred for Earthmen was rife among the Venusians, and Black's assignment seemed to be doomed before it started—until he came across that small, insignificant man in the gray suit whose name was Yzz-Five. In a suspense-filled story of war-hysteria that could have destroyed a whole dimension of life, Earthman Alexander Black teams up with a green-haired Venusian girl and a creature from another dimension to save two planets from destruction—though a ghastly sacrifice is demanded before peace is restored." Entertaining space opera, with satirical touches.

VEKTIS BRACK (House pseudonym)

A19. *Castaway from Space,* (author unidentified). London: Gannet Press, October 1953, 109 + 19 p., 1/6d. Cover by Ray Theobald.

Roton, a Vegantian space explorer, crash-lands on Earth. The inhabitants of this new planet are physically similar to him, but savage in other respects. Earth was decimated during a time the Vegantians called the Great Madness, and only small pockets of civilization survived. Roton joins forces with Maxwell Hunter, who is trying to unite the remaining population, but first they must fight Laramore, who is trying to take over as dictator of the world. The book includes an anonymous and very mediocre nineteen-page short story, "The Terrors of Marinda."

A20. *Odyssey in Space,* (by BRUNO G. CONDRAY). London: Gannet Press, 1954, 127 p., 1/6d. Cover by Gerald Facey.

SEE: LESLIE G. HUMPHRYS for synopsis.

A21. *The "X" People,* (author unidentified). London: Gannet Press, June 1953, 128 p., 1/6d. Cover by Gerald Facey.

Mysterious acts of sabotage lead Earthcontrol Chief Mark Theling to ask Dr. Alec Crane to investigate. The saboteurs are destroying seemingly impregnable machines and can pass through solid walls. The search for the "X" people, as the saboteurs are nicknamed, sends Crane and his team, including the irascible Professor Cartwright, to Venus. While in space, they are contacted by an alien race who first take Cartwright and then Crane. The aliens intend to invade Earth by putting everyone under hypnotic control. Before the climax is reached, the reader is likely to have fallen asleep; this story is *dull!*

MATTHEW C. BRADFORD—see: John Jennison

ARNOLD BREDE (Pseudonym?)

A22. *Sister Earth.* London: Scion Ltd., October 1951, 112 p., 1/6d. Cover by George Ratcliffe.

An expedition into space leads to the discovery that Earth has a twin planet with an identical orbit, forever hidden by the Sun. A second voyage is launched, which lands on the planet after an uneventful trip. A series of advance camps are set up, then one advance group meets up the the world's inhabitants, the Helenians. Pedantic, puerile narrative.

GEORGE SHELDON BROWN—see: Dennis Hughes

GEORGE SHELDON BROWNE—see: John Jennison

JOHN (Kilian Houston) BRUNNER, 1934-

John Brunner was born in Preston Crowmarsh, Oxfordshire, on September 24, 1934, the son of Egbert Sidney Houston Anthony Brunner (a sales representative) and Amy Phyllis Ivy Felicity Whitaker (a model). He was hooked on SF from the age of six, when he read *War of the Worlds* and *The Time Machine*.
He tried writing his first story in 1943, and his first novel at the age of ten. He collected his first rejection slip in 1947, and sold his first novel to Curtis Warren, Ltd. in 1951, while studying at Cheltenham College. He made his first sales to magazines in the United States in 1952, and many more followed, including *Astounding*. He entered National Service in 1953 as a Pilot Officer in the Secretarial Branch of the Royal Air Force, leaving in 1955 to become technical abstractor for a magazine edited by John Christopher (Samuel Youd). In 1956 he became editor under John Burke for the Paul Hamlyn publishing group. He left in 1958 to marry and become a full-time writer. Since then, he has written over 80 science fiction and mystery novels and collections of poetry. Possibly his best known book is *Stand on Zanzibar* (1968), which won the Hugo Award, British SF Award and the Prix Apollo. Brunner has become one of the most respected British SF authors ever. He also wrote four books in the 1960s as KEITH WOODCOTT.

as GILL HUNT, *house pseud.*

A23. *Galactic Storm.* London: Curtis Warren, November 1951, 110 p., 1/6d. Cover by Ray Theobald.

Sharpe, a young meterologist, uses the super-computer Charlie to run a thirteen-hour program, and discovers that the Earth's temperature is gradually rising, threatening to melt the ice caps. A team of scientists is sent to the South Pole, where they discover an alien hideout. Sharpe and his friends Paul and Honey are captured and become prisoners of an advance force from Venus who are artificially increasing the temperature and carbon dioxide levels in the atmosphere, preparing Earth for colonization. Ignored for years before Brunner's authorship was known, it is now a collector's item.

H(enry) K(enneth) BULMER, 1921-

(Henry) Kenneth Bulmer was born in London on January 14, 1921, son of Walter Ernest Bulmer (a chemist) and Hilda Louise Corley. He became interested in SF at an early age, and was a well-known fan in London, issuing a fanzine, *Star Parade*, in 1941. During World War II, he served in the Royal Corps of Signals, serving in

Africa, Sicily, and Italy. He married Pamela Kathleen Buckmaster on March 7, 1953 and has three children.

His first work in the SF field was for the paperback novel market, writing a number of books for Hamilton's, Pearson's (TIT-BITS), and Comyns; his first short story ("First Down") appeared two years later in the April 1954 issue of *Authentic*. His rate of output has not slackened since those early days; he later sold many novels to Ace Books, Robert Hale, and DAW Books, most notably the popular DRAY PRESCOTT series, first as ALAN BURT AKERS, and subsequently as DRAY PRESCOT.

Using his own name and 23 pseudonyms (including TULLY ZETFORD), he has produced over 120 novels and as many short stories. Included among books are science fiction, Viking adventures, a western, historicals, thrillers, U-Boat novels, and pirate stories. He also edited the *New Writings in SF* series after the death of *Ted Carnell*. He wrote all of his "Void" period works as H. K. BULMER, before becoming KENNETH BULMER in his later career.

A24. *Challenge.* London: Curtis Warren, November 1954, 160 p., 1/6d. Cover by Gordon C. Davies.

A well-written, low-key novel of early space exploration and the struggles of pioneer spacemen. Similar in theme to Fredric Brown's *Project Jupiter*, except that Bulmer's protagonists aim for Saturn. The second to last Curtis SF to be issued—and for which Bulmer did not receive any payment!—it has now become something of a collector's rarity.

A25. *Empire of Chaos.* London: Hamilton & Co. ("Panther" #69), November 1952, 158 p., 1/6d. Cover by John Richards.

"When Captain Lance is offered, by a millionaire politician, a job as astrogater aboard a ship engaged in illegal trafficking, he realizes that he has blundered into something big that could end freedom in the Galaxy. From there on, the story moves rapidly, out from the solar system to the far planets of Martell and Loris, on which Lance struggles, side-by-side, with flame-haired beauty, Rusty Purcell, against the machinations of the hated aliens." Pirate story set in outer space, moderately entertaining.

A26. *Encounter in Space.* London: Hamilton & Co. ("Panther" #29), November 1952, 128 p., 1/6d. Cover by Gordon C. Davies.

"One puny Earthman against a colossus of metal, one man with only his fists and his brain pitted against a seeking, destroying shape of death, fashioned with all the skill of alien minds. And Man's very brain, his most powerful weapon, which had brought him from the mud to the stars, was the thing that drew the Destromech on!" Interstellar war story in typical Bulmer vein.

A27. *Galactic Intrigue.* London: Hamilton & Co. ("Panther" #60), June 1953, 160 p., 1/6d. Cover by John Richards.

Entertaining space opera telling of the complications and political machinations arising from the misuse of the invention of a matter transmitter.

The book is enhanced by a memorably baroque cover, showing a "humpty-dumpty" monstrosity being reassembled through a faulty transmitter.

A28. *Space Salvage.* London: Hamilton & Co. ("Panther" #37), January 1953, 143 p., 1/6d. Cover by Gordon C. Davies.

The adventures of a space salvage corps on the outer planets is unmemorable early Bulmer space opera, redeemed only by the author's evident knowledge of early maritime history, on which he is an expert. In later years, he would write genuine maritime historical novels, such as the "Adam Hardy" series.

A29. *The Stars Are Ours.* London: Hamilton & Co. ("Panther" #48), March 1953, 158 p., 1/6d. Cover by John Richards.

"...in this story, not one man, but the whole of the Earth is in the grip of fear of the unknown. Who...? What...? Where...? Those were the questions people were asking themselves as they witnessed incredible events that led them to believe that their own minds were deranged. How would you react if somebody told you that your best friend was a robot? What would you do if somebody you have always admired and respected tried to murder you for no apparent reason?" One of Bulmer's best early efforts, with a new slant on the Fortean concept that "we are property."

A30. *World Aflame.* London: Hamilton & Co. ("Panther" #159), November 1954, 144 p., 1/6d. Cover by John Richards.

"A shadow people, subtly different from normal mankind in their strange, alien power, living on the Earth, rubbing shoulders daily with ordinary folk—such is the incredible truth that faces Michael Halliday, atomicist at the Atomic Energy Establishment at Barwell...How Halliday reacts to the problems of divided loyalties; how he struggles to perfect an atomic space drive that will free men from the shackles of the erupting Earth—all this enacted against the Judgement Day volcanic upheaval of the world, combine to produce a powerful, fast-moving story." Probably the best of Bulmer's early novels.

as PHILIP KENT

A31. *Home Is the Martian.* London: C. A. Pearson (TIT-BITS no #), November 1954, 64 p., 9d. Cover by Ronald Turner.

After futilely chasing a Druvan spaceship which has entered the solar system, Space Rangers Conroy and Miller, on the *Antietam*, are returning to Pluto when their rockets begin acting erratically. With the *Antietam* out of action, the Druvans return to destroy it, but Conroy outwits them. Upon returning to Pluto, the Rangers discover a new job awaiting them—to track down Dr. Kern Fliess, who has fled to Cha-Inroth, the fifth planet of the Druvan system. With him, he has taken the secret of the Martians' ancient power source, only recently rediscovered after millennia of secrecy.

A32. *Mission to the Stars.* London: C. A. Pearson (TIT-BITS no #), April 1954, 64 p., 9d. Cover by Ronald Turner.

Captain Matlin is recalled to the moon from his exile on Venus, where mutants carry out continual bombing raids on "normal" humans. He is given sealed orders to be opened only when he reaches Callisto, where Earth is still at war with the Jovian Satellite Federation. "The job is the most important undertaking one man can perform for Earth. You are expendable." It is nothing more than a suicide mission...or is it?

A33. *Slaves of the Spectrum.* London: C. A. Pearson (TIT-BITS no #), July 1954, 64 p. 9d. Cover by Ronald Turner.

Commander Railton had already experienced the deep space beyond Jupiter. Now he was on a special assignment; special enough to have been given command of the newest vessel out the the shipyards...before it had even been put through any trial flights. A previous mission to Saturn, led by Captain Dolan on the *R.7* had resulted in the return of a deathship...the whole crew had perished. Railton takes the new *R.13* to Saturn, where alien life is encountered. An unidentified spaceship appears and Railton watches helplessly as the *R.13* is destroyed, leaving him marooned on Titan with no way to escape. This book has a promising beginning that falls away into a routine action story.

A34. *Vassals of Venus.* London: C. A. Pearson (TIT-BITS no #), May 1954, 64 p., 9d. Cover by Ronald Turner.

Captain Devlin, a space salvage expert, is asked to recover records from a spaceship that has crashed into the Great Ring Swamp of Venus. The economy of Earth depends on the return of these files. After kidnappings and other adventures, he finds more than just the rocket in the swamp.

as KARL MARAS, *house pseud.*

A35. *Peril from Space.* London: Comyns (Publishers) Ltd., December 1954, 128 p., 1/6d. Cover by Ronald Turner.

Not up to Bulmer's usual standards, this is an unsuccessful attempt to create a futuristic detective. Arnold Denton is meant to be a cross between Philip Marlowe and James Bond, but comes across as a bit of a wimp. The SF elements are few and far between, and just used as ciphers. The story itself concerns a political struggle on the Jovian moons, which have been colonized, and is no more than a routine adventure story.

A36. *Zhorani.* London: Comyns (Publisher) Ltd., December 1953, 128 p., 1/6d. Cover by Ronald Turner.

By far the best of Bulmer's two stories for this publisher. The Zhorani are a race of alien invaders who have subjugated Earth (and most of the galaxy) without having ever been seen. Only one man, Mallory, has glimpsed the invaders, but has had his memory of them wiped, after they have extracted from his mind the information which enabled them to effect a conquest.

Mallory joins with a group of freedom fighters, and the story builds nicely to an interstellar *dénouement* that only old SF hands would have seen coming.

with A. V. CLARKE

A37. *Cybernetic Controller.* London: Hamilton & Co. ("Panther" no #), August 1952, 112 p., 1/6d. Cover by Gordon C. Davies.

A final, cataclysmic war, fought with atomic bombs and bacteriological disease, drives the surviving remnants of Mankind into underground city blocks, away from plague and deadly radioactive rains. A distrust of the leaders who led them into war leads to the acceptance of a new government under advanced cybernetic machines. The society erected by the machines is based on a system that grades people based on their level of intelligence demonstrated at birth. But with the emergence of a mutant strain, the system begins to break down...

A38. *Space Treason.* London: Hamilton & Co. ("Panther" no #), May 1952, 112 p., 1/6d. Cover by Gordon C. Davies.

Idealistic Space Police Commander Steve Manning gets stranded on Venus with Janine Anderley, daughter of a missing scientist and a member of the rebellious Insurgents. He discovers a secret Space Police prison camp, and realizes the SP leadership is just as corrupt as the Insurgents claim, but also that the Insurgents' leaders are in league with a high-ranking SP official. After a series of chases, captures, and escapes, the solar system is saved (along with the hero and heroine) by means of the matter-transmitter which Janine's father has been developing from his hideout. Fast-paced and trivial. The first professional effort for Clarke.

JOHN (Frederick) BURKE, 1922-

John Frederick Burke was born in Rye, Sussex on March 8, 1922, son of Frederick Goode Burke (a Police Chief Inspector) and Lilian Gertrude Sands. He was educated at Holt High School in Liverpool. He worked for Museum Press, Ltd. for many years as associate editor (1953-1956) and production manager (1956-1957), and then became editorial manager for the Books For Pleasure group (1957-1958). He later joined Shell International Petroleum, where he was their public relations and publications executive until 1963, after which he became the London editor for 20th Century-Fox.

He received the Rockefeller Atlantic Award for Literature in 1947 for his novel *Swift Summer* (published 1949); his first SF story, "Chessboard," was published in *New Worlds*, in January 1953. He has subsequently written many novels and stories as JOHN BURKE. He was involved heavily in fandom during the 1930s, especially in Liverpool, and was a close friend of CHARLES ERIC MAINE (David McIlwain) and JOHN CHRISTOPHER (Christopher Samuel Youd). During the 1960s, through his association with 20th Century-Fox, he was the author of many book adaptations of films, among them *Dr. Terror's House of Horrors* (1965), *The Hammer Horror Omnibus* (1966), and *The Second Hammer Horror Omnibus* (1967). He also edited three volumes of horror stories in the "Tales of Unease" series (1966-

1976). His "Void" period works were written as JONATHAN BURKE. His other pseudonym is ROBERT MIALL, which he used on four adaptations in the 1970s.

as JONATHAN BURKE

A39. *The Dark Gateway.* London: Hamilton & Co. ("Panther" #94), January 1954, 223 p., 2/-. Cover by John Richards.

A gateway is opened in Wales into another dimension, and conflict develops between Earth and the alien plane. A blending of science fiction and the supernatural, with Lovecraftian overtones.

A40. *Deep Freeze.* London: Hamilton & Co. ("Panther" #144), March 1955, 144 p., 2/-. Cover by Ronald Turner.

All the men on the planet Demeter are destroyed, and only women and children are left to establish a feminist utopia. Conflict develops as the male children mature.

A41. *The Echoing Worlds.* London: Hamilton & Co. ("Panther" #103), February 1954, 159 p., 1/6d. Cover by John Richards.

"The basic idea is parallel worlds, both in the present. What we know as our world is in an even worse state than it is now, though war has been abolished. There is something stultifying about perpetual peace, apparently, and young men of Earth who are not fit enough for space travel find life most dull. They get themselves to parallel worlds and there find war aplenty, together with romance, adventure, and a certain amount of soul searching. The critical point, of course, comes when intercourse between the two worlds is attempted." Occasionally lapses into space opera, but written with remarkable restraint in places. Not a first-class novel, but shows the promise in technique that Burke has since reached.

A42. *Hotel Cosmos.* London: Hamilton & Co. ("Panther" #135), July 1954, 142 p., 1/6d. Cover by John Richards.

"It was a place where travelers from all the inhabited galaxies met—a junction of the great space routes. But it was also close to a penal colony, and when a Uranian escaped from the colony, the guests at the hotel had reason to be alarmed. Uranians are disturbing creatures. They have great powers of imitation. The face that seems to be the face of someone you know may be a deception. The criminal you want to track down may wear an appearance that rightly belongs to somebody else. You've got to suspect everybody." The harassed hotel detective attempts to identify the real criminal. The plot appears to be based on Burke's short story, "Detective Story," in *Science Fantasy.*

A43. *Revolt of the Humans.* London: Hamilton & Co. ("Panther" #192), May 1955, 141 p., no price. TWILIGHT #2. Cover by John Richards.

Mankind overcomes his parasitical alien oppressors in this excellent and suspenseful sequel to *Twilight of Reason* (#A44). The ironic ending is very satisfying. Both novels are well worth reading.

A44.   *Twilight of Reason.* London: Hamilton & Co. ("Panther" #118), April 1954, 159 p., 1/6d. TWILIGHT #1. Cover by John Richards.

"...Here is the record of the first onslaught of a strange disease that dropped on Mankind from the skies. It is the story of an alien plague that worked too swiftly to be counteracted by human science—a plague that did not so much drive men out of their minds as steal the minds from them...you will see what it is like to be an exile on the face of your own world, threatened by an enemy who cannot be fought with ordinary weapons, an enemy who may take possession of you without warning and without pity." An interesting novel of the successful alien takeover of the Earth, and an early major exploration of the symbiosis theme. See also the sequel, *Revolt of the Humans* (#A43).

BERL CAMERON (House pseudonym)

A45.   *Black Infinity,* (by David O'Brien). London: Curtis Warren, June 1952, 127 p., 1/6d. Cover by Ray Theobald.

SEE: *David O'Brien* for synopsis.

A46.   *Cosmic Echelon,* (by John Glasby and Arthur Roberts). London: Curtis Warren (TERRAN EMPIRE series), August 1952, 128 p., 1/6d. Cover by Gordon C. Davies.

SEE: *John Glasby* for synopsis.

A47.   *Destination Alpha,* (by Brian Holloway). London: Curtis Warren, March 1952, 127 p., 1/6d. Cover by Gordon C. Davies.

SEE: *Brian Holloway* for synopsis.

A48.   *Lost Aeons,* (by Dennis Talbot Hughes). London: Curtis Warren, January 1953, 159 p., 1/6d. Cover by Gordon C. Davies.

SEE: *Dennis Talbot Hughes* for synopsis.

A49.   *Photomesis,* (by David O'Brien). London: Curtis Warren, May 1952, 127 p., 1/6d. Cover by Gordon C. Davies.

SEE: *David O'Brien* for synopsis.

A50.   *Solar Gravita,* (author unidentified). London: Curtis Warren, May 1953, 159 p., 1/6d. Cover by Gordon C. Davies.

"Silent, swift and terrible in its super-mechanical cunning, the 'visitor' from Space made its attack during one of the opening years of the 21st Century—an attack that threatened the very existence of Mankind...The next stage begins with the flight of Captain Ferguson and his crew from an Earthly satellite station on Man's first sunwards spaceflight, to the mist-shrouded planet that is Earth's nearest neighbor. Here, they meet their opponents—strange creatures of an age-old civilization, advanced in scientific achievement, yet the brains behind a plan savage in its merciless inhumanity." Action-packed, and written with considerable panache.

A51.   *Sphero Nova,* (by Arthur Roberts & John Glasby). London: Curtis Warren, 1953, 159 p., 1/6d. Cover by Ray Theobald.

SEE: *John Glasby* for synopsis.

H(erbert) J(ames) CAMPBELL, 1925-

Campbell was born in London on November 18, 1925, and was educated at the University of London, where he received his B.S. in 1955 and a Ph.D. in 1957. Campbell began as a chemical research worker and later became a senior lecturer in the Department of Psychiatry at his alma mater.

He first started writing scientific articles, and then branched out to science fiction. He was a member of "The London Circle," and became Technical Editor for *Authentic Science Fiction* and then Editor for the 38 issues between December 1952 and January 1956, during which time the magazine improved considerably. He resigned from writing to return to research work, and has since written a number of scientific books. His novels for Hamilton & Co. are among the best of the early 1950s books, drawing on his considerable scientific knowledge. He also wrote under the house byline ROY SHELDON for Hamilton/Panther, and probably heavily influenced or edited the other SF books published by Hamilton & Co. during this period, particularly the stories attributed to JON J. DEEGAN (pseudonym of Robert Sharp), among them the OLD GROWLER series.

A52.   *Another Space—Another Time.* London: Hamilton & Co. ("Panther" #67), July 1953, 158 p., 1/6d. Cover by John Richards.

"Two universes interlocked at the point of contact in time. And the path is clear for the invasion of Earth. Science is suspect. Controlled by the mailed mist of S.S.—Science Security. Steen, an S.S. operative, a paid snooper, a servant of the law, fighting against the brain of a resurgent scientist who won't bow to the controlling hand of S.S. Jaky, Steen's beautiful wife and invaluable aide, a pawn in a game...the results of which might mean a death-grip on Earth. Meg, a creature from Another Space—Another Time. Polymorphallactic—able to change his, or its, form at will." An interesting precursor to Jack Finney's *Invasion of the Body Snatchers.*

A53.   *Beyond the Visible.* London: Hamilton & Co., November 1952, 189 p., 2/-d. Cover by Vann.

"All around us are invisible things. We become aware of them when we switch on the radio. The invisible things are electro-magnetic waves. But—maybe there are other things...our eyes are sensitive to only a narrow band of the electro-magnetic spectrum that we call light. Beyond that band on either side are many other radiations we cannot see. Perhaps, in these radiations, there are things that some people would rather not see." One man tries to convince others that invisible creatures are driving Mankind's destiny, and Man towards his doom. A pure parallel of Eric Frank Russell's *Sinister Barrier*, which Campbell greatly admired.

A54.   *Brain Ultimate.* London: Hamilton & Co. ("Panther" #86), November 1953, 157 p., 1/6d. Cover by John Richards.

"It was a rigid dictatorship of the planets...an iron control...but it nursed a dreamer at its bosom, and the dreamer was dangerous. On Asteroid Twenty Two, the scientist's dream took shape, and only he and his assistant knew its frightening nature...that dream that gave vent to power through the disembodied brains of murdered men." The novel ends on a Stapledonian note, with the establishment of an interstellar gestalt. By turns scientific and mystical, it is one of Campbell's better efforts.

A55.   *Chaos in Miniature.* London: Hamilton & Co. ("Authentic" #18), February 1952, 109 p., 1/6d. Cover by George Ratcliffe.

One of Campbell's satires, seeded with in-jokes concerning contemporary fans and authors, *Chaos* features Willy Grant, Irish SF publisher, investigating the disappearance of the Houses of Parliament. He visits the "Black Mare" (White Horse), where "the main topic of conversation was the disappearance of the moon. One lean man who had spent his life working towards the fulfillment of the moon rocket wept quietly into a glass of orange juice."

A56.   *The Last Mutation.* London: Hamilton & Co. ("Authentic" #11), July 1951, 105 p., 1/6d. Cover by George Ratcliffe.

Campbell's controversial *tour de force*, and a much sought-after collector's item. The story is told in the second person from the viewpoint of Mu, a mutant of the future who is raised in a colony of all kinds of monstrosities, looked after by human warders. But an advanced scientific paper written by Mu—who is outwardly human—leads to his release, to work alongside Professor Lumet. Outside, Mu works towards a shocking Final Solution, aimed at replacing Humanity with others of his kind. His plot fails, and with the crushing realization of defeat comes the revelation that, in any case, mutants are biologically incompatible, and so unable to breed. Mu is shot, but dies with the realization that it would be possible to correct the incompatibility—a fine, ambiguous ending!

A57.   *Mice—or Machines.* London: Hamilton & Co. ("Authentic" #22), June 1952, 109 p., 1/6d. Cover by Gordon C. Davies.

This novel is set in a complex, low-key future society that is based on the abolition, for the most part, of mechanization. An illegal teleporter device has extra energy fed into it at the transmission stage, which results in the duplication of objects. An underground group transmits vending machines to every house in the country to dispense rebellious literature. This group, the Scientific Mechanics, overthrows a woman Prime Minister and restores machines to society. A short story idea stretched uncomfortably to novel length.

A58. *The Moon Is Heaven.* London: Hamilton & Co. ("Authentic" #16), December 1951, 110 p., 1/6d. Cover by George Ratcliffe.

Another of Campbell's satires with London fans as characters. This one is written in the second person, and is a fast-paced story of the first Lunar voyage. The chief character is one Atah Kark, an expert on astronautics.

A59. *Once upon a Space.* London: Hamilton & Co. ("Panther" #160), November 1954, 142 p., 1/6d. Cover by John Richards.

"Earth was very old and very tired. A few men dominated the masses, imposed upon them an odious regime that amounted to slavery. There was no freedom of thought, no freedom of action. Transgressors underwent total annihilation, represented by the dread word REDISTRIBUTION. One man, a high official, had a change of heart. He rebelled—and found himself in the midst of murder and torture by two opposing groups. He was caught in the crossfire of rival power-seekers. And there was a girl, clever, shrewd, and daring. The man did not know where she stood amongst his enemies, or even if she was an enemy at all." Typical Campbell dystopia, filled with disturbingly grim and realistic medical and scientific details.

A60. *The Red Planet.* London: Hamilton & Co. ("Panther" #77), September 1953, 159 p., 1/6d. Cover by John Richards.

"They were wrecked together in space—a scientist and a man from the engine room—and the planet they found themselves on seemed to be a crazy one, dominated by the red grass. They had no fuel to get them off the red planet of Bokez. The food they had would last a few days only, and after that there was only the red grass. But to eat the sacred red grass of Bokez was to bring sharp and vengeful destruction at the hands of the planet's inhabitants. The scientist and his companion could expect only death by starvation or execution. But a scientist will never admit defeat, and in this stirring drama of ideas, it is the resource and courage of Petersmith, the Earth scientist, that finally overcomes the menace of the Red Planet." An intriguing adventure story.

A61. *World in a Test Tube.* London: Hamilton & Co. ("Authentic" #8), April 1951, 106 p., 1/6d. Cover by D.L.W.

A mutant genius and his daughter experiment on normal humanity, causing worldwide cataclysms culminating in the Earth breaking free from its orbit following a series of contrived nuclear explosions. Catastrophe is averted when the mutants realize that Mankind is not the inferior species they had thought.

as ROY SHELDON, *house pseud.*

A62.   *Atoms in Action.* London: Hamilton & Co. ("Panther" #47), March 1953, 159 p., 1/6d. SHINY SPEAR #6. Cover by Gordon C. Davies.

Dirk Manners and Shiny Spear, now joined by the telepathic girl, Aylees (introduced in *The Plastic Peril*), are sent on a mission to investigate strange pulsations from the Spican system. They discover a system of three worlds, Alpha, Beta, and Gamma. The usual colorful aliens are encountered—an underground telepathic race on Alpha is being threatened by the monolithic Betans, who reproduce by fission. As usual, the Terrans wipe out the entire planet of Beta.

A63.   *Beam of Terror.* London: Hamilton & Co. ("Authentic" #13), September 1951, 110 p., 1/6d. SHINY SPEAR #3. Cover by George Ratcliffe.

Shiny Spear and Dirk Manners search Saturn's moons, looking for a missing ship, one of several that have vanished on the trade line to Uranus. Nearing Japetus, they experience some sort of mental compulsion urging them to remain, promising a utopian paradise, before they are pulled down to the moon's surface. They find Japetus inhabited by a Saturnian colony, the ancestors of which had left Saturn 300 million years ago. As usual, Spear and Manners get embroiled in xenophobic, shoot-'em-all-up adventures, which read somewhat distastefully by present-day standards.

A64.   *Energy Alive.* London: Hamilton & Co. ("Authentic" #7), April 1951, 101 p., 1/6d. SHINY SPEAR #2. Cover by D.L.W.

An imaginative space opera in which Spear and Manners head an interstellar expedition to the hub of the galaxy, and encounter "the Source," an intelligent cloud of primal energy. As usual in this series, the plot complications are resolved by violence.

A65.   *House of Entropy.* London: Hamilton & Co. ("Panther" #59), June 1953, 160 p., 1/6d. SHINY SPEAR #7. Cover by John Richards.

"Children behaving like adults, and adults playing like children—this is what Spear and Manners find on the faraway planet of Lindos. This planet is ruled by a Brain whose decisions control the life of every inhabitant. Earth and the Galactic Empire are threatened by the plans of this fabulous Brain. There is an adventure of conflict and action for Shiny Spear and his companions before they finally penetrate the grisly secret of the *House of Entropy*." A highly ingenious and entertaining story—the last and best of the SHINY SPEAR series.

A66.   *Mammoth Man.* London: Hamilton & Co., February 1952, 110 p., 1/6d. PREHISTORIC #1. Cover by George Ratcliffe.

This was the beginning of a fascinating, short-lived series featuring the adventures of Magdah, caveman, together with his friend Garo. The smoothly-written story describes how Magdah takes a mate, Lena, hunts, fights rival cavemen, and escapes a herd of rampaging mammoths. The background details of the flora and fauna are smoothly integrated, and appear utterly convincing, as befits author Campbell's real-life scientific knowledge.

A67. *The Menacing Sleep.* London: Hamilton & Co. ("Authentic" #16), August 1952, 126 p., 1/6d. Cover by Gordon C. Davies.

This SF detective story offers a future where interplanetary travel is commonplace, and where a large proportion of Earth's food supply comes from hydroponic Lunar farms. A private eye returns from Mars to find the population of Earth utterly debilitated due to causes unknown. The hero is called in by the Authorities to solve the mystery, in collaboration with the official sleuth—an obligatory beautiful girl. The two travel to the Moon, where the mystery is eventually solved. The plot is basically sound, and the author plays fair in the solution of the mystery. While there is a commendable absence of "thud and blunder," generally shallow writing and feeble characterization make for a disappointingly mediocre novel.

A68. *Moment out of Time.* London: Hamilton & Co., 1951, 111 p., 1/6d. Cover by J. Pollack.

Nine men and four women, including amongst them criminal elements from the year 2050, are marooned by a one-way time trip to the Jurassic Era. Battling variously against dinosaurs, giant dragonflies, alligators, and each other, the party eventually comes to terms with their situation.

A69. *Phantom Moon.* London: Hamilton & Co. ("Authentic" #6), March 1951, 117 p., 1/6d. SHINY SPEAR #1. Cover by D.L.W.

The opening story in the series introduces Shiny Spear and Dirk Manners, operatives in the Earth Space Force. They become embroiled in utterly fantastic adventures on Saturn's moons Phoebe and Themis, encountering two alien races, the crustacean-like Ligidia, and globe-like Saturnians. Manners releases a nova-like weapon which destroys both races, setting the xenophobic tone for the series.

A70. *The Plastic Peril.* London: Hamilton & Co. ("Authentic" #25), September 1952, 109 p., 1/6d. SHINY SPEAR #4. Cover by J. Pollack.

Spear and Manners are sent to do a geological survey on a newly-discovered planet, Grisette, one of the planets of Algol. During the preliminary survey, they open sealed orders which tell them that the planet is possessed of entirely new lifeforms which may be hostile. They discover huge monoliths and swarms of parasites that can eat everything, including stone, metal—and people!

A71. *Star of Death.* London: Hamilton & Co. ("Authentic" #27), November 1952, 108 p., 1/6d. SHINY SPEAR #5. Cover by Gordon C. Davies.

This story sends Manners and Spear to a planet with a methane atmosphere, inhabited by giant, intelligent dinosaurs, and a smaller "servant" race.

A72.   *Two Days of Terror.* London: Hamilton & Co. ("Panther" no #), May 1952, 112 p., 1/6d. PREHISTORIC #2. Cover by Ronald Turner.

Two Days continues the primitive adventures of Magdah, his mate Lena, and their friend Garo, who eventually dies tragically and realistically. A device at the beginning and end of the story, Professor Echert's "time probe," attempts to put the story into an SF frame, but it is essentially a simple adventure story, and none the worse for it.

DEE CARTER—see: Dennis Hughes

MILES CASSON (Pseudonym)

A73.   *Time Drug.* London: Curtis Warren, October 1954, 159 p., 1/6d. HERITAGE #1. Cover by Gordon C. Davies.

A borderline SF thriller set against a background of hospital medical research into a new form of anesthetic which has a "time slip" side effect, the story concentrates more on the private lives and relationships of the medical doctors and their wives and girlfriends than on the fantasy elements. The main characters, Dr. Alan Heritage and Dr. David Owen, are also featured in the sequel, *The Seeing Knife* (see below).

as CRAWLEY FENTON

A74.   *The Seeing Knife.* London: Curtis Warren, November 1954, 159 p., 1/6d. HERITAGE #2. Cover by Gordon C. Davies.

A typical "late series" Curtis production, this competent but unspectacular borderline medical SF thriller is a sequel to *Time Drug*, featuring the same main characters, Drs. Heritage and Owen. In *Knife* the medical invention is electronic surgery using laser technology—quite prophetic and scientifically accurate. This last-published Curtis SF novel is also the rarest title in that series, a true collectors' item.

WILLIAM CAUSETT—see: Erroll Collins

NEIL CHARLES (House Pseudonym)

A75.   *Beyond Zoaster,* (by Dennis Talbot Hughes). London: Curtis Warren, May 1953, 159 p., 1/6d. Cover by Gordon C. Davies.

SEE: *Dennis Talbot Hughes* for synopsis.

A76.   *The Land of Esa,* (by Dennis Talbot Hughes). London: Curtis Warren, October 1952, 128 p., 1/6d. Cover by Ray Theobald.

SEE: *Dennis Talbot Hughes* for synopsis.

A77.   *Para-Robot,* (by John W. Jennison). London: Curtis Warren, February 1952, 112 p., 1/6d. Cover by Ray Theobald.

SEE: *John Jennison* for synopsis.

A78.   *Planet Tha*, (by Brian Holloway). London: Curtis Warren, March 1953, 159 p., 1/6d. Cover by Gerald Facey.

SEE: *Brian Holloway* for synopsis.

A79.   *Pre-Gargantua*, (by Dennis Talbot Hughes). London: Curtis Warren, June 1953, 159 p., 1/6d. Cover by Gordon C. Davies.

SEE: *Dennis Talbot Hughes* for synopsis.

A80.   *Research Opta*, (by Dennis Talbot Hughes). London: Curtis Warren, October 1953, 160 p., no price. Cover by Gordon C. Davies.

SEE: *Dennis Talbot Hughes* for synopsis.

A81.   *Titan's Moon*, (by Brian Holloway). London: Curtis Warren, March 1952, 112 p., 1/6d. Cover by Ray Theobald.

SEE: *Brian Holloway* for synopsis.

A82.   *Twenty-Four Hours*, (by Dennis Talbot Hughes). London: Curtis Warren, July 1952, 128 p., 1/6d. Cover by Gordon C. Davies.

SEE: *Dennis Talbot Hughes* for synopsis.

A83.   *World of Gol*, (by Dennis Talbot Hughes). London: Curtis Warren, August 1953, 159 p., 1/6d. Cover by Gordon C. Davies.

SEE: *Dennis Talbot Hughes* for synopsis.

A(ubrey) V(incent) CLARKE

A London fan, Aubrey Vincent Clarke has been a regular contributor to and editor of fanzines, as well as writer of the "Inquisitor" column for the *Vargo Statten SF Magazine*. He only collaborated on two novels with *Kenneth Bulmer*, and says of them:

> "I was sharing his [Bulmer's] flat at the time (the Epicentre in Drayton Park, London...a famed fan residence of the fifties) and someone—I think it was Bert Campbell—suggested we might try writing something for him; he was hoping some experienced fans might turn out something better than the rubbish he was receiving. We sat down and tried it out. I seem to recall that on one book I wrote alternate chapters with Ken, and on the other I wrote the first half and Ken the second. I never did read either book in its completed form. I found out that I didn't have the storytelling urge and that fanning was more fun. Ken was far more ambitious. He ploughed on, made a success of his authorship, and is still ploughing on, I'm happy to say."

with H. K. BULMER

A37.   *Cybernetic Controller.* London: Hamilton & Co. ("Panther" no #), August 1952, 112 p., 1/6d. Cover by Gordon C. Davies.

        SEE: *Henry Kenneth Bulmer* for synopsis.

A38.   *Space Treason.* London: Hamilton & Co. ("Panther" no #), May 1952, 112 p., 1/6d. Cover by Gordon C. Davies.

        SEE: *Henry Kenneth Bulmer* for synopsis.

ERROLL COLLINS

Collins also wrote two hardcover novels for Lutterworth Press, *Mariners of Space* (1944) and *Submarine City* (1946). He has also written books under numerous pseudonyms, some listed below.

A84.   *Conquerors of Space.* Brighton, Sussex: S. Baker (FANTASTIC SCIENCE THRILLER #5), 1954, 60 p., 0/9d. Cover uncredited.

        "At dawn, January 1, 2054 A.D., Earth's scientific experts exploded their latest Super-Hydrogen bomb. In less than a minute, Planet Earth was blown to radioactive dust, and all life on it ceased." The 100-strong crew of the Brand expedition, exploring Mars, are spared and set off on an interstellar odyssey, calling at a myriad of new planets, including Nievia (planet of snow), Hestia (planet of fire), and Elysia ("the poisoned paradise"). Finally, on the planet Solaris, they encounter the ubiquitous Martians! Mercifully, this title marked the end of this awful series which has gone to deserved oblivion.

as WILLIAM CAUSETT

A85.   *Pirates in Space.* London: S. Baker (FANTASTIC SCIENCE THRILLER #2), 1953, 63 p., 9d. Cover uncredited.

        Strange events befall a regular supply ship after leaving Space Station Four. Crossing the orbit of Mars, it begins to whirl at a fantastic speed; when rescued by another ship, it is discovered that the cargo of "atomic spirit" has vanished. Meanwhile, the captain of Station Four receives a visit from a mysterious girl (named Skrunch!) who threatens to blow up the station unless her planet, Nordhen, is supplied with "atomic spirit." The story becomes even sillier after this point. Unlike the better titles issued by Scion Ltd. and Hamilton & Co., the Baker titles were of such an inferior quality that nobody collected them. As a consequence, copies are almost impossible to find today...which is something of a blessing!

as CLYDE MARFAX

A86.   *Planets of Peril.* London: S. Baker (FANTASTIC SCIENCE THRILLER #4), November 1954, 62 p., 9d. Cover uncredited.

Passing Jupiter while taking part in the Spacemen's Derby race, the *Astronaut* is threatened when the Red Spot tears itself free in a whirlwind of flame and red hot stones. To outrun the debris, Captain Allard crashes the ship though the light barrier. The crew find themselves in an absurd "reverse" universe (where suns shed "rays of darkness") and battling against Vampire Men and Antmen. The reader has been warned! The author's credit on the title page reads "Marfay."

as JOSEPH MOIS

A87. *A Spot on the Sun.* Richmond, Surrey: S. Baker (FANTASTIC SCIENCE THRILLER #3), May 1954, 62 p., 9d. Cover uncredited.

Schoolteacher Paul Dagod tries to solve the mystery of atmospheric disturbances which have caused a scalding hot rain and have left a circular depression suggestive of a flying saucer visit. Is there a connection with a flying saucer and a sunspot growing so large that it threatens to snuff out the sun and extinguish all life? Is there a connection between this story and good SF? Juvenile crud that has justifiably passed into oblivion. Copies of this series are almost impossible to obtain, for the simple reason that nobody seems to have collected them!

as SIMON QUERRY

A88. *Adventures on the Planets.* London: S. Baker (FANTASTIC SCIENCE THRILLER #1), June 1953, 64 p., 9d. Cover uncredited.

This daft story must rank in the top five worst SF novels published. Aliens are being killed by blue light, leaving only two Earth denizens left. They land on a mysterious planet by magnetically attracting themselves via a robot strapped to their spaceship, and meet humanoids who claim that the mystery planet is also called Earth. The movement of a second Universe has caused Planet "X" to explode, causing changes in gravitational influence throughout both universes and threatening the survival of the Earths. The plot deteriorates from this point, if one can believe it!

BRUNO G. CONDRAY—see: Leslie Humphrys

RICK CONROY (Pseudonym)

Rick Conroy is credited with two SF novels and a western, *Injun Justice* (Hamilton & Co., 1951). His style is similar to that of LEE STANTON (q.v.), and STANTON and CONROY are probably pseudonyms of the same author.

A89. *Martians in a Frozen World.* London: Hamilton & Co. ("Authentic" #26), October 1952, no p., no price. Cover by J. Pollack.

This ludicrous adventure is set in Antarctica, where a scientific expedition encounters ten-foot-high beautiful Martian women (wearing saris!) and their revolting servitor race, the Cagoras (a cross between an elephant and an octopus). The Martians have landed on Earth to mine lead, which they use for atomic power. Fully as absurd as it sounds, but quite well written.

A90.   *Mission from Mars.* London: Hamilton & Co. ("Panther" no #), August 1952, 112 p., 1/6d. Cover by J. Pollack.

A young Martian and his girlfriend desire to reform Earth to a point where the more thoughtful Martians no longer feel it necessary to exterminate Mankind in self-defense. They bring with them a gadget that destroys all metals except gold, and after trying the device on a few battlefields, succeed in destroying all the metal in most of Europe. This stops the major European war, but starts a civil war in England, with the Nobs and Spivs on one side, and the Reds (Working Classes) on the other. This minor brawl reveals facets of character in Homo sapiens which the other Martians accept as sufficient reason to allow him to survive. Essentially a light-hearted satire, an oddity for this period.

ADAM DALE—see: Arthur Woolf

JON J. DEEGAN—see: Robert G. Sharp

ASTRON DEL MARTIA (House pseudonym)

"ASTRON DEL MARTIA is the pen name of an American scientist who has become recognized as an authority on certain aspects of interplanetary travel. He is also a brilliant storyteller, who uses his specialist knowledge of astrophysics in the writing of imaginative tales set in that never-never land beyond the Earth's atmosphere." The first of a vast army of exotic pen names concocted to byline British SF during the 1950s, this one was invented by Stephen Frances, who eventually appeared under it with *One Against Time* (Mayflower, 1969), which was a reprint of the HANK JANSON SF novel that appeared in 1956.

A91.   *Dawn of Darkness,* (author unidentified). London: Gaywood Press, 1951, 98 p., 1/6d. Cover by Leroi (Osborne).

"Flying Saucers have apparently spent enough time looking at Earth. Now they come lower and lower, and the government gets worried when aircraft are unable to shoot them down. One man suspected what the Saucers really were and the government gave him instructions to fight the Saucers. But it was a considerable shock when the Saucers fought back, aimed their lethal radiation rays at the laboratory, and kidnapped the crew!" It is a pity their rays hadn't been aimed at Gaywood Press before this book was published.

A92.   *Interstellar Espionage,* (by Franz Harkon). London: Gaywood Press, 1952, 100 p., 1/6d. S.E.C. #3. Cover by Leroi (Osborne).

SEE: *Franz Harkon* for synopsis.

A93.   *Space Pirates,* (by Franz Harkon). London: Gaywood Press, February 1951, 112 p., 1/6d. S.E.C. #1. Cover by Leroi (Osborne).

SEE: *Franz Harkon* for synopsis.

A94.   *The Trembling World,* (by John Russell Fearn). London: S. D. Frances, June 1949, 128 p., 1/6d. Cover by Philip Mendoza.

SEE: *John Russell Fearn* for synopsis.

LEE ELLIOTT (House pseudonym)

A95. *Bio-Muton,* (by Dennis Talbot Hughes). London: Curtis Warren, October 1952, 128 p., 1/6d. Cover by Gordon C. Davies.

SEE: *Dennis Talbot Hughes* for synopsis.

A96. *Overlord New York,* (author unidentified). London: Curtis Warren, September 1953, 159 p., 1/6d. Cover by Gordon C. Davies.

"Time and speed, according to Professor Carlton, are merely two different aspects of the same thing. If a spaceship exceeds the velocity of light, it will travel through time instead of space." America is overrun by the Asian Alliance, and four men launch a spaceship to escape in the hope that they can return 200 years in the future. On landing, they discover that Earth is now the home of mutated aliens, while all living Earthmen are rulers of the alien homeworld, Sanic, ruled over by the Overlord, who has reduced the human race to non-thinking zombies through "moral organization." Unusual and quite well-written.

A14. *The Third Mutant,* (by William Bird). London: Curtis Warren, October 1952, 160 p., 1/6d. Cover by Gordon C. Davies.

SEE: *William Bird* for synopsis.

GERALD EVANS, 1910-

Gerald Evans was born in Fforestfach, Swansea, and educated at Gors Cockett. In 1938, he entered the G.P.O. as a Night Telephonist, and retired from them in 1969 as a Telecommunications Traffic Officer. During his time with them, he was on the Executive of the National Guild of Telephonists, and editor of *The Telephonist*. He became interested in Life Extension in 1964, and became a coordinator for the Life Extension Society of Washington. Through this work he has made several television appearances, once in an interview with David Frost. He started writing at the age of nine, and wrote SF stories for *Thrilling Wonder Stories*, and also for Gerald Swan, but was never a prolific author. He sold a story to John Spencers, and followed it with a novel, which appeared under a pseudonym. He has also published a collection of his short stories, *Shadows in Landore* (Morfa, 1979).

as VICTOR LA SALLE, *house pseud.*

A97. *The Black Sphere.* London: John Spencer, October 1952, 108 p., 1/6d. Cover by Norman Light.

A flying saucer intercepts an airplane and kidnaps four of the passengers. They are taken to Saturn, where the Saturnians use them as guinea pigs in the hopes of finding an easy way to take over the Earth and exterminate the population. The prisoners find the rings of Saturn are not what they seem—not solid, but the massed forces of millions and millions of spaceships. So how can the four captives hope to escape back to Earth...or destroy their enemies?

JOHN FALKNER—see: E. F. Gale

R(obert) LIONEL FANTHORPE, 1935-

Born in Dereham, Norfolk on February 9, 1935, son of Robert Fanthorpe (a shopkeeper) and Greta Christine Garbutt (a teacher), Robert Lionel Fanthorpe left school at the age of fifteen and became a dental prosthetics technician earning £1 a week. He later worked as a journalist and a lorry driver before becoming a schoolmaster at Dereham Secondary School in 1958. He attended Keswick College in Norwich from 1961-63, where he received Distinctions in Theology and Merit in English, and returned to Dereham Secondary until 1967, before moving on to Gamlingay Village College. He spent two years as Battalion Rock Climbing Instructor to the Territorial Army and three years as an industrial training manager at the Phoenix Timber Company in Essex. In 1979 he became headmaster at a high school in South Ely, near Cardiff, and has been recently ordained as a priest.

At the age of sixteen, Fanthorpe launched himself as an author for John Spencer & Co., which was to last until 1966, during which time he had written 120 novels and nearly 300 short stories. Since then, Fanthorpe's incredible output (he regularly wrote a 50,000-word novel each week, using a tape recorder, with his family typing it out for him) has dropped to almost nothing, although he has published the first part of a proposed trilogy in 1979, under his own Greystoke Mobray imprint. *The Black Lion* was written in collaboration with his wife, Patricia. Although his most prolific period was in the early 1960s, he published his first novel in 1953 under the VICTOR LA SALLE byline. Essentially, however, his career as a writer did not really begin until after the period covered by this history.

as VICTOR LA SALLE, *house pseud.*

A98.   *Menace from Mercury.* London: John Spencer, March 1954, 128 p.,
       1/6d. Cover by Ray Theobald.

> Giving no hint of the flood of productivity which was to follow just a few
> years later, Fanthorpe's first novel, written when he was only eighteen, appeared under this Spencer housename. Fanthorpe recalls it thus:
> "Basically, the peaceful co-existence of a solar system trading civilization
> is broken by something unpleasant invading from Mercury, which had previously been thought too hot to sustain life. The hero of this trading
> group, Rex Malone, leaves with a Jupiterian expedition to explore the
> planets circling Sirius, and there encounters a medieval warrior society on
> the planet Krall. Their leader is a 'Black Lion' type called Valkas who,
> after many adventures, leads his unconquerable barbarians to rescue our
> solar system from the Mercurians. It all ends happily."

JOHN (Francis) RUSSELL FEARN, 1908-1960

Fearn was born on June 5, 1908 in Worsley, near Manchester, son of John Slate Fearn (a cotton salesman) and Florence Rose Armstrong (a secretary). Shortly thereafter his family moved to Blackpool, where Fearn lived most of the rest of his life. He became one of the most prolific authors ever to write science fiction—a taste for which he acquired at an early age, crystallizing when he discovered the American pulps in 1931. He immediately wrote a serial for *Amazing* called "The Intelligence Gigantic," which was published in the June/July 1933 issues.

Throughout the 1930s and early 1940s Fearn contributed over a hundred stories to all of the leading American pulp magazines, employing a number of pseudonyms. Fearn became the first British SF writer to turn professional, relying only on his sales to the American magazines and the occasional British contender. In 1944 he began writing a highly successful series of detective novels under the bylines JOHN SLATE and HUGO BLAYN, while continuing to write SF for the American magazines *Startling* and *Thrilling Wonder Stories* as a sideline. By 1946 his output had branched again to include westerns, which, along with the appearance of the MARTIAN series (Hamilton & Co.), prompted a rival publisher, Scion Ltd., to put Fearn under exclusive contract.

Fearn had many problems with the American market (these have been detailed in *Vultures of the Void*), and his only stable market was the *Toronto Star Weekly*, for whom he was writing the highly popular GOLDEN AMAZON series. The turning point came when he offered Scion an SF novel—and VARGO STATTEN was born. An exclusive contract with Scion was signed in November 1950, and Fearn rapidly became Britain's most prolific and popular paperback SF author. Many of his novels were also translated in Europe. His remarkable output involved writing 5,000 words per day, seven days a week: "I will write for anybody just as long as it sells," he once wrote. "But it only pays if you are *prolific*. It also demands that you must hop with nimble ease from a western to destroying the Universe, or equally rapidly switch to solving a complex murder."

Fearn followed this policy for many years with great success, but because of their vast numbers, his books are often assumed to be simplistic hackwork. However, his best SF, consisting of extremely imaginative action/adventure stories *à la* the Golden Age American pulp magazines, has gradually gained recognition, and a number of his stories have been anthologized.

After his marriage in 1956, he turned increasingly to more serious work, including stage plays and television and radio scripts. On September 18, 1960 he collapsed while attending church with his wife, was rushed to a hospital, and was pronounced dead of a heart attack on arrival. His widow submitted his last novel, the Golden Amazon adventure *Earth Divided* (completed just the previous day), to his Canadian publisher, *The Star Weekly*, where it appeared posthumously in 1961. He also left behind many other unpublished manuscripts, including novels, short stories, and plays, which only came to light when Philip Harbottle was appointed Literary Executor of his estate in 1982. Some of these have subsequently been published, including a supernatural crime thriller, "No Grave Need I" (Harbottle, 1984), and an SF novel, *The Slitherers* (Harbottle, 1984). Other western and detective novels have been published in translation in Italy, where Fearn still enjoys a vast posthumous popularity.

A99. *Emperor of Mars.* London: Hamilton & Co., October 1950, 127 p., 1/6d. MARTIAN SERIES #1. Cover by Terry Maloney.

Compelled by an unknown power to climb a Lake District peak, Earthman Clay Drew is captured by Martians. He is amazed to learn from them that he is the rightful ruler of Mars by descent from ancient Atlantis, and must now discharge his duties in this capacity. He also discovers himself betrothed to the lovely Princess Thalia, but soon finds himself thrown into conflict with the evil Lexas, brutal Warlord of Mars.

A100. *Goddess of Mars.* London: Hamilton & Co., November 1950, 126 p., 1/6d. MARTIAN SERIES #4. Cover by Terry Maloney.

Clayton Drew and Princess Thalia escape from the microcosm to face the final conflict with the Warlord Lexas, whose plans include the transfer of his own evil brain into the body of the Princess. Lexas fails and is spectacularly destroyed. A rather disappointing conclusion to the series.

A101. *Operation Venus!* London: Scion Ltd., May 1950, 128 p., 1/6d. Cover by Ronald Turner.

A jetliner crashes into the Brazilian jungle, and the two pilots confront a madman scientist who has discovered an ancient Venusian El Dorado, complete with relics that he plans to use for his own evil ends. This is an expanded version of "Queen of Venus" (*Marvel Stories*, November 1940).

A102. *Red Men of Mars.* London: Hamilton & Co., November 1950, 127 p., 1/6d. MARTIAN SERIES #3. Cover by Terry Maloney.

For the first time in generations, Mars is at peace. Under the combined rule of Clay Drew and Princess Thalia, the Warlord Lexas has been overthrown, but not yet destroyed. The action expands to include Quornal, leader of the hidden race of red-skinned Martians. Subplots are derived from "Red Heritage" (*Astounding*, January 1938). The best work in this series.

A103. *Warrior of Mars.* London: Hamilton & Co., October 1950, 127 p., 1/6d. MARTIAN SERIES #2. Cover by Terry Maloney.

Clay Drew and Princess Thalia bring about the downfall of Lexas and his followers, and bring peace to the underground kingdom of Mars. But Lexas, far from beaten, is determined to destroy Earth itself by stealing most of its air and water.

as HUGO BLAYN

NOTE: Fearn's popular detective pseudonym and character, Chief Inspector Garth, had been previously featured on novels published by Stanley Paul in hardcover: *Except for One Thing* (1948), *The Five Matchboxes* (1948), *Flashpoint* (1950), and *What Happened to Hammond?* (1951). *The Silvered Cage* is a scientific detective novel.

A104. *The Silvered Cage.* London: Dragon Books, March 1955, 144 p., 2/-. CHIEF INSPECTOR GARTH #1. Cover uncredited.

"For an illusionist to make a woman vanish from a cage is merely stock in trade, because it is just that—an illusion. But when the woman concerned really vanishes, in full view of the audience, Scotland Yard is forced to call in a specialist in scientific jigsaws, who finally solves the mystery." This book reintroduces Inspector Garth and Doctor Carruthers (for another book in this series, see *Vision Sinister* [#A119]).

as ASTRON DEL MARTIA, *house pseud.*

A94. *The Trembling World.* London: S. D. Frances, June 1949, 128 p., 1/6d. Cover by Philip Mendoza.

A series of violent earthquakes all over the planet leads the World Council to ask Rob Driscoll, astronomer, if there are any cosmic disturbances causing the destruction. In the course of his investigations Rob is forced to fly with his wife, Mona, to Buenos Aires during a storm, and crashes in Brazil. Here, they discover a valley of statues, where Mona enters a trance and recites a fantastic tale. Many centuries before a scientific outpost was based on Earth. The Aldebarran researchers had built a projector capable of sending itself via the fifth dimension to Sirius in a matter of hours. It returned with a sample of the star's atmosphere, a grey gas which turned all it touched to stone, leaving behind a weird heritage of scientific knowledge which saves Earth from destruction. A superior Fearn effort, well worth seeking out.

as VOLSTED GRIDBAN, *house pseud.*

A105. *The Dyno Depressant.* London: Scion Ltd., June 1953, 128 p., 1/6d. Cover by Ronald Turner.

The world of 1985 is plunged into a chaos of riots and public disorder when an abnormal form of electrical energy—the Dyno Depressant—neutralizes all other energy, resulting in total darkness, without heat, without sound. Scientists become involved in a race against time to overcome the threat before Mankind is destroyed. A fascinating variant of A. Conan Doyle's *The Poison Belt.*

A106. *Exit Life.* London: Scion Ltd., October 1953, 128 p., 1/6d. Cover by Ronald Turner.

Returning to Earth after a two-year voyage of exploration among the planets, the crew—two married couples—are horrified to discover all human and animal life has mysteriously vanished, leaving behind only their domestic chattels and strangely malevolent scorch marks. An exciting, ultimately downbeat novel that keeps the reader guessing.

A107. *The Frozen Limit.* London: Scion Ltd., March 1954, 128 p., 1/6d. Cover by Ronald Turner.

When Dr. Robert Cranston and his partner, Dr. Campbell, perfect a system of deep-freeze surgery, the Medical Council frowns on their experiments and the original volunteer cannot oblige. But a motion picture stunt girl willingly takes his place, and the doctors find themselves facing a murder charge when they cannot revive the girl from a state of suspended animation. Amusing, semi-farcical comedy.

A108. *The Genial Dinosaur.* London: Scion Ltd., February 1954, 128 p., 1/6d. GENIAL DINOSAUR #2. Cover by Ronald Turner.

Herbert, the frisky dinosaur, returns to many and varied adventures, overcomes a threat to condemn him to death as a menace to society, and becomes the kingpin in Earth's battle against a race of mental wizards from Venus who are bent on denuding the Earth of its most valued possessions. An engagingly humorous novel in the style which Fearn most enjoyed writing, but for which publishers gave him few opportunities. See also the first book in the series, *A Thing of the Past* (#A116).

A109. *I Came—I Saw—I Wondered.* London: Scion Ltd., April 1954, 128 p., 1/6d. Cover by Ronald Turner.

Life for Arthur Tredgard, an author, and his wife Lucy, changes dramatically when they play host to the strange Seacombe, who turns out to be a Martian visiting Earth incognito. This quite amusing novel satirizes, amongst other things, SF movies.

A110. *The Lonely Astronomer: An Adam Quirke Adventure.* London: Scion Ltd., May 1954, 128 p., 1/6d. ADAM QUIRKE #2. Cover by Ronald Turner.

Perched on top of a two-mile high column stands the great Metropolitan Observatory. One night, Dr. Henry Brunner, a brilliant astronomer, is found with his head battered in and strangulation marks on his neck, leaving behind a number of suspects, all of whom have reasons to hate him. These include his immediate assistants, Calhoun, the police chief's suspect, and the janitor, Joe, who owns a fantastic Venusian spider as a pet. Adam Quirke is called in to solve the puzzle. The *dénouement* derives from Fearn's short story, "Death at the Observatory" (1938). The first book in the series is *The Master Must Die* (#A112).

A111. *The Magnetic Brain.* London: Scion Ltd., July 1953, 128 p., 1/6d. Cover by Ronald Turner.

Timothy Arnside is severely injured in a spaceship crash on Mars, and the Martians use him as a guinea pig. With the help of a new wonder metal, niridium, the planet's greatest surgeon effects a trepanning operation on the victim's brain. In doing so, he endows the hitherto shy and diffident Arnside with the dangerous gift of being able to read the innermost thoughts of his fellow mortals. An interesting beginning that falls away with careless inconsistencies, probably due to hasty writing.

A112. *The Master Must Die.* London: Scion Ltd., November 1953, 128 p., 1/6d. ADAM QUIRKE #1. Cover by Ronald Turner.

Gyron De London, an utterly ruthless and powerful industrialist in the year 1990, is warned that he will die on a given date. De London takes elaborate precautions, including sealing himself in a steel cube which is totally radiation proof. Yet, on the given date, he dies as predicted. An Adam Quirke SF detective story in the best "locked room mystery" tradition. See also the second book in the series, *The Lonely Astronomer* (#A110).

A113. *Moons for Sale.* London: Scion Ltd., May 1953, 128 p., 1/6d. Cover by Ronald Turner.

Hall Paget, one of London's greatest brain specialists, uses his infant son as a guinea pig in an experimental operation designed to enhance the child's mental capacity by five-fold. The operation appears to be a success, but before Paget can guide his son through the early years of his development, he is killed in the War of 1985, leaving his child a homeless refugee, unaware of the mental powers that will eventually see him locked in battle with the ruler of Mars.

A114. *The Purple Wizard.* London: Scion Ltd., January 1954, 128 p., 1/6d. Cover by Ronald Turner.

Sent back in time, two young time travelers from 1967 find themselves in danger of being executed as necromancers by the dull-witted folk of 828 A.D., who remain unconvinced of such marvels as television and radio. How they extricate themselves and cause an upheaval in the court of the king (who wants to believe them but dares not) form the basis of this new approach to time travel. An amusing variant on Mark Twain's *A Connecticut Yankee in King Arthur's Court.*

A115. *Scourge of the Atom.* London: Scion Ltd., September 1953, 128 p., 1/6d. Cover by Ronald Turner.

Doctor Martin Bond has an intriguing theory. By re-creating on Earth the prototype of a section of Mars, he hopes to piece together the history of the racial descent of the Martians and learn what happened to Mars's extinct civilization. His experiment is a success even beyond his wildest dreams, and he becomes the witness to the end of the human race. The grim ending derives from Fearn's short story, "After the Atom" (1948).

A116. *A Thing of the Past.* London: Scion Ltd., September 1953, 128 p., 1/6d. GENIAL DINOSAUR #1. Cover by "Ferrari" (Philip Mendoza).

Routine mining excavations to level a basalt hill on the outskirts of London uncover a Jurassic-age fissure which plunges into the bowels of the Earth. The miners discover a heritage from a prehistoric era 80,000,000 years old. The sinister remnants of that age become a menace to modern civilization and lead to a terrifying excursion into the past. This novel introduces Herbert, who is also featured in *The Genial Dinosaur* (#A108).

as GRIFF, *house pseud.*

A117. *Liquid Death.* London: Modern Fiction, August 1953, 126 p., 1/6d. Cover by Ray Theobald.

"With English gold sovereigns at their present high value, it doesn't take long for the wide boys to supply the demand in this direction, the difference being that they make their sovereigns to order, establishing a far-reaching racket in counterfeit coins and involving many innocent men and women in their toils." A detective thriller story with SF elements, including a scientist villain and the transmutation of base metals to gold.

as CONRAD G. HOLT

A118. *Cosmic Exodus.* London: C. A. Pearson (TIT-BITS no #), August 1953, 64 p., 9d. Cover by Ronald Turner.

Out of the aftermath of a world war arises a new scientific regime dominated by a mysterious girl. Rayburn Cloud, humanitarian President of a corrupt government, learns the truth about her interplanetary background while fighting to avert global suicide. A complex and very satisfying thriller by Fearn that deserves to be much better known.

as NAT KARTA, *house pseud.*

A119. *Vision Sinister.* London: Dragon Books, November 1954, 144 p., 2/-. CHIEF INSPECTOR GARTH #2. Cover uncredited.

"Could two young women, in full possession of their faculties look through a slide in a door and see a girl being murdered—and yet find the room beyond completely empty when they come to enter it with the police?" Reintroduces Fearn's Chief Inspector Garth of Scotland Yard, who had previously appeared in novels written under the pseudonym HUGO BLAYN (to which one should refer for more details). One of several superior "locked room mysteries" written by Fearn. See also *The Silvered Cage* (#A104).

as PAUL LORRAINE, *house pseud.*

A120. *Dark Boundaries.* London: Curtis Warren, January 1953, 159 p., 1/6d. Cover by Gerald Facey.

"When Commander Herries of the Space Line began to sell the water of Mars as a 'potion' for lengthening life, he had no idea that he was going to create the world's greatest thirst and produce havoc among the two social grades of Earth—the Intelligentsia and the Normals. But produce it he did. Amongst the confusion thus produced, one man thinks clearly, for his own ends—Vance Unthra, the leading scientist of the world, and he sees in the crisis which has hit Earth a way to be rid of all those who do not measure up to what he thinks is an intellectual standard. By his orders, two synthetic worlds are created—Alpha and Omega—and to these are ruthlessly evacuated all the victims of the Martian water, there to rebuild their shattered fortunes and never cross 'The Dark Boundaries' which exist between these worlds and Earth." An ingeniously complex space opera involving intrigue on Mars, Venus, and Jupiter, in addition to the synthetic worlds. The longer format of the Curtis line compared to that of Scion's (160 p. vs. 128 p.) enabled Fearn to produce a more detailed plot than in most of his *"Vargo Statten"* novels.

as LAWRENCE F. ROSE

A121. *The Hell Fruit.* London: C. A. Pearson (TIT-BITS no #), September 1953, 64 p., 9d. Cover by Ronald Turner.

A superior space opera featuring the exploits of Earmar Brown, son of Terrestrial and Martian parents, who operates as a kind of interplanetary "Saint." He and his confidential secretary, Vanita, fight to smash a Venusian conspiracy to flood Earth with a Venusian fruit—the Tropica Cherry—which is addictive. The action includes trips to both Mercury and Venus. Fearn had intended this book to be the first of a series, but when he renewed his *Vargo Statten* contract, he was unable to write SF for any other British publisher outside of Scion Ltd.

as JOHN RUSSELL

A122. *Account Settled.* London: Paget Publications, November 1949, 128 p., 1/6d. Cover by Oliver Brabbins.

A fascinating crime thriller that readily qualifies as SF. An inventor perfects a self-sinking bomb, a device which magnetically polarizes atoms so that all their electrons lie flat, in the same plane, so that substances can pass through one another. The same basic idea was used by Fearn in his *Vargo Statten* novel, *The G-Bomb*, and, as in that novel, the inventor is murdered by a ruthless industrialist seeking to exploit the invention. The development in this earlier story is completely different, however, moving along conventional mystery-thriller lines as the inventor's daughter goes undercover to bring the murderer to justice with the help of an FBI agent.

as BRIAN SHAW, *house pseud.*

A123. *Z Formations.* London: Curtis Warren, March 1953, 159 p., 1/6d. Cover by Gerald Facey.

"Using the secret motive power of a lost flying saucer, physicist Michael Arnott, three companions, and an escaped convict are flung into the void at eight times the speed of light, to eventually land, after the oblivion of acceleration, upon a world that is both extraordinary and terrifying...To the hazards of the mystery world, which include a race of synthetic, friendly people, another race of highly skilled, and yet, pagan scientists, and the advent of a Deluge, is also added the riddle of why the travelers constantly become younger..." An excellent story, one of Fearn's best. The author's byline is listed as BRYAN SHAW on title page.

as VARGO STATTEN

The most popular SF pseudonym of the 1950s paperback writers, STATTEN sold over five million copies of his books, and became the launching pad from which all other SF pseudonyms sprang.

A124. *Across the Ages.* London: Scion Ltd., August 1952, 96 p., 1/6d. Cover by Norman Light.

A chance meeting with a stranger who disappears before his very eyes enables Jeffrey Collins to gain an ancient secret which destroyed Atlantis—a bizarre legacy which enables him to become dictator of the solar system throughout future centuries. Previously published without the last-page epilogue as "Glimpse," in *Star Weekly* (21 February 1952) as by *John Russell Fearn.* A superb piece of storytelling and one of the best in the STATTEN series.

A125. *Annihilation.* London: Scion Ltd., May 1950, 128 p., 1/6d. Cover by Ronald Turner.

The failure of the solar cycle results in the loss of Earth's magnetic field, which eventually leads to the complete destruction of Mankind. Addressing a science fiction convention in 1952, *Fearn* stated this was his best novel. It had originally been written for the American book market in 1949.

A126. *The Avenging Martian.* London: Scion Ltd., January 1951, 128 p., 1/6d. Cover by Ronald Turner.

In the remote past, the evil super-scientists of Venus had totally destroyed Mars to ensure their planet's survival. But the doomed Martians set in motion events involving the sending of two of their race to Earth, which results in their being avenged by a present-day descendant. This is an expanded and rewritten version of "Red Heritage," which appeared in *Astounding*, January 1938, as by *John Russell Fearn.* An archetypal STATTEN novel which was reprinted in the United States as *Survivor of Mars* (*Two Complete Science Adventure Books*, Spring 1953).

A127. *The Black Avengers.* London: Scion Ltd., June 1953, 128 p., 1/6d. Cover by Ronald Turner.

Unjustly banished to Jupiter's penal colony, Dayton Rastor escapes to become the mastermind behind a band of interplanetary outlaws—and solves the mystery of the asteroids.

A128. *Black Bargain.* London: Scion Ltd., December 1953, 128 p., 1/6d. Cover by Ronald Turner.

At first it just looked like a harmless cloud, but then it appeared that every man, woman, and child was doomed through its poisonous influence. From Jupiter comes a strange woman and an antidote—but she demands a horrible price.

A129. *Black-Wing of Mars.* London: Scion Ltd., March 1953, 128 p., 1/6d. Cover by John Richards.

The first explorers on Mars bring back to Earth samples of everything they find, including living specimens of the last surviving life on Mars, the giant Martian moth, and unwittingly threaten Earth with destruction. Previously published as "Winged Pestilence" in *Star Weekly*, 23 May 1953, as by *John Russell Fearn.*

A130. *Born of Luna.* London: Scion Ltd., March 1951, 128 p., 1/6d. Cover by George Ratcliffe.

Cliff Saunders's wife is affected by strange radiations which cause her to build a rocket and pick up an embryo from the moon. The last man of Luna has a mission to save Earth and the descendants of his ancient race from a great meteorite storm which destroyed the moon many millions of years ago.

A131. *Cataclysm!* London: Scion Ltd., February 1951, 128 p., 1/6d. Cover by Zero (Philip Mendoza).

A fantastic interstellar adventure involving the destruction of this universe and the creation of another, *Cataclysm!* is a much-expanded and rewritten version of the plot in "The Devouring Tide," which first appeared in *Thrilling Wonder Stories*, Summer 1944, as by POLTON CROSS. One of the best STATTEN novels.

A132. *The Catalyst.* London: Scion Ltd., December 1951, 112 p., 1/6d. Cover by Ronald Turner.

Scott and Nancy Andrews bring back a small cinder rock from Mercury, not knowing that it is a catalyst which will turn water into gold. It is lost in the sewers of London, and Earth is threatened. An ingenious SF re-working of the King Midas legend.

A133. *The Cosmic Flame.* London: Scion Ltd., October 1950, 128 p., 1/6d. Cover by Ronald Turner.

The inhabitants of a synthetic world beyond the orbit of Pluto come to the aid of Earth when renegade scientists utilize a natural cosmic lens to back up an ultimatum to the world. An entertaining space opera.

A134. *Creature from the Black Lagoon.* London: Dragon Books, September 1954, 176 p., 2/-d. Cover by John Richards.

This novelization of the Universal International Pictures film concerns the discovery of the Gill Man, the half-man, half-fish survivor of another geological era, in a lagoon off the Amazon River. An excellent adaptation of a classic film, but seemingly unknown to film historians, not one of whom has ever mentioned it in a film reference book, *Creature* is now hard to find both in this paperback edition and in the identical hardcover version released from the same publisher. This is now the single most collectible (and valuable!) item of all the British pocket books from this era.

A135. *Deadline to Pluto.* London: Scion Ltd., March 1951, 128 p., 1/6d. Cover by Ronald Turner.

To prevent a catastrophe from disrupting the planetary equilibrium of the solar system, a spaceship races from Earth to Pluto to destroy a gigantic meteorite that has crashed on the planet. A desperate race against time and human nature ensues as the crew rebels against the iron discipline of the ship's captain.

A136. *Decreation.* London: Scion Ltd., October 1952, 96 p., 1/6d. Cover by Roger Davis.

Esau Jones was just a wandering tramp who loved his beer and the country air. But Esau also had the ability to work miracles, which led to problems. A humorous variation of H. G. Wells's "The Man Who Could Work Miracles," and one of the best STATTEN novels.

A137. *The Devouring Fire.* London: Scion Ltd., September 1951, 112 p., 1/6d. Cover by Ronald Turner.

The first spaceship to venture beyond the atmosphere should have been the beginning of a new era for Mankind, but instead, it was to be the trigger for the fiery holocaust which left Earth an almost sterile globe, with only a handful of survivors to start anew.

A138. *The Dust Destroyers.* London: Scion Ltd., February 1953, 127 p., 1/6d. Cover by John Richards.

Amateur inventor Timothy Brown's machine that totally eliminates dust seemed to be a boon, but it started a chain reaction that threatened to destroy life on Earth by allowing harmful radiation to reach the surface unhindered. The basic idea for the novel derived from Fearn's "The Man Who Stopped the Dust," which appeared in the March 1934 issue of *Astounding* under his real name, but with completely different characters. The original novelette on which the novel was based has been acknowledged by SF historians as a genuine classic, but *The Dust Destroyers*, because of its STATTEN association, continues to be overlooked.

A139. *Earth 2.* London: Dragon Books, August 1955, 128 p., 1/6d. Cover by John Richards.

Into a world armed to the teeth there suddenly comes a strange gospel of disarmament. The shedding of weapons has reached almost dangerous proportions when it is realized that clever interplanetary trickery is to blame—trickery from the fantastic Earth 2, an exact duplicate of our own world.

A140. *The Eclipse Express.* London: Scion Ltd., April 1952, 112 p., 1/6d. Cover by Ronald Turner.

The construction of a special stratoplane to enable astronomers to follow the track of a solar eclipse leads to the discovery of a new planet hidden behind the moon, and lays bare the secrets of a vanished lunar civilization. This novel incorporates in modified form much of "Eclipse Bears Witness," which appeared in the March 1940 issue of *Science Fiction*, as by EPHRIAM WINIKI; and also "Valley of Pretenders," as by DENNIS CLIVE, originally published in *Science Fiction* in March 1939. An amazingly prophetic story which forecasts the worldwide televising of the first moon journey (contrary to the repeated assertion by so-called "experts" that "SF got it wrong"), and uncannily describes an actual scientific experiment (the filming an eclipse from the stratosphere) carried out by Concorde decades later.

A141. *The G-Bomb.* London: Scion Ltd., June 1952, 112 p., 1/6d. Cover by Ronald Turner.

Twice thwarted in their attempts to make the nations of Earth destroy themselves, the elders of Mars make one more attempt by making available to the warmongers the ultimate weapon of destruction—the Gravity Bomb. The novel incorporates "The Last Secret Weapon," published in *Marvel Stories* in April 1941 as by POLTON CROSS, with a different interplanetary angle as new material. One of the best STATTEN novels.

A142. *The Grand Illusion.* London: Scion Ltd., January 1954, 128 p., 1/6d. Cover by Ronald Turner.

Dudley Carnforth, gifted beyond the norm with the gift of the gab, and a jack-of-all-trades scientific but master of none, decides it is time to use his abilities to make his mark on the world, and masterminds a trip to Mars—a different sort of trip... A drawn-out novel that would have been better as a short story.

A143. *I Spy.* London: Scion Ltd., April 1954, 128 p., 1/6d. Cover by Ronald Turner.

By 1970 television has reached the peak of perfection, incorporating both color and 3D technologies. TV engineer Curtis Drew, by combining X-rays and television signals, invents the Z-ray...by means of which he can see through walls and spy on any scene. This enables him to learn the secrets of the warlords and their hidden crimes. However, nothing is immune to the merciless Z-ray, not even Drew himself!

A144. *Inferno!* London: Scion Ltd., December 1950, 128 p., 1/6d. Cover by Ronald Turner.

Dick Blake is the sole survivor of a fifty-man expedition to Pluto. On his return, he creates an intrigue which only the super science of a lost Atlantean race can resolve. A grandiose interplanetary adventure.

A145. *Inner Cosmos.* London: Scion Ltd., January 1952, 112 p., 1/6d. Cover by Ronald Turner.

The experiments of a long-dead race lead to an invasion from the microcosm, and ultimately the creation of life on Earth and the origin of the comets. Based on "Worlds Within," which was published in the March 1937 issue of *Astounding* under *Fearn*'s own name.

A146. *The Interloper.* London: Scion Ltd., September 1953, 128 p., 1/6d. Cover by Ferrari (Philip Mendoza).

A power-mad armaments baron fans the flames of war between Earth, Mars, and Venus for his own evil ends, but finds himself pitted against a power even greater than his own—a power which is setting out to preach a new philosophy of trust and understanding between the planets. Sub-plots are derived from "Face in the Sky," which *Fearn* wrote for *Amazing Stories*, September 1939, as by THORNTON AYRE.

A147. *The Last Martian.* London: Scion Ltd., July 1952, 96 p., 1/6d. Cover by Norman Light.

An engrossing interplanetary saga encompassing the mystery of cosmic rays and the interference by ancient Martians interested in evolution.

A148. *Laughter in Space.* London: Scion Ltd., May 1952, 96 p., price. Cover by Ronald Turner.

Banished into outer space for the crime of murder, a scientist seeks revenge by manipulating of a cloud of poison gas in space to threaten the extinction of life on Earth. The novel is expanded from "Laughter out of Space," which appeared in the July 1939 issue of *Future Fiction*, as by DENNIS CLIVE. An inventive and surprisingly downbeat story.

A149. *The Lie Destroyer.* London: Scion Ltd., November 1953, 127 p., 1/6d. Cover by Ronald Turner.

Concerned by the fact that his son is a compulsive liar, and that society is built on sham and pretense, a scientist develops a machine which destroys the ability to lie. Severe repercussions follow when criminals are quick to see the possibilities, and the police are powerless to intervene—because *everyone* has a secret to hide!

A150. *The Man from Tomorrow.* London: Scion Ltd., April 1952, 112 p., 1/6d. Cover by Ronald Turner.

A scientist from the future travels back in time to the present day to carry out historical research, and becomes embroiled in human affairs. Previously published with a slightly more complex ending as "Stranger in Our Midst" which appeared in *Star Weekly* on September 2, 1950, as by *John Russell Fearn.*

A151. *Man in Duplicate.* London: Scion Ltd., April 1953, 128 p., 1/6d. Cover by John Richards.

Playboy Harvey Bradman finds himself involved in many strange adventures when an extraterrestrial from Andromeda creates a duplicate of him. It seems the alien wants to further his experiments in creating a new race from the test tube.

A152. *Man of Two Worlds.* London: Scion Ltd., October 1953, 128 p., 1/6d. Cover by Ronald Turner.

While walking in the Peak District, Walter Cardish is caught in the epicenter of a violent storm and struck by strange electrical forces, becoming two people...one existing on Earth, while an exact duplicate of himself is transmitted to Mars—where Martian super scientists are planning an invasion of his home planet.

A153. *The Micro Men.* London: Scion Ltd., June 1950, 128 p., 1/6d. Cover by Ronald Turner.

Attempts to create eternal life result in the invasion and conquest of Earth from the sub-universe and the coming of the micro men.

A154. *The Multi Man.* London: Scion Ltd., June 1954, 128 p., 1/6d. Cover by Ronald Turner.

As a result of his experiments in cellular biology, Jeoffrey Dexter creates a being that is capable of endless reproduction, but which has none of the reservations of a normal human being. Soon, along with his wife and research partner, Dexter falls prey to the ruthless Multi Man, a creature seemingly unstoppable in its quest for absolute power.

A155. *Nebula X.* London: Scion Ltd., November 1950, 128 p., 1/6d. Cover by Ronald Turner.

By a multimillion-to-one fluke of physics, a long-dead woman, Nebula, is re-created during a laboratory experiment. Beautiful, amoral, and totally evil. she sets out to avenge her dead race. The basic plot of this story is based on "The Multillionth Chance," which appeared in the September 1946 issue of *Thrilling Wonder Stories*, as by **John Russell Fearn**.

A156. *The New Satellite.* London: Scion Ltd., October 1951, 112 p., 1/6d. Cover by Ronald Turner.

The total destruction of the solar system seems assured when the moon begins to disintegrate, leaving a new satellite racing around the Earth, an enigmatic Copper Globe constructed by a mysterious and ancient alien race. Pilot Frank Hurst discovers the strange plans, and makes a space flight to the Copper Globe, only to be accused of planning an invasion of Earth, and of being an alien himself.

A157. *The Odyssey of 9.* London: Scion Ltd., July 1953, 128 p., 1/6d. Cover by Ronald Turner.

From time immemorial the figure nine has had a strange influence on Mankind. Ward Jackson, the ninth son of a ninth son, sets out on an incredible odyssey that takes him from Stonehenge to all nine planets in the solar system, in pursuit of a solution to the cosmic significance of nine.

A158. *1,000-Year Voyage.* London: Dragon Books, November 1954, 128 p., 1/6d. Cover by Ronald Turner.

Rigilius 1, absolute ruler of Earth and the Solar System, is banished along with his despotic retinue on a voyage of no return to the system of Alpha Centauri, where, upon their arrival 1000 years later, his descendants meet their fate.

A159. *Petrified Planet.* London: Scion Ltd., August 1951, 112 p., 1/6d. Cover by Ronald Turner.

A man and his wife, returning from a maiden voyage to Venus, discover that the Earth and everything on it has been suspended in a single moment in time. A well-written and fascinating exploration of the "frozen time" theme, usually confined to short stories.

A160. *Pioneer 1990.* London: Scion Ltd., August 1953, 128 p., 1/6d. Cover by Ronald Turner.

From the ether come mysterious messages announcing that a hitherto unknown Englishman has conquered space, flown to Venus, and is now on his way back to Earth. But is he? An ace reporter sets out to uncover the truth. Expanded from "He Conquered Venus," published under *Fearn*'s own name in the February 1940 issue of *Astonishing Stories*, plus new material and a different ending.

A161. *The Red Insects.* London: Scion Ltd., March 1951, 128 p., 1/6d. Cover by Zero (Philip Mendoza).

A scientist's evil experiment with ants and termites places the Earth in deadly peril which only science from the remote future can overcome. Fearn's sub-plots derive from "Lords of 9016," which appeared under the author's own name in the April 1938 issue of *Thrilling Wonder Stories*.

A162. *Renegade Star.* London: Scion Ltd., December 1951, 112 p., 1/6d. Cover by Ronald Turner.

When the Solar System is doomed to absolute destruction by the close passage of a renegade star, super scientist Evelyn Stokes is Earth's only chance of survival. An audacious novel that sends Earth on a titanic voyage through the universe, the story is a slightly expanded and rewritten version of "The Blue Infinity," which was published in the September 1935 issue of *Astounding* under *Fearn*'s own name.

A163. *Science Metropolis.* London: Scion Ltd., November 1952, 128 p., 1/6d. Cover by Philip Mendoza.

Set in a future when time traveling is commonplace, Fearn's novel tells the story of a population in deadly peril from a Jovian super scientist who has vowed vengeance upon Humanity for the destruction of his home world. This old-fashioned super-science extravaganza does not read well today. The book is actually an abridged version of "Zagribud," which was a three-part serial appearing in *Amazing Stories* from December 1937-April 1938 under *Fearn*'s own name, and which was a sequel to the novel *Liners of Time* (*Amazing Stories*, May-August 1935), published by World's Work in

1947. Both novels were originally written by *Fearn* in 1933 in a pseudo-scientific proto-style which he soon abandoned.

A164. *Space Warp.* London: Scion Ltd., February 1952, 112 p., 1/6d. Cover by Ronald Turner.

A fault in the ether causes temperatures to rise to record levels all over the world as the endless day gets under way. The lives of a number of people are affected in different ways by this strange and terrifying metamorphosis in nature.

A165. *The Sunmakers.* London: Scion Ltd., December 1950, 128 p., 1/6d. Cover by Ronald Turner.

The London Planetarium of 2000 A.D. is perfect in every way except for the model of the sun, but a dangerous experiment in physics to create a sun in miniature results in a strange invasion from the fourth dimension. The first half of this novel is partly based on "Metamorphosis," which appeared under *Fearn*'s own name in *Astounding*, January 1937.

A166. *A Time Appointed.* London: Scion Ltd., March 1954, 126 p., 1/6d. Cover by Ronald Turner.

Thirty million miles out on her maiden voyage to Venus, a space liner encounters the baleful power of a long-extinct race of scientists, a power that destroys the liner without warning, and threatens the Earth with a dreadful legacy that will destroy the Solar System unless it can be stopped in time. The sub-plots derive from "Mystery of the Martian Pendulum," a collaboration between *Fearn* and Ray Palmer, as written by THORNTON AYRE and A. R. STEBER, in the October 1941 issue of *Amazing Stories*.

A167. *The Time Bridge.* London: Scion Ltd., March 1952, 112 p., 1/6d. Cover by Ronald Turner.

A girl is plunged into a state of non-time by a jealous suitor, to be revived five hundred years in the future, where she is a central figure in averting an interplanetary war. The novel is expanded from *Fearn*'s POLTON CROSS story entitled "Prisoner of Time," which was published in *Super Science Stories* in May 1942. Ingenious and well-written.

A168. *The Time Trap.* London: Scion Ltd., September 1952, 96 p., 1/6d. Cover by Roger Davis.

A group of people are faced with a grim struggle when their car suddenly passes into the fourth dimension, including the prospect of never being able to return to their normal way of life. Some adapt to the situation better than others.

A169. *To the Ultimate.* London: Scion Ltd., December 1952, 128 p., 1/6d. Cover by Gordon C. Davies.

A sample of metal from an artificial world discovered fifteen million miles from the sun has strange powers that plunge three scientists into an incredible journey to the dawn of creation through the magic of mathematical and mental metaphysics. The novel is based on the classic "Mathematica" and "Mathematica Plus," both by *Fearn*, respectively appearing in the February 1936 and May 1936 issues of *Astounding*.

A170. *2,000 Years On.* London: Scion Ltd., September 1950, 112 p., 1/6d. Cover by Ronald Turner.

A modern man mentally projects himself into the future to become the linchpin of interplanetary politics and alien oppression. The opening chapter derives from "Wanderer of Time," which was published as by POLTON CROSS in the Summer 1944 issue of *Startling Stories*.

A171. *Ultra Spectrum.* London: Scion Ltd., January 1953, 128 p., 1/6d. Cover by Ronald Turner.

Struggling to repair overhead power lines during a violent storm, Sidney Cassell, an engineer, takes the opportunity to avenge a grudge by murdering his partner. But fate takes a hand when he touches a 100,000 volt cable and survives to become a glowing outcast, the pawn of ruthless businessmen who want to find the secret of cold light.

A172. *Wanderer of Space.* London: Scion Ltd., August 1950, 128 p., 1/6d. Cover by Ronald Turner.

Deep in space a son is born to the Queen of Earth, while back on the politically unstable homeworld, an exact twin is created by synthesis, giving rise to interplanetary intrigue and adventure. An SF variant of Alexandre Dumas's *The Man in the Iron Mask*.

A173. *Wealth of the Void.* London: Scion Ltd., February 1954, 128 p., 1/6d. Cover by Ronald Turner.

The discovery of a planetoid of almost pure gold gives rise to greed and avarice in a group of people, overcoming their finer sentiments as they try to capitalize on the discovery. An SF variant on *The Treasure of the Sierra Madre*. *Fearn* also made a sound film of the story using amateur actors.

A174. *Worlds To Conquer.* London: Scion Ltd., June 1952, 96 p., 1/6d. Cover by Norman Light.

The invention of a matter transmitter leads to murder, avarice, interstellar conflict, and finally, to its inventor's own destruction, but not before he has saved Earth from an invasion from space. An entertaining SF morality tale.

A175. *Zero Hour.* London: Scion Ltd., May 1953, 128 p., 1/6d. Cover by Ronald Turner.

If it were possible to see into the future, could it be possible to avoid death by knowing of fatal accidents in advance? Scientific guinea pig Gordon Fryer knows his doom and sets out to avoid his fate. Previously published as "Deadline," which appeared under *Fearn*'s own name in the December 13, 1952 issue of *Star Weekly*. A well-written human interest story, brilliantly plotted.

as EARL TITAN

A176. *Anjani the Mighty*. London: Scion Ltd., May 1951, 128 p., 1/6d. AN-JANI THE MIGHTY #2. Cover by Ronald Turner.

The lost city of Akada is rediscovered and Tocoto obtains the Jewel from vast stores of treasure left behind by a vanished race. This gives him the power he has always been seeking. Anjani has fallen in love with Rita Perrivale, the widow of the explorer who located the lost city. Another city, Monango, is encountered, which is inhabited by a savage tribe ruled over by the utterly ruthless and beautiful Mea, the last of a once-powerful race. In Anjani, she sees a man worthy of continuing her race, and orders the death of Rita.

A177. *The Gold of Akada*. London: Scion Ltd. (ANJANI THE MIGHT #1), May 1951, 128 p., 1/6d. Cover by Ronald Turner.

Mark Hardnell and his wife are on safari in Africa in search of a legendary lost city. En route, they are deserted by their native guides and murdered by hostile Monango tribesmen. The lives of their twin babies, born during the expedition, are spared. Years pass and the children are brought up by separate native tribes. "Anjani," meaning "White God," is the name given to one twin for his tremendous strength and aptitude for jungle life. His identical twin becomes the ruthless and self-seeking Tocoto, who is searching for the legendary Jewel of Akada, which would give him power over the superstitious natives. Anjani and Tocoto are unaware of each other, and even after meeting, they do not realize that they are of the same family. Instead, they become deadly enemies. *Fearn*'s homage to Edgar Rice Burroughs's *Tarzan and the Jewels of Opar* is obvious. Both novels are now collectors' items commanding high prices.

CRAWLEY FENTON—see: Miles Casson

R(alph) L(eslie) FINN, 1912-

Ralph Leslie Finn was born on January 17, 1912 at London, son of Alec Finerman (an architect) and Leah Lev (a school teacher), and was educated at Oxford University (B.A. 1933) and London University. A freelance writer for many years, he was feature writer for *Reynolds News* (1937-1940), *People* (1941-1945), *Cavalcade* (1946-1948), and *Daily Mail* (1953-1955), and *Sporting Review* (1953-1954). He was also senior copywriter for L.N.P. (1955-1958), and creative director for various advertising firms from 1955. Finn is the author of many novels and screenplays, and won awards for his short stories in 1943 and 1946. Amongst his many books are a number about soccer, and three science fiction novels, none of which he particularly considers worthy. The two books listed below were commissioned by

Gaywood at their high rate of £2 per thousand words, twice that paid to other writers. He also wrote the hardcover *Time Marches Sideways* for Hutchinson (1950).

A178. **Captive on the Flying Saucers.** London: Gaywood Press, January 1951, 123 p., no cover price. Cover by Leroi (Osborne).

Gerard Hanson is wrongly accused of dereliction of duty when his laboratory was destroyed by a flying saucer. By building a machine to capture a flying saucer he hopes to prove his case, but instead, finds himself captive aboard a vast spaceship populated by the Visians, dwarf-like inhabitants of Venus. Their population is declining through the impotency of their males, and Hanson is chosen to mate with the Queen of the Vis—but only after he has gone through the ritual of delight to test his virility. An obscene, unpleasantly sadistic novel with absurd SF elements.

A179. **Freaks Against Supermen.** London: Gaywood Press, December 1950, 123 p., 1/6d. Cover by Leroi (Osborne).

Herbert Jenkins is a scientist who has lived a virtual recluse. He thus survives when the world's population is decimated by the Sickness, and later finds a female companion and a child. Through them he populates the city with mutant Supermen, the New Race of Earth, whose brilliance and inventiveness far exceed that of their "father." But the New Race creates a second and more servile race to perform all their menial tasks, and eventually the servants (the Freaks) rebel. Surprisingly readable and competently written, with the erotic content appropriate to the context of the story.

LEONARD G. FISH

This author also wrote at least one gangster novel for John Spencer Ltd. as LANNY ROGERS, and short SF stories as L. G. FISH and DAVID CAMPBELL. Nothing is known of his personal life.

as FYSH

A180. **Planet War.** London: Archer Press, 1952, 96 p., 1/6d. Cover by Gerald Facey.

Captain John Forrest and a select crew volunteer for a hazardous trip to Jupiter, knowing that other spaceships making the journey have vanished without a trace. Fifty million miles from their destination, the crew suddenly find themselves orbiting a huge planet—but it is not Jupiter! They learn that they have been transported there by aliens who are at war with their neighboring planet. The Cironians want help from the Earthmen, and they show Forrest something which helps form his decision: the true history of the birth of Mankind. An action-packed space opera with good ideas marred by an unfortunate juvenile style.

as CLAUD(E) HALEY

A181. **Beyond the Solar System.** London: Arc Press, 1954, 141 p., 1/6d. Cover by Norman Light.

"The Venusians were a peaceful race; they did not know the first thing about war. So they probably did not know what hit them. They were utterly wiped out, dying in their millions at the touch of the dreadful ray the Mercurians used, their furry bodies scorched to nothingness. The Mercurians could have only one object—to occupy the planet with members of their own race...And Earth was certainly next on the list." Captain Steven Raine and a crew of 500 scientists escape the destruction in the FTL spaceship *Triton*, and start a search for a new home. A routine adventure; the refugees, predictably, eventually return to Earth.

as VICTOR LA SALLE, *house pseud.*

A182. *After the Atom*. London: John Spencer, April 1953, 108 p., 1/6d. Cover by Norman Light.

An atomic war has reduced the human population to a scattering of feuding communities, forever fighting over food stocks. There is little to live for, and it is easy for the invading Dorians to take control. Physically they resemble huge floating brains, mentally superior and telepathic. But John Marsh and Roger Craig discover a weakness: the Dorians cannot employ their powers over long distances or through the Earth—so they know nothing about the people who have moved underground to escape the atomic holocaust.

as JOHN RAYMOND, *house pseud.*

This byline was later credited with a 1957 war novel from John Spencer, and a supernatural story, "The Incredulist," in *Supernatural Stories 2* (July 1954), which was actually written by *R. Lionel Fanthorpe*.

A183. *Zamba of the Jungle*. London: John Spencer (NEW JUNGLE STORIES no #), November 1951, 114 p., 1/6d. Cover by Barry.

Jacob P. Smirkle is a rich man, used to getting everything he wants. And he wants a zoo. So, he meets Kevin Burgess, recognized as Britain's Number One big game hunter, and arranges an expedition to Africa. In the jungle, they catch more than the lion-trap was intended to catch—they catch Athea, white queen of the African tribes and mate of their god, Zamba, the jungle man. Jealousy within the ranks of the expedition leads Van Gort, the surly Dutch explorer, to break away and to tell the tribes that Burgess is taking their queen. Only Zamba can stop the attack on the white men, but he is many miles away, and Van Gort has set out to kill him... A tongue-in-cheek pastiche of Burroughs, and as such, a collector's item.

B. (i.e., William David) FLACKES, 1921-1993

Better known as Billy Blackes, Flackes was born in Burt, County Donegal, Ireland. He began a career in journalism in the Irish country papers during World War II. His first political assignment was reporting the proceedings of the Stormont Parliament for the *Belfast Newsletter* in 1945. In 1947 he moved to London and represented the Press Association at Westminster for ten years. He returned to Ireland in

1957, and in 1964 became the local political correspondent for the BBC, a position he retained until 1982. A consummate reporter, he was awarded an OBE in 1981. Among his other works are three editions of *A Political Directory to Northern Ireland*, and (as co-author) a biography of Viscount Montgomery of Alamein.

A184. *Duel on Nightmare Worlds.* London: Hamilton & Co. (Stafford), January 1952, 112 p., 1/6d. Cover by George Ratcliffe.

This very mediocre space opera, mostly set on Venus features "Tall, wiry, gray-haired, Dr. Rex Kyle," who battles to prevent the occupation of Venus by the Mercurians, as well as conquering Mercury itself. This he proceeds to do after much juvenile adventuring and flashing of colored rays.

as CLEM MACARTNEY

A185. *Dark Side of Venus.* London: Hamilton & Co., 1951, 111 p., 1/6d. Cover by George Ratcliffe.

The opening sentence in this peculiar book reads: "Rocket-Squadron Commander Dan Fury, one of the most distinguished and most decorated young pilots in the British Air Command, looked at the instruments of his ramjet supersonic fighter." After this not-so-promising beginning, the story can only get *worse*! A terribly juvenile jingoistic clap-trap involving hackneyed, belligerent Martians laying plans for an Earth invasion from Venus [sic]. The invaders are foiled by young Dan Fury and his chums, including the inevitable "Professor." The author seems to have derived his SF inspiration from juvenile magazines and comics such as the English *Rover* and *Wizrd*, rather than from *Astounding*.

A186. *Ten Years to Oblivion.* London: Hamilton & Co. ("Authentic" #12), August 1951, 109 p., 1/6d. Cover by George Ratcliffe.

One of MACARTNEY's learned "Professor" characters announces to an Astronomical Assembly that the newly discovered planet Menis "is at this moment more than three hundred million miles away, and it is moving towards us at the rate of a thousand miles a second. And ten years from now, it will approach to within thirteen thousand miles of our planet, and that will mean disaster for everyone." Macartney's abilities as a science fiction writer are about on par with his mathematical skills, since according to his own figures it will only take the planet a little over three days to arrive! One of the characters examines "a wall-sized map of the Solar System" which shows the Earthlike planet, Prima, which exists "between Earth and the Magellanic Cloud." It had been colonized by a spaceship "using the unlimited power derived from solar radiation...after a five-year journey." An eight-man team from "the Galactic Exploration Bureau," operating out of Prima, which Menis is due to pass before threatening Earth, is summoned to fly to the planet Menis and either blow it up or divert it. This novel deservedly sank into oblivion in considerably less time than ten years!

STEPHEN (Daniel) FRANCES, 1917-1989

Stephen Daniel Frances is best known for his creation of the pseudonym HANK JANSON, under which name he became the most popular of the 1950s' American gangster story writers. Born in London, he struggled against poverty (his father died 18 months after his birth) and illiteracy to become a writer. During World War II he was a conscientious objector, issuing a magazine, *Free Expression*, and launching his own publishing company, Pendulum Publications, which issued a number of SF books and the first three issues of *New Worlds* under the editorship of John Carnell. He later founded S. D. Frances (Publisher) Ltd., and wrote many JANSON novels—as well as initiating the ASTRON DEL MARTIA byline—until 1952, when he sold the pen name and moved to Spain. He continued to write as JANSON occasionally until the mid-1960s, as well as penning many more books under a score of pseudonyms.

Frances had a keen interest in science fiction, and wanted to write under the DEL MARTIA byline. Eventually, he penned three HANK JANSON "specials" with SF backgrounds, and a fourth, a reprint of *One Against Time*, was issued in 1969 as ASTRON DEL MARTIN. Frances also worked with W. Howard Baker and published two books in the 1960s under the byline PETER SAXON. He died in 1989.

as HANK JANSON, *house pseud.*

A187. *Tomorrow and a Day.* London: Alexander Moring, 1955, 159 p., 2/6d. Cover by Reginald C. W. Heade.

This is a realistic story of post-holocaust life, with the handful of survivors fighting each other for the few stocks of food remaining. A complex society built by multi-billionaire H. L. R. Dalston, survives, including a vast underground city, planned to withstand the attack. Dalston's dream was to save enough people and technology to repopulate the Earth, to allow the survivors to build a new, free society. But he fails to reckon with such basic human instincts as greed or the lust for power. Here there is also the possibility for one strong man to rule the whole world!

A188. *The Unseen Assassin.* London: Top Fiction Press, October 1953, 142 p., 2/-. Cover by Reginald C. W. Heade (girl's figure only) and Ronald Turner (background city).

The aliens known as the Outsiders unexplicably appear above Earth in their spaceships. They hover in orbit without communicating, silent and ominous, and then, without ever having communicated, depart, leaving behind a deadly legacy. From all over the Earth come reports of a mystery illness. The first symptom is an irritation on the skin, a rash which spreads, then the first drop of blood, then continual bleeding until the victim finally loses consciousness and is finally claimed by death, as his cellular structure slowly breaks down. The novel is marred by shaky plotting and a sleazy undercurrent.

JULIAN E. FRANKLYN, 1899-1970

Born near the Elephant and Castle, Franklyn was an expert on speech forms, writing such works as *The Cockney: A Survey of London Life* (1953) and *A Directory of Rhyming Slang* (1960). His fiction writing started in the 1930s, and included *The Gutter Life* (1935). During the 1950s he worked for Scion Ltd. as an editor. It has been said that he reworked a number of rejected manuscripts, and may be responsible for the birth of VECTOR MAGROON. There is a chance that he submitted his manuscripts to Scion under the byline KARL VALLANCE, but this is not an indication that Franklyn is the author of the novel which appeared under that name. Rather it seems more likely that it was used by Gannet Press (an offshoot of Scion) because the director remembered the name and thought it "hard" enough.

STEVE FUTURE (Pseudonym)

Steve Future may have been the pen name of a contemporary SF fan, Steve Gilroy. Gilroy had a "How to Write SF" article published in a fanzine called *Operation Fantast*, but no work appeared under his own name.

A189.   *Doomed Nation of the Skies!* London: C. A. Pearson (Tit-Bits no #), November 1953, 64 p., 0/9d. Cover by Ronald Turner.

> Reporter Ben Wilkie is sent to the New Forest to investigate a crashed flying saucer which is believed to be from Mars. A missile thrown from the saucer contains a Martian, who takes Wilkie and Pam Collins back to Mars, where the population is slowly dying. The people there are little more than automatons, incapable of emotion—all but a few throwbacks, one of whom intends to take over the red planet, using an invading alien race...

A190.   *Slave Traders of the Sky.* London: C. A. Pearson (Tit-Bits no #), December 1954, 64 p., 0/9d. Cover by Ronald Turner.

> This story opens promisingly on a terraformed Venus, with tensions between colonists from Earth and Venusian natives. However, it quickly deteriorates into a rather routine detective story, albeit set in outer space.

FYSH—see: Leonard G. Fish

E. F. GALE

as JOHN FALKNER

A191.   *Overlords of Andromeda.* London: Hamilton & Co. ("Panther" #193), April 1955, 144 p., 1/6d. Cover by John Richards.

> "Earth was just a slave-state, and the Andromedians were the Masters. But an Earth-native remembered the days when his people owned their planet. He resolved to win it back for them. But the Andromedians had so much and the natives had nothing at all—nothing except courage and brains and determination and the will to obey. They turned to the past, to the 20th

Century, for bloodless weapons with which to fight. The Overlords replied with a massacre. It was cosmic-ray disintegrators against bare hands, and endurance against evil cunning, until the heavens, prompted by man, brought their mighty forces to bear on the conflict." An interesting story, but not very well written.

A192. *Untrodden Streets of Time.* London: Hamilton & Co. ("Panther" #136), December 1954, 143 p., 1/6d. Cover by John Richards.

A man is projected into the future in an attempt to save contemporary humanity, but becomes involved with helping Mankind of the future to survive. An ambitious story, but disappointingly handled.

ROLF GARNER—see: Bryan Berry

MARCO GARRON (House pseudonym)

This house name was used by Curtis Warren for two series of books. The first was a Tarzan pastiche called AZAN, and the second was a "straight" jungle adventure series written by *Dennis Talbot Hughes* as "MARCO GARON." The author of the AZAN series remains unidentified, but it was probably *David Griffiths*.

The AZAN series hero is "Group Captain Donald Chanders, D.F.C. Missing, presumed dead. Solo flight. Lagos-Aden, June 1944." After a plane crash, Chanders is found and nursed back to health by a native whom he names Spitfire. Suffering from amnesia, he makes the jungle his home, and, after six years, has become a legend among the African tribes. This series is, in places, well written and sometimes more credible than the source of its inspiration.

A193. *Jungle Fever,* (author unidentified). London: Curtis Warren, March 1951, 128 p., 1/6d. AZAN #3. Cover by Terry Maloney.

Scaling a mountainous crag to rescue a native child snatched by a giant eagle, Azan kills the bird and rescues the child. While on high, he notices a flying saucer streaking across the sky. Shortly thereafter, he encounters two parties; one Russian and one British, who have abandoned geological research to track down the jungle base of the flying saucers, now very much in evidence in the skies. After a series of the usual jungle-type adventures, the saucers are discovered to come from a man-made base, manned by international conspirators and renegade scientists.

A194. *King Hunters,* (author unidentified). London: Curtis Warren, March 1951, 112 p., 1/6d. AZAN #6. Cover by Terry Maloney.

A party searching for the Tombs of the Kings faces danger from hostile tribes, wild beasts, and less native enemies—two ex-Nazi criminals. Azan captures the Germans, but one escapes. During the hunt for the renegade, Azan is captured by a mad scientist, Yastoda, and forced to become part of a bizarre experiment. Meanwhile, the leaderless party is drawn into a trap set by Rantika, beautiful queen of Zolkani, who wants to find the Tombs for her own purposes.

A195. *The Lost City*, (author unidentified). London: Curtis Warren, November 1950, 128 p., 1/6d. AZAN #2. Cover by Terry Maloney.

This novel begins with Azan at the height of his powers, accompanied by Spitfire, his faithful native companion. They are asked by a dying village wise man to return an enormous ruby which, as a young man, he had stolen from the Lost City of Shalmyra. The wise man goes in and out of a coma, but believes he cannot achieve the release of death until the sacred ruby is returned. An American party is also searching for the city, and events bring them together when the city is found. Azan is acclaimed a hero in Shalmyra when he helps the city fight off an attack on the palace during a bloody civil war. Azan then leads an expedition to the Region of Eternal Darkness, separated from the city by an ancient wall. The region comprises a subterranean jungle, teeming with prehistoric survivors, including the Balyus, a tribe of ape men. After numerous adventures, the party returns with the usual promise not to divulge the location of the city. Enjoyable hokum.

A196. *The Missing Safari*, (author unidentified). London: Curtis Warren, November 1950, 128 p., 1/6d. AZAN #1. Cover by Terry Maloney.

The news of a party of whites on safari attracts Azan, especially when he finds that they intend to pass through the dangerous B'fani country. His warnings are ignored, and he narrowly escapes death in saving them. More adventures befall the group in Ghazala, where Azan hopes to find news of John Cumberland and Bruce Redbourne, leaders of a previous safari which has disappeared, and the reason behind this second trek into the jungle.

A197. *Tribal War*, (author unidentified). London: Curtis Warren, January 1951, 112 p., 1/6d. AZAN #5. Cover by Terry Maloney.

Azan discovers that Edward Robinson and his daughter have been kidnapped. He saves Jean from horrible death in the hands of Zimbao tribesmen, after she has escaped her original captors, Portugese gun runners who are supplying Mohiga, witch doctor of the Bastao, with weapons to make him supreme leader of all the surrounding lands. He uses the stolen treasure as payment. The Treasure of Tahato belongs to the Naganno, whose Queen orders a war with the Bastao to regain what is rightfully theirs.

A198. *White Fangs*, (author unidentified). London: Curtis Warren, January 1951, 128 p., 1/6d. AZAN #4. Cover by Terry Maloney.

White Fangs is a leopard raised by Azan and Spitfire from a cub; the cat remains loyal to Azan but wild and ferocious to their enemies, a good advantage in the remaining novels. The vigorous and complicated plot revolves around a party of six people of mixed nationalities whose plane crashes in the jungle. Hostile natives intend to use them as sacrifices to abate the wrath of a killer-leopard which is terrorizing the tribe, but Azan rescues them. The party then becomes embroiled in a fantastic adventure involving the usual war between mythical jungle races, the Thatorans and the Kalkulans, whose wicked Queen, Jamorca, commands an army of giant apes. Fast-moving hokum in the Edgar Rice Burroughs style.

JOHN (Stephen) GLASBY, 1928-

Glasby was born on September 23, 1928 at East Retford, Nottinghamshire, son of Edgar Stuart Glasby (a locomotive engineer) and Elizabeth Alice Hempsall, and was educated at King Edward VI Grammar School and Nottingham University, where he graduated with an honors B.S. degree in chemistry in 1952. Since that time he has been employed by I.C.I. as a research chemist. Always a keen astronomer, he joined the British Astronomical Society in 1958, becoming head of the Variable Star Section in 1965, and is the author of several textbooks, beginning with *Variable Stars* (1968).

During the 1950s, he wrote many science fiction books for the paperback publishers, and many short stories for John Spencer magazines. His connection with Spencers lasted many years, and Glasby later wrote westerns, crime, romance, supernatural thrillers, and war novels for them.

Although his output must rank him as one of the most prolific authors in this volume, his stories are redeemed by a natural flair for writing. His SF is very good, capable of standing on its own even today (allowing for recent scientific discoveries), and his style is very fluent, occasionally suspenseful and chilling. The influence of A. E. van Vogt can be seen in some of his stories (*Satellite B.C.* [as RAND LE PAGE] and *Zenith-D* [as PAUL LORRAINE]). Glasby is one of the few authors we invite you to seek out based on story merit rather than novelty value. His later output included works under such pseudonyms as JOHN ADAMS, B. L. BOWERS, J. B. DEXTER, JOHN C. MAXWELL, JOHN MULLER, and J. L. POWERS among, no doubt, many others, as well as one book published under his own name in 1971 called *Project Jove*.

as VICTOR LA SALLE, *house pseud.*

A199. *Dawn of the Half Gods.* London: John Spencer, October 1953, 128 p., 1/6d. Cover by Ray Theobald.

> They came out of the void, from Venus, only to find there was no answer to their radio signals. Earth was dead, and on the moon, Man's greatest achievement, the Lunar Military Base, was a mass of rubble and blasted wreckage. Here, the crew of the *Stellar Polaris*, led by Commander John Forrest, discovered one sole survivor—but he was mad! To their questions he could only answer that the children had destroyed the armed might of the military base. When they finally reached Earth they found that what he had said was true. The children *had* taken over control of the world. But then, these were no ordinary children—and their little weapons were almost enough to overthrow the armed superiority of the *Stellar Polaris* herself!

A200. *Twilight Zone.* London: John Spencer, February 1954, 130 p., 1/6d. Cover by Ray Theobald.

> In the remote future, the sun has cooled and brought another Ice Age to Earth. Mankind is trapped in huge shells in the twilight zone of Mercury. Man becomes regimented, with the Overlords holding sway over the remnants of the human race. The Sun restores itself, but the knowledge is kept from the humans; when the truth is finally learned, a revolt breaks out.

as A. J. MERAK

MERAK was John Glasby's most popular byline, one thought by many to have been a real name. It was used mostly in the John Spencer magazines, and later on five novels for Badger books between 1959-1960. One early SF novel was also published under this name for Hamilton & Co.

A201.   *Dark Andromeda.* London: Hamilton & Co. ("Panther" #95), January 1954, 159 p., 1/6d. Cover by John Richards.

"Earth was threatened with attack from the huge space fleets of the Hundred Suns of Andromeda—an attack that the Terran Fleet could not hope to defeat. Only one chance remained, and that was the chance that a skilled and experienced saboteur might just have time to strike his blow before the enemy could launch his attack. It was Captain Blair whose mission this became, and it was this ace-saboteur who raced against death on planet after planet, as the zero-hour approached when Earth would face the attacking fleets of Dark Andromeda."

as KARL ZIEGFRIED, *house pseud.*

A202.   *Dark Centauri.* London: John Spencer, April 1954, 130 p., 1/6d. Cover by Ron Embleton.

Entertaining space opera adventures for the crew of the *Stellar Crusader*, who are projected to Alpha Centauri by a Hyperspatial Transmitter. There, they discover an alien race of apparent primitives using the remnants of an advanced technology. They eventually establish that the technology is the legacy of an ancient race who had progressed to such a high peak of evolution that there was nothing more for them to discover. Eventually, they began to regress, to drop back along the scale of evolution and revert to beast-like state. One of Glasby's best stories.

A203.   *The Uranium Seekers.* London: John Spencer, December 1953, 128 p., 1/6d. Cover by Ray Theobald.

In the remote future, Earth's despotic rulers face annihilation when the solar system's supply of radioactive materials nears exhaustion, and all life-support machinery beings running down. They hope to defeat their fate by using a time machine, created in 1974, whose young inventor is suddenly pitched into the future. There he becomes embroiled in a series of inventive adventures, featuring all manner of Martians and Venusians *et al.*

with Arthur Roberts as BERL CAMERON, *house pseud.*

A46.   *Cosmic Echelon.* London: Curtis Warren (TERRAN EMPIRE series), August 1952, 128 p., 1/6d. Cover by Gordon C. Davies.

"The vast federation of outworld states that formed the Terran Empire smarted under the unjust, evil influence of the Emperor Jrun. Daily, his tax gatherers swooped down on the member planets, wringing the people dry of money and goods...But away from the decadent shell that Jrun had built up, out among the lonely suns of the Edge, a new power is growing. It has fallen on Kelda, the young star-king of Zandyr, to form the union known as the Cosmic Echelon. A fleet of ships that dared to match the armed might of Imperial Terra." A peculiar mixture of Asimov and van Vogt that doesn't quite work.

A51. *Sphero Nova.* London: Curtis Warren, 1953, 159 p., 1/6d. Cover by Ray Theobald.

"They came out of the star-strewn wilderness around Sol, these alien creatures. And their object was the vicious, total destruction of the Federation of Worlds. Earth was one of the last planets to be attacked, and here they were opposed by the Earth Council; six men who held the destinies of a hundred billion in their hands. But in the end, there remained only one man out of the six to fight against them. Velga Dorne...and he himself was a hunted man. Death and terrible destruction followed him across the wastes of space in the search for the crazy, nightmare planet that had spawned the creatures."

with Arthur Roberts as RAND LE PAGE, *house pseud.*

A204. *Satellite B.C.* London: Curtis Warren, May 1952, 127 p., 1/6d. Cover by Gordon C. Davies.

A rather uneven first novel, this book is a mixture of A. E. van Vogt's *Space Beagle* and Eric Frank Russell's "Jay Score" stories. Some episodes are successful, especially the opening segment where the crew of the interstellar exploration ship *Ultima Thule* is menaced by a brain-eating alien. Later episodes, which include the discovery of a world inside a sun, are less gripping.

A205. *Time and Space.* London: Curtis Warren, August 1952, 128 p., 1/6d. Cover by Gordon C. Davies.

"There were many reasons why the Time Kings sent their warrior hordes back through the endless corridors of Time. The ancient spaceships had been destroyed by the wrath of a people smarting under the aftermath of Galactic War. But though the lanes of space were deserted to them, the Time Kings possessed a weapon more deadly than any other—the Amphichron. Sweeping through the gray ages, the warriors destroyed and pillaged the peaceful eras of the past." A strange mixture of space opera and sword & sorcery fantasy, with touches of Asimov and van Vogt, but vitiated by a conventional "shoot 'em up" plot line.

A206. *Zero Point.* London: Curtis Warren, October 1952, 128 p., 1/6d. Cover by Gordon C. Davies.

"Over the long years, ships of the Interplanetary Confederation had scoured the empty wastes surrounding Sol, searching desperately for a sister planet, a companion for the isolated worlds of the Solar System. Of the ships that were sent out, many returned. But the answer was the same. There were no planets! The worlds of Sol were alone in the Great Dark that swirled across the boundless heavens. It was not until Steve Rane and Nick Brodine reached across the yawning gulf of light years to Sirius that they found the strange planet that rotated on its complicated orbit around the twin sun. It was a discovery that plunged the planets of Sol into the greatest race of all time. For whoever controlled the alien planet controlled the solar system." One of Glasby's better early efforts.

with Arthur Roberts as PAUL LORRAINE, *house pseud.*

A207.   *Zenith-D.* London: Curtis Warren, December 1952, 159 p., 1/6d. Cover by Gordon C. Davies.

"To the crew of the Exploratory Ship *Canopus*, outward bound on the first intergalactic voyage to the flaring suns of mighty Andromeda, the evil whisperings spilled out of the nebula into deep space came as a warning. This was something far beyond their previous experience. Nor were they the only ones to come under the malignant influence of the alien intelligence. In the empty, murmuring void, virtually halfway between the two galaxies of stars, a solitary sun streaked away from Andromeda, dragging its lonely, ammonia-ridden planet with it. And it was here that the explorers gained their first glimpse of the black horror that lay straddled across the intergalactic darkness." Action-packed Glasby homage to van Vogt's *Voyage of the Space Beagle*.

CHARLES GREY—see: E. C. Tubb

VOLSTED GRIDBAN (House pseudonym)

This was originally *E. C. Tubb*'s personal pseudonym, invented by Scion Ltd., for whom *Tubb* wrote three novels. He then wrote two for Milestone under this pseudonym, before Scion got an injunction to stop their use of the name. The name was then given to *John Russell Fearn*, who wrote all subsequent GRIDBAN novels and short stories.

A208.   *Alien Universe,* (by E. C. Tubb). London: Scion Ltd., November 1952, 94 p., 1/6d. Cover by George Ratcliffe.

SEE: *E. C. Tubb* for synopsis.

A209.   *De Bracy's Drug,* (by E. C. Tubb). London: Scion Ltd., February 1953, 1/6d. Cover by John Richards.

SEE: *E. C. Tubb* for synopsis.

A105.   *The Dyno Depressant,* (by John Russell Fearn). London: Scion Ltd., June 1953, 128 p., 1/6d. Cover by Ronald Turner.

SEE: *John Russell Fearn* for synopsis.

A106.   *Exit Life,* (by John Russell Fearn). London: Scion Ltd., October 1953, 128 p., 1/6d. Cover by Ronald Turner.

SEE: *John Russell Fearn* for synopsis.

A107.   *The Frozen Limit*, (by John Russell Fearn). London: Scion Ltd., March 1954, 128 p., 1/6d. Cover by Ronald Turner.

SEE: *John Russell Fearn* for synopsis.

A210.   *Fugitive of Time*, (by E. C. Tubb). London: Milestone Publications, February 1953, 112 p., 1/6d. Cover by Ronald Turner.

SEE: *E. C. Tubb* for synopsis.

A108.   *The Genial Dinosaur*, (by John Russell Fearn). London: Scion Ltd., February 1954, 128 p., 1/6d. GENIAL DINOSAUR #2. Cover by Ronald Turner.

SEE: *John Russell Fearn* for synopsis.

A109.   *I Came—I Saw—I Wondered*, (by John Russell Fearn). London: Scion Ltd., April 1954, 128 p., 1/6d. Cover by Ronald Turner.

SEE: *John Russell Fearn* for synopsis.

A110.   *The Lonely Astronomer: An Adam Quirke Adventure*, (by John Russell Fearn). London: Scion Ltd., May 1954, 128 p., 1/6d. ADAM QUIRKE #2. Cover by Ronald Turner.

SEE: *John Russell Fearn* for synopsis.

A111.   *The Magnetic Brain*, (by John Russell Fearn). London: Scion Ltd., July 1953, 128 p., 1/6d. Cover by Ronald Turner.

SEE: *John Russell Fearn* for synopsis.

A112.   *The Master Must Die*, (by John Russell Fearn). London: Scion Ltd., November 1953, 128 p., 1/6d. ADAM QUIRKE #1. Cover by Ronald Turner.

SEE: *John Russell Fearn* for synopsis.

A113.   *Moons For Sale*, (by John Russell Fearn). London: Scion Ltd., May 1953, 128 p., 1/6d. Cover by Ronald Turner.

SEE: *John Russell Fearn* for synopsis.

A211.   *Planetoid Disposals Ltd.*, (by E. C. Tubb). London: Milestone Publications, January 1953, 112 p., 1/6d. Cover by Ronald Turner.

SEE: *E. C. Tubb* for synopsis.

A114.   *The Purple Wizard*, (by John Russell Fearn). London: Scion Ltd., January 1954, 128 p., 1/6d. Cover by Ronald Turner.

SEE: *John Russell Fearn* for synopsis.

A212. *Reverse Universe,* (by E. C. Tubb). London: Scion Ltd., December 1952, 128 p., 1/6d. Cover by John Richards.

SEE: *E. C. Tubb* for synopsis.

A115. *Scourge of the Atom,* (by John Russell Fearn). London: Scion Ltd., September 1953, 128 p., 1/6d. Cover by Ronald Turner.

SEE: *John Russell Fearn* for synopsis.

A116. *A Thing of the Past,* (by John Russell Fearn). London: Scion Ltd., September 1953, 128 p., 1/6d. GENIAL DINOSAUR #1. Cover by Ferrari (Philip Mendoza).

SEE: *John Russell Fearn* for synopsis.

GRIFF (House pseudonym)

GRIFF was a house pseudonyms used on some fifty gangster novels, the majority of which were the work of Ernest McKeag and F. Dubrez Fawcett. The novel listed here is borderline SF.

A117. *Liquid Death,* (by John Russell Fearn). London: Modern Fiction, August 1953, 126 p., 1/6d. Cover by Ray Theobald.

SEE: *John Russell Fearn* for synopsis.

DAVID (Arthur) GRIFFITHS

David Arthur Griffiths, London fan and author, was a regular attendee at the White Hart. He scouted manuscripts there for Curtis Warren, where he was employed as a reader. He wrote a few novels for them himself to supplement his wages, books which exhibit considerable knowledge of standard SF conventions, based around uninspired Ray Theobald covers. While most of the plots are hackneyed, Griffiths showed a certain amount of vigor and occasional ingenuity. *Task Flight* (as KING LANG) is probably his best work.

Griffiths left Curtis Warren to join the Army Catering Corps, and appears not to have written any more SF stories. There is also a good chance that he was the author behind the "Azan the Apeman" series, under the byline MARCO GARRON. Griffiths had great potential. It is a pity he did not develop it.

as GILL HUNT, *house pseud.*

A213. *Fission.* London: Curtis Warren, January 1952, 111 p., 1/6d. Cover by Ray Theobald.

William Harding is recalled from holiday by an old friend who has, he claims, invented a time machine. His heart condition prevents him from testing the machine himself, so Harding sets off into the future to collect samples of a radioactive isotope that could solve the world's energy crisis.

He travels faster and faster through the centuries, past a world devastated by atomic war, past a future invasion by telepathic aliens, and further, until he discovers that he cannot return, and his only hope is to find some future race with the power to help him. One of Griffiths' best novels—quite imaginative and written with a light touch. Possibly influenced by Eric Frank Russell and Leslie J. Johnson's novelette, "Tomorrow" (1937).

A214. *Vega.* London: Curtis Warren, October 1951, 111 p., 1/6d. Cover by Ray Theobald.

In the 26th century, Gilbert Bradley receives a message from an old friend to join him at a secret government research base in Germany. As he approaches there is a tremendous explosion. Calvin, head of research, suspects sabotage, which has ruined the last stage of experiments designed to produce a force field of negative energy. Then, Calvin dies, apparently of natural causes. On Pluto there are more disturbing problems—an invisible barrier surrounds the planet, allowing nothing to pass. A well-written and complex story of alien invasion, nicely understated.

as KING LANG, *house pseud.*

A215. *Astro Race.* London: Curtis Warren, February 1951, 112 p., 1/6d. Cover by Ray Theobald.

Astro Race is a reasonably entertaining space opera whose starting point centers on the commercial intrigues of rival development corporations who are mining on Jupiter and competing to get their shipments back to Earth first. The plot develops nicely with the discovery of a new "galactic drive," and ends with the establishment of a human colony on a planet in the Sirius star system. Theobald's cover, however, is really awful!

A216. *Gyrator Control.* London: Curtis Warren, January 1951, 112 p., 1/6d. Cover by Ray Theobald.

This adventure story is set in the far future after a war between Earth and Mars. Stanley Leinster—whose discoveries led to space travel—was hailed as "Saviour of the Race," when Earth spaceships successfully concluded the war and contained it in space. When he perfects his ramifications of the "Leinster Principles," he fears that his new discoveries may lead to further wars, so he translates his work into ancient Greek. His intention is to entrust copies of the translation to younger friends for eventual release to the world when it is ready. Meanwhile, the Martians plot to rise again to overthrow their Terra-strial conquerors. Vaughan, one of Leinster's assistants, steals the secrets of the "Gyrator Control" and offers it to the Martian warlords. Theobald's cover work is still atrocious.

A217. *Projectile War.* London: Curtis Warren, September 1951, 111 p., 1/6d. Cover by Ray Theobald.

The Procyonics—a human-type race from the Procyon star system—have established beachheads on the outer planets of the solar system and are intent on taking the inner worlds. Richard Douglas, a young atomic physicist, is recruited into military service to become an undercover agent. Once captured by the Procyonics—who have a secret plan for which they are recruiting captured Earth scientists and technicians—Douglas must somehow get the information back to Earth. A routine adventure, competently handled. Theobald's cover work at its daftest.

A218. *Rocket Invasion.* London: Curtis Warren, August 1951, 111 p., 1/6d. Cover by Ray Theobald.

Chan Houston, of the Terrestrial Space Force, discovers a wrecked spaceship. A baited trap, it leads to his own ship and crew being transported to the planet of the Meciti, a humanoid race who plan to invade Earth. The Meciti are destroyed at the eleventh hour by the release of an influenza virus (à la *War of the Worlds*) against which they have no defense. *Rocket Invasion*, like all of the Curtis titles, had its own built-in handicap in that it had to be written around a dreadful (Theobald) cover.

A219. *Task Flight.* London: Curtis Warren, February 1951, 112 p., 1/6d. Cover by Ray Theobald.

A Militiaspatial Command spaceship follows a smuggler to Centauri 54 and lands on the airless planet. Then *something* happens, the ship shivers, and the crew experiences a momentary blackness, only to awaken on a different planet, Quin'atr. Natives tell them of the dead land of M'hor, where the three survivors travel. They journey to a deserted city, where they are contacted by telepathic voices. Earthmen discover their galactic heritage in an interesting space opera.

as DAVID SHAW

A220. *Laboratory "X".* London: Curtis Warren, November 1950, 128 p., 1/6d. Cover by Terry Maloney.

This book is a ham-fisted space opera treatment of an interesting SF concept...what happens when terrestrial civilization encounters an alien race who are the embodiment of exactly the *reverse* characteristics of Humanity? The germ of a good idea is swamped in a hackneyed adventure treatment.

A221. *Planet Federation.* London: Curtis Warren, November 1950, 150 p., 1/6d. Cover by Ray Theobald.

Stephen Holland and two companions return to Earth after several years on the *Stardust*, the first ship to explore interstellar space, to find Earth has been conquered by the Kelpi and the population has been placed under hypnosis. They meet resistance fighters from Mars and eventually overcome the Kelpi by destroying their base on the Moon, and by blowing up their hypnotic ray machine. Very bad space opera, with the Kelpi being depicted as the usual one-eyed, green, slimy, bug-eyed monsters, complete with tentacles. Theobald excelled himself with a nude cover of dubious taste.

A222. *Space Men.* London: Curtis Warren, January 1951, 128 p., 1/6d. Cover by Ray Theobald.

Blood and guts are on the spaceways as Captain Jerry McLaughlin single-handedly captures thirty renegade spacemen on the planet Zovana, despite intensive radiation exposure. (He apparently gains immunity by eating a native Zovanian meal rich in iron and silicon!)

VON GRUEN—see: Brian Holloway

CLAUD(E) HALEY—see: Leonard G. Fish

FRANZ HARKON (Pseudonym)

A223. *Spawn of Space.* London: Scion Ltd., November 1951, 112 p., 1/6d. S.E.C. #2. Cover by Ronald Turner.

The crash landing of a spaceship on a Pacific island leads to unexpected danger for Space Express Security (S.E.C.) man Dog and his friends. While investigating the cause of the crash, he becomes the first to see one of the huge monsters that later become known as Zimmos. He suspectsd that there is a connection between the Zimmos and the increasing tension between Earth and the dying planet of Mellanya. Dog travels to the planet to discover how the Mellanyas are introducing rampaging Zimmos and crashing Earth ships—an event that becomes all too real for Dog when his own return trip turns into disaster. Indeed, the entire novel is a disaster.

as ASTRON DEL MARTIA, *house pseud.*

A92. *Interstellar Espionage.* London: Gaywood Press, 1952, 100 p., 1/6d. S.E.C. #3. Cover by Leroi (Osborne).

"A journey through Space is a hazardous undertaking at the best of times. But when the Space Express Company's expedition is planned to look for supplies of Crystonium—the new element which counteracts gravitational pull—then it is full of peculiar perils of its own. Foreign powers are just as anxious to find Crystonium, and not all of them are above smuggling their own agents aboard the company's spaceship. But the job has its more attractive aspects—as 'Dog,' S.E.C. security officer, discovers when he meets Mena Diamenter, the female scientist who is to lead the expedition on its perilous journey to Nebulae Sixty-Six." The same characters appear in the novel, *Spawn of Space*, by FRANZ HARKON. Abject rubbish.

A93. *Space Pirates.* London: Gaywood Press, February 1951, 112 p., 1/6d. S.E.C. #1. Cover by Leroi (Osborne).

"After the prototype space ships have stood the tests of their journeys out into the great voids, regular scheduled services operate between Earth, Mars, and Venus. This entails large, Earth-manned bases on the latter two planets, and these are not easy to build. First one space ship full of scientists, technicians, and valuable equipment goes astray between Earth and the planetary bases. Then another...and another...They have all gone somewhere...but where? The only way to find out where a kidnapper keeps his hostages—is to get kidnapped yourself! That is what the company's detective did..." The first of this author's S.E.C. series of three boring, mediocre novels.

PETER HAWKINS, 1924-

Peter Hawkins is a London-born SF fan. He only wrote one novel, under the house name KARL MARAS, and about a dozen short stories, all of which appeared in *New Worlds* and *Science Fantasy* (under his own name). He is no longer active in the field, although he still reads SF from time to time.

as KARL MARAS, *house pseud.*

A224. *The Plant from Infinity.* London: Paladin Press, 1954, 128 p., 1/6d. Cover by Ronald Turner.

This unjustly-overlooked novel is extremely well written, and is further enhanced with a quite superb Turner cover painting which illustrates an incident in the story. The opening background and several of the characters are borrowed from Jack Williamson's *Legion of Space*, with a Space Academy and Space Marines. However, the story that is developed is highly original and realistically low-key; it is to be regretted that *Hawkins* did not continue as a novelist. The title describes alien seed spores drifting into the solar system, which take root on all of the planets in the solar system, many of which have been terraformed.

GEORGE (i.e., Oswyn Robert Tregonwell) HAY, 1922-

George Hay was born in Chelsea, London in 1922. "Childhood reading of John Russell Fearn's *Liners of Time* and Arthur Eddington's *The Nature of the Physical* instilled into me a deep distrust of linear time, as opposed to lived time. I gobbled up SF's 'Golden Age' in search of something like genuine thought and metaphysics.

"After three hard-labor years in wartime Army depots serving in the Ordinance corps, I went happily over the water into Normandy and then Brussels, where I learned French and the delights of conversation in a land where even (especially?) the layabouts talked philosophy. I went on thus for two years on the bum in Paris and Vienna. In the former, I read Korzybski's *Science and Sanity* in the Sorbonne Library, and Jack Williamson's *The Humanoids*, purchased monthly with trembling hands the *Astounding* serializations as it came to the stands in Brentano's. In the latter, I discovered Vienna actually lived up to its image for charm and irresponsibility.

"Back in England, I took up writing for Hamilton & Co. and as a secretary for the Dianetic Association, invited L. Ron Hubbard to the U.K. Unhappy with the general British dilettante approach to Sf, I founded the Science Fiction Foundation and helped edit early issues of its journal with the hope that this would encourage actual *application* of the subject. Only litcrit emerged, but at least it was good litcrit. Recent cash cuts are now forcing the Foundation to admit that there is a demand for SF as a lateral thinking generator. My own actions have insured that a Foundation Library and other resources will now be available for any schools or researchers that wish to use them."

As an author, George Hay wrote a few novels in the 1950s, but stopped in 1951 (SEE ROY SHELDON for details). As a promoter of SF, he has edited a number of anthologies, including *Hell Hath Fury* (1963), *The Disappearing Future* (1970), *Stopwatch* (1974), *The Edward De Bono Science Fiction Collection* (1976; an anthology of stories illustrating De Bono's lateral thinking theories). More recently, he edited the original series PULSAR, which sadly lasted only two editions (1978-1979).

A225. *Flight of the Hesper.* London: Hamilton & Co., December 1951, 112 p., 1/6d. Cover by George Ratcliffe.

A highly original story of a giant starship heading into deep space on an exploratory mission on the "generation ship" principle, *Flight* describes how tensions develop between the original crew and the second generation. An attempted landing and colonization of an extra-solar planet is doomed because the crew suffer from agoraphobia. The climax of the story, when one man battles against the ship computer, which is sentient and is controlling the human captain, is a foreshadowing of Arthur C. Clarke's HAL in *2001: A Space Odyssey.*

A226. *Man, Woman—and Android.* London: Hamilton & Co. ("Authentic" #10), June 1951, 106 p., 1/6d. Cover by George Ratcliffe.

Hay's first novel revealed a thorough familiarity with SF and a definite panache. Much of the action takes place on the artificial world of Paradise, where "a man could taste any pleasure the universe held, and many it did not—at a price." The concept of an artificial pleasure world has been much imitated since. The plot concerns the machinations of ancient Martian "watchers" who interfere in the destiny of Mankind when they see the danger of war with the androids, a servitor race.

A227. *This Planet for Sale.* London: Hamilton & Co., October 1951, 110 p., 1/6d. Cover by George Ratcliffe.

An appealing, and at times amusing, space opera detailing the struggle of Federal forces against Starways Inc., a tyrannical private organization spread across the galaxy. One of the central characters is an android named Pomfret, a prototype model created by an advanced race who then descended back into barbarism and feudalism.

as KING LANG, *house pseud.*

A228. *Terra!* London: Curtis Warren, January 1952, 112 p., 1/6d. Cover by Ray Theobald.

Terra! is an amusing tale of alien invasion and red-tape bureaucracy. Morgan Lee fights single-handedly against the multi-tentacled Vegans with the help of his spaceship, *Spacebug*. He runs into trouble when a warrant is put out for his arrest, and launches a one-man revolt against the Federation of Planets, eventually leading to the formation of a new Democratic Union of Planets, bringing peace between Terra and the aliens.

IRVING HEINE—see: Dennis Hughes

BRIAN HOLLOWAY

Holloway wrote a number of SF adventures for Curtis Warren, none of which are particularly memorable. He also penned foreign legion and western novels for Curtis Warren under other house names, including Adam Dale, Bentley Gerrold, John Karn, and Cal Scott. Nothing is known of his personal life.

as BERL CAMERON, *house pseud.*

A47.   *Destination Alpha.* London: Curtis Warren, March 1952, 127 p., 1/6d. Cover by Gordon C. Davies.

A unique example of post-war British SF mediocrity is to be found in this story, in which the main action and dialogue is obviously based on the author's then recent wartime experiences in the R.A.F. A Martian invasion is successfully repelled, and the Earth arms itself to the teeth in readiness to repel any future extraterrestrial invasion, building what are described as "Super-titanic flying air-craft carriers [sic]."—huge space fortresses that are equipped with officers and ratings and an entire space fleet. True to the traditions of British pulp SF, a new planet, Alpha, is discovered between Mars and Jupiter, and the Martians, signatories to a non-aggression and mutual aid pact with Earth, claim to have been attacked by Alphians. The Earth's armada is sent to Alpha, leaving the Martians free to launch a second invasion against Earth (they have, obviously, invented the Alphian attacks). Then, in the words of the blurb: "How the Alphians help to avert a second interplanetary conflagration is the theme of this scientific story of the Outer Reaches of space, by America's Master of Science Fiction." Pass the barf bag...

as NEIL CHARLES, *house pseud.*

A78.   *Planet Tha.* London: Curtis Warren, March 1953, 159 p., 1/6d. Cover by Gerald Facey.

"Momentary carelessness on the part of an otherwise unimportant technician sent the rocket-ship Ventura blasting on her way to the planet Tha just twenty-four hours ahead of schedule. Commander Blair thus found himself not only short of crew, but saddled with a company of three civilians, one of them a woman. In due course, Ventura touched down on Tha, which proved to be inhabited by a vastly superior race of corporate beings. But they were creatures with a problem; creatures who were planning to evacuate their world and invade another." Plodding style and shaky science.

A81.   *Titan's Moon.* London: Curtis Warren, March 1952, 112 p., 1/6d. Cover by Ray Theobald.

A runaway planet which has jumped its orbit heads for Earth. A spaceship manned by scientists heads for Titan, as the planet has been named, and discovers that it is inhabited by a peace-loving race whose science is far in advance of our own. All hard labor is undertaken by robots, and the Titanians devote their time to experimentation; they had already split the atom, and had attempted to split the neutron, with devastating results for their planet. The usual Holloway mediocrity, filled with ghastly pseudo-science derelictions.

as VON GRUEN

A229. *The Mortals of Reni.* London: Curtis Warren, April 1953, 159 p., 1/6d. Cover by Gordon C. Davies.

"For over two hundred years, the distant planet of Reni had been occupied and colonized by troops and technical experts from Earth. The gentle-natured Renians had always trusted the Earth powers; their beautiful women intermarried with the stalwarts from Earth and a state of friendship existed which it seemed nothing could destroy. Nothing but threatened calamity, that is. And a terrible Fate threatened the Renian world when its sun's light and warmth suddenly ceased, bringing the planet back into the Ice Age almost overnight. Evacuation, the World Council ordered; bring back all troops, all material, all technicians—and leave Reni to its fate." An ambitious allegory of racial exploitation, vitiated by the author's dreadfully ponderous style.

as KING LANG, *house pseud.*

A230. *Trans Mercurian.* London: Curtis Warren, February 1952, 112 p., 1/6d. Cover by Ray Theobald.

Professor Kendell, on the first expedition to Mercury, receives an incomplete message saying that one of the crew is a spy. Cliff Dawson, minerologist, is revealed to be a drug addict, but is he the spy? On Mercury they discover Sodium Uranyl, but make an even bigger discovery when they relaunch the ship: a planet between the Sun and Mercury—the legendary Vulcan! They start back to Earth, but as they near it, the spy makes his move... As silly as it sounds.

as RAND LE PAGE, *house pseud.*

A231. *"A" Men.* London: Curtis Warren, March 1952, 127 p., 1/6d. Cover by Gordon C. Davies.

"For fifteen years Professor Julian Baxter was a prisoner of a strange race of creatures that inhabited the planetoid Amor, one of the smallest of the myraid asteroids. After nine years of more-or-less benign captivity, he managed to send a message to Earth. Quite by chance, a prospector, hunting for uranium deposits with the aid of a Geiger counter and a discredited space-flyer, Bart Kennedy, locates the ship from Amor—and as a consequence, a secret expedition leaves Earth for Amor, with the avowed intention of rescuing the Professor from the sub-human creatures who have no intention of letting him go." They just don't write them like this any more...thank God!

as ARN ROMILUS, *house pseud.*

A232. *Beyond Geo.* London: Curtis Warren, March 1953, 159 p., 1/6d. Cover by Gerald Facey.

Professor Spurling leads a search for a planet where evolution is only just beginning in the hope of discovering how life arose on Earth. He and the crew of *Terra 1* land on three planets far beyond Pluto. On Terra Nova, they find a civilization centuries behind our own; on Secundus, they find a civilization that has solved the secrets of time travel and which already knows the fate of the spaceship and the problems the crew will face when they finally land on the third, the primeval planet, Zyxen. *Beyond Geo* contains some imaginative ideas, but as usual is ruined by the author's plodding and repetitive style.

as BRIAN SHAW, *house pseud.*

A233. *Lost World.* London: Curtis Warren, July 1953, 159 p., 1/6d. Cover by Gordon C. Davies.

"The mind of Theophilus Rhenstein was very like a critical mass; it required so very little to set off a chain reaction that could not be countered. For Theo Rhenstein had a plan for ending strife by splitting the Earth literally in two; one half to be given to those who supported one form of ideology, the remaining hemisphere for those who disagreed. The trouble was that Theo could actually *do* what he planned—which was the reason for the planet Cassio suddenly becoming a lost world in the infinite cosmos." Plodding narrative, very weak science, absurd flowery conversations.

as BRIAN STORM

A234. *Red Storm.* London: Curtis Warren, March 1952, 112 p., 1/6d. Cover by Ray Theobald.

In 2195 the Moon is invaded by aliens and an Expeditionary Force is launched against the enemy. A scouting crew captures a creature that exits a huge sphere—a swog. The swogs are the slaves of the hostile women of Venus, who need space for colonization. This somewhat involved, mediocre mishmash of a story is probably loosely adapted by the author from his own experiences in the Armed Services, with ludicrous results.

EDWARD R. HOME-GALL

A235. *The Human Bat.* London: Mark Goulden Ltd. (FANTASY LIBRARY #1—"Caught in the Spider's Web"), 1950, 128 p., 1/6d. HUMAN BAT #1. Cover by Roland G. Davies

Written by a noted writer of boys' stories, this book is a weird mixture of high camp juvenile adventuring and chilling violence. The "hero" is The Human Bat, a costumed psychotic who makes *Batman* appear almost normal. Mechanical batwings give him the power of flight, and from his fingers he is able to project energy beams. His mission in life is to save young boys from a life of crime. Here, he smashes a criminal mastermind (masquerading as a robot spider!) who recruits boy thieves by poisoning their minds with "kleptotoxin."

A236. *The Human Bat vs. the Robot Gangster.* London: Mark Goulden Ltd. (FANTASY LIBRARY #2), 1950, 128 p., 1/6d. HUMAN BAT #2. Cover by Roland G. Davies.

More spectacular high camp, and even more violence (dead policemen everywhere!), as the sinister Dr. Syntax sends out a gigantic armed robot to commit jewel robberies. The robot is accompanied by a schizophrenic schoolboy controlled by the disembodied brain of his twin, who has been dismembered by his mad scientist father. By turns hilarious, repellent, and oddly fascinating.

CONRAD G. HOLT—see: John Russell Fearn

DEN(N)IS (Talbot) HUGHES

Dennis Talbot Hughes is the mystery man of British SF, one who sadly remains untraced by these authors. His earliest known works are 24- and 32-page pulp western, crime, and romance stories dating from the late 1940s. He seems to have worked mainly for a small number of companies: Hamilton & Co. and its offshoots, Curtis Warren, and Grant Hughes, with most of his work going to the former of the two.

His full output will probably never be known, but he wrote at least seventy-five books under a profusion of pennames (his own name was usually shortened to DENIS HUGHES), many of which were science fiction. His writing shows a remarkably fast and flowing quality, although his speed and style allowed no more than cardboard characterization and hackneyed plots. His SF completely disregards standard astronomical conventions ("solar system," "galaxy," "universe," "planet," and "star" are used and misused interchangeably), and his early work under such names as GILL HUNT and GEORGE SHELDON BROWN rate as some of the worst SF novels ever published; but his later science-fantasy stories from the second half of his short career show that he could be a capable and sometimes excellent writer. Characterizations in these books improved, the allegorical-dream-fantasy sequences are far above his SF sections (he sometimes mixed both styles in the same book), and some of the later novels are quite readable (*Blue Cordon*, as DEE CARTER; *Twenty-four Hours*, as NEIL CHARLES; and *House of Many Changes*, as VAN REED).

Hughes vanished from the writing scene when Curtis Warren folded in November 1954, although his appearance with Brown Watson later that year may indicate that he continued to write for them under other, unknown house names. Below are listed the books he wrote as *Den(n)is Hughes.*

A237. *The Earth Invasion Battalion.* London: Curtis Warren, October 1950, 128 p., 1/-. Cover by George Ratcliffe.

The world's ruling council is threatened by civil war unless vital material resources can be found. An expedition is sent to Venus in two spaceships, led by Commander Fortis. But even before the launch, there is trouble—someone sabotages one of the ships. In space, there is a confrontation, and Shaw Capel and his companions find themselves stranded in the void while the sinister metallurgist, Vultan, takes over the other ship and continues the voyage to Venus. Capel's ship is repaired and then it is a race to save Fortis from Vultan and the strange inhabitants of the shrouded planet. Competently written, but altogether an uninspired and mediocre action story.

A238. *Formula 695.* London: Curtis Warren, November 1950, 128 p., 1/6d. Cover by Terry Maloney.

A normal space run from Earth to Venus turns into a deadly adventure when the liner, piloted by Wayne Dorman and Pete Shorn, is dragged off course by some mysterious force. Landing on Phraetiles 78, they discover they are not the first explorers there. They are captured by Doctor Truffi, a brilliant scientist and formerly one of their passengers. They are to be the guinea pigs in an experiment which Truffi hopes will prove the power of his time-distorting drug, Formula 695. He sends Shorn, Dorman, and Sonia Baylis into Earth's future to collect information on the latest ray-gun developments from a secret government scientific laboratory. On arrival, they discover an apparently petrified world with no sound or movement. A surprisingly well-written and quite imaginative story.

A239. *Moon War.* London: Curtis Warren, January 1951, 128 p., 1/6d. Cover by Ray Theobald.

While on a routine patrol of the "outer galaxy" [sic], Rekel has seen a vast force of spaceships on a course that would bring them to Terra. Soon after he arrives back on Terra, he is sent to check further reports sent by Dr. Tondell on the Moon, and discovers that an advance party of aliens from Gamma 7 has taken the base with the intention of launching an attack on Terra. Rekel and four survivors escape imprisonment and try to warn Terra. A second spaceship crashes on the Moon, and while trying to save the crew, Rekel and and his companions are recaptured, not knowing whether or not their messages have reached Terra. A ghastly space opera mish-mash.

A240. *Murder by Telecopter.* London: Curtis Warren, October 1950, 127 p., 1/-. Cover by George Ratcliffe.

A futuristic mystery thriller, with the SF element being a television gizmo which can view either the past or the future—the Telecopter (from "televising optic"). This book was trashed by the fan reviewers at the time of publication (one suspects due to the uninspiring cover) and has remained in publishing limbo ever since. To be fair, it is quite well written and successful within its own modest canvas, and certainly much better than some of Hughes's space operas which immediately followed.

A241. *Warlords of Space.* London: Curtis Warren, November 1950, 128 p., 1/6d. Cover by Ray Theobald.

A book that is so shockingly bad that it's almost enjoyable! This wild and woolly tale of an Interplanetary Federation of Terrans, Venusians, Martians, and (God help us) Uranians features a fabulously rare mineral called "Molgamium," which is discovered on the planet Branium. A trading route is opened, but when ships begin mysteriously to disappear, interplanetary salvage operators Bellamy and Horton are called in to solve the problem—which they do, after a series of utterly ludicrous adventures. For some reason (perhaps the publisher's insistence) Hughes, a talented writer, deliberately wrote in a dreadful, mechanically pulp style, peppered with outrageous astronomical errors. And yet...the plotting shows a refreshing ingenuity.

as MARVIN ASHTON

A242. *People of Asa.* London: Curtis Warren, June 1953, 159 p., 1/6d. Cover by Gordon C. Davies.

"A moonlit bay, sailing in a boat on calm waters with a beautiful girl seemed perfect to Ashton; but the calm of the evening is soon disturbed by the surfacing of a huge black sphere. A sudden storm heralds their first meeting with the People of Asa, who plan to rise from their underwater home and conquer the surface with a far-superior technology." An oddly appealing and original story of conflict with an inhuman enemy.

as RAY BARRY

A243. *Blue Peril.* London: Curtis Warren, March 1952, 128 p., 1/6d. Cover by Gordon C. Davies.

"Gregory Conrad was a doomed man, though right until the end he still imagined he could escape. Even the significance of Brooking's remark about using his brain failed to register. So Conrad perished and Brooking's dream came true: the monster was created. The trouble began, of course, when Brooking discovered that the Thing his genius had made not only possessed a will of its own, but superhuman powers as well. There followed a reign of terror during which people died and the peace of the world was threatened." One of Hughes's best efforts.

A244. *Death Dimension.* London: Curtis Warren, February 1952, 112 p., 1/6d. Cover by Ray Theobald.

Robert Varden nearly died when his plane was caught in an electrical storm, but somehow he survived and awoke in the hospital in a single bed. But someone else was in the bed with him, someone that nobody else could see, that nobody else could hear, someone who said his name was Robert Varden! An extraordinary and chilling fantasy.

A245. *Gamma Product.* London: Curtis Warren, April 1952, 127 p., 1/6d. Cover by Gordon C. Davies.

"Dr. James Marshal's Gamma Transference Process was aimed at providing the key to practical travel in space. By it, he intended to bridge the gap between planets, to open the void to human movement. The planet Venus was his first target. But the process failed in its object, and its failure was beset by unexpected results." The process opens a tunnel into a strangely unreal world inhabited by even stranger monsters who hold many humans captive for study.

A246. *Humanoid Puppets.* London: Curtis Warren, May 1952, 127 p., 1/6d. Cover by Ray Theobald.

Gina inherits the house of her Great-Aunt Tabitha, and sets out to discover the truth behind the stories of the puppets; she breaks the seal of Thaa-an and releases the four spirits embodied in the puppets: Jealousy, Hate, Lust, and Fear, imprisoned there many years ago by the gods. Now, with their Master freed from his restraint in a mortal body, Gina and her fiancé Martin have to save themselves from their imprisonment as humanoid puppets in the hands of the Master. An intriguing fantasy, reminiscent of A. Merritt's *Burn, Witch, Burn.*

A247. *Ominous Folly.* London: Curtis Warren, February 1952, 112 p., 1/6d. Cover by Ray Theobald.

Jane and Diana find themselves on a road that never ends. Eventually, they sink into a deep sleep, only to awaken on an island where time stands still. The small community there is ruled by a time traveler they call the Master. The girls meet Alvarez and Ellery, who also want to escape the island. But the only way is to ask the Satyr to guide them through the Ring of Storms! Entertaining dimensional fantasy.

as GEORGE SHELDON BROWN

A248. *Destination Mars.* London: Edwin Self, 1951, 128 p., 1/6d. Cover by Ronald Turner.

"GSB here tells the story of the spaceship *Aphid*, built in the Western Hemisphere of the world of the future to conquer space and make the adventurous journey to the planet Mars. Sabotage and interference from the Eastern Hemisphere delay the start of the space explorers, but finally their ship takes off across the millions of miles of space on their hazardous journey to Mars. The explorers reach their destination with the intention of claiming it for the Western Hemisphere, but find unexpected opposition to their plans from the Martians, who have themselves perfected a spaceship of an advanced type." A "fantastic and horrifying" novel in Hughes's most mechanical vein. One of his worst.

A249. *The Planetoid Peril.* London: Edwin Self, March 1952, 128 p., 1/6d. Cover by Terry Maloney.

"Two dauntless space explorers, Ted and Johnny Stevens, traveling through the dark, unmapped emptiness of the galaxy, strike hidden peril and horrors far beyond the imaginations of ordinary men. Forced down on an unknown planet, they are helpless against the might of the terrible Mist People of Bekel, and how they struggle to prevent the evil designs of these inhuman beings, aided by the beautiful Princess of Bekel and the intrepid

space explorer, Nick Dannert, makes a fantastic and horrifying story."
Absolute drivel from beginning to end.

as BERL CAMERON, *house pseud.*

A48. *Lost Aeons.* London: Curtis Warren, January 1953, 159 p., 1/6d. Cover
by Gordon C. Davies.

The crew of a space station falls captive to a strange power—an uncontrolled alien spaceship racing towards an unknown destination where a
cosmic mystery unfolds. One of the best of the "straight" SF novels written by Hughes.

as DEE CARTER

A250. *Blue Cordon.* London: Curtis Warren, September 1952, 128 p., 1/6d.
Cover by Ray Theobald.

"When Lieutenant Thomas Savage of the Polar Warfare Research Station
found the frozen corpse of a woman from another age, he little knew into
what fearful realms her supernatural influence would lead him. By taking
the Blue Cordon from her mummified body, he opened the way to a journey through Fear and the Land of Eternal Dark. His companion was a girl
whose uncanny likeness to the dead woman—the fabulous Ingrid, Winter
Princess of the Northern Night—only added to his own tribulations.
Imagine, for instance, the thoughts of the man who, loving a human girl,
and in turn being desired by one of the immortal spirits, is called on to
chose between them, only to find that in every respect, the two are apparently identical." An extraordinary fantasy, loosely based on Norse mythology.

A251. *Chloroplasm.* London: Curtis Warren, December 1952, 159 p., 1/6d.
Cover by Gordon C. Davies.

"In A.D. 2043, the world seemed doomed to suffer the impact of total war
on a hitherto undreamt of scale...But it is only a handful of men and
women, living and working in the underground dumps of destructive force,
who fully appreciated the danger. They feared for their fellow beings; but
when the war itself was due to start, the blow came...not from a mortal enemy, but from a far more terrible foe. There was nothing partisan in its
onslaught, for the enemy was a being without emotion or mercy, an alien
Intelligence." An ingenious mixture of realistic SF and surreal fantasy,
written around a gloriously bad-taste B.E.M. cover!

A252. *Purple Islands.* London: Curtis Warren, January 1953, 159 p., 1/6d.
Cover by Gerald Facey.

"To leave the Earth in a vessel designed to ride the emptiness of outer
space would certainly demand of its crew the very highest qualities and
determination. But if the journey was to be a one-way trip, with the object
of establishing an offshoot of the human race on a distant world, then every
mortal quality would have to be considerably strengthened. Such was the

project launched by Doctor Helenus Smith. He selected his crew with apparently small regard for the obvious essentials, but in doing so had his own reasons. The trouble began when a nameless world interposed itself on their course, appearing from nowhere. They landed because they had no choice, and it was then the hands of fantasy were laid upon them." Another weird blend of SF and outright fantasy.

as NEIL CHARLES, *house pseud.*

A75.   *Beyond Zoaster.* London: Curtis Warren, May 1953, 159 p., 1/6d.
        Cover by Gordon C. Davies.

"From the dying world of Ginya the wisdom of Zahn, its ruler, reached out and viewed the Earth with covetous eyes. Here, he realized, his race would prosper and be safe from certain extinction. The peoples of Earth were decadent, sunk in idle complacency. Conquest was assured. And conquest achieved." A small group of Earthmen, based on Zoaster, plan to free the Earth using a synthetic army of supermen, but do not reckon on the intervention of Zoaster's inhabitants. Superior Hughes fantasy, with a weird eroticism unique to this author.

A76.   *The Land of Esa.* London: Curtis Warren, October 1952, 128 p., 1/6d.
        Cover by Ray Theobald.

The whole thing started as a joke played by Noel and his wife Prega on Gately, a crashing bore with a theory about reincarnation. They told him about the long-dead civilization buried beneath the waters around Capri. When Gately saw through the joke, he gave Prega a strange reward...the Golden Clasp of Zedae—a clasp that opens up a gateway to the Land of Esa, where Noel is plunged into desperate battle to save the people of Esa from the evil Zadae. One of Hughes's better fantasies, albeit somewhat bloodthirsty!

A79.   *Pre-Gargantua.* London: Curtis Warren, June 1953, 159 p., 1/6d. Cover
        by Gordon C. Davies.

"Man is established on Kliron XIV, a dark, bleak, barren little globe used solely as a base for spatial patrol ships. Life on Kliron is no bed of roses...for the first time in their lives, men find themselves confronted by an enemy against which no weapon can prevail. Worse even than the Master Entity, the Gargantua, are its slaves, evil Flowers of Darkness that bloom where no life can exist. It is a peril that extends to Earth itself..." A weird mixture of SF and outright fantasy.

A80.   *Research Opta.* London: Curtis Warren, October 1953, 160 p., no price.
        Cover by Gordon C. Davies.

"It was a daring experiment, made possible through the medium of advanced instruments which offered scope in the realms of micro-dissection...life-forms had been created by means of chromosomic manipulation. But the impact of the resulting entities was to have a disturbing effect on the man who made them." A measurement of the cerebral potential of the microscopic organisms shows that they are capable of superhuman intelligence, and thanks to a synthetic growth accelerator, potential masters of Man. Imaginative fantasy.

A82. *Twenty-Four Hours.* London: Curtis Warren, July 1952, 128 p., 1/6d. Cover by Gordon C. Davies.

"Fate's selection of Nick and Pat for the task of preserving the world is one of those problems which will always remain unsolved. Outwardly, they were hardly a suitable pair. One was liable to be branded a traitor; the other was incurably ill. And yet to them fell the colossal responsibility of doing what they did—destroying the alien threat at terrible sacrifice to themselves." A man and woman have twenty-four hours in which to save Earth from invasion and enslavement. They are subjected to physical and psychological torture, but come through unflinchingly, finally turning the tables on their tormentors, but destroying themselves in the process. A fine, at times almost surrealistic, thriller in Hughes's best vein.

A83. *World of Gol.* London: Curtis Warren, August 1953, 159 p., 1/6d. Cover by Gordon C. Davies.

"When James Gellen managed to talk his way into skippering the schooner, *Blue Chihuahua*, he little knew what kind of weird events he was destined to meet. The purpose of the voyage was to find out if lovely Maxine MacIntyre was dead or alive...But even before the passage began, Gellen had to face the mystery of men who died of fear, of a crew that deserted *en masse*, and a stranger who presented him with the Seal of Freedom. But on Miriloa itself, there were stranger things, for Miriloa was the gateway to Gol, and Gol was the underworld of evil more terrifying than anything hitherto known to Man." Surreal fantasy.

as LEE ELLIOTT, *house pseud.*

A95. *Bio-Muton.* London: Curtis Warren, October 1952, 128 p., 1/6d. Cover by Gordon C. Davies.

"The aims of Laurie Paton and his colleagues was a goal which no other scientists had ever attained...the creation of a living entity by means of synthetic biological structure. But working on their isolated island base, they unleashed a force for which they had never bargained, and against which they were powerless. They created, not the entity they aimed at, but a window in Time, and unexpectedly a channel through which the forces of Darkness assailed them." Compelling fantasy, with realistic characters, woven in Hughes's unique style.

as IRVING HEINE

A253. *Dimension of Illion.* London: C. A. Pearson (TIT-BITS no #), March 1955, 64 p., 0/9d. Cover by Ronald Turner.

A pilot named Franklin Braun loses consciousness for one minute while flying his plane over Texas, and awakens to find he has traveled over seven thousand miles during his "blank." Later, Braun is taken via flying saucer to meet Illion the First, Mind Supreme and ruler of the alien inhabitants of another dimension. Braun is given a strange order: to save Earth from self-destruction through propaganda—or by force, if necessary.

as GILL HUNT, *house pseud.*

A254. *Elektron Union.* London: Curtis Warren, June 1951, 112 p., 1/6d. Cover by Ray Theobald.

The newly opened route between Earth and Tanus is an attractive business proposition to a number of small companies, including Elektron Union, headed by Pete Conner and Jim Baylis. The Union has operated on the margins even during the best of times, and Pete and Jim suspect a rival company when their ships being disappearing on the new route. A fiery meeting with Moira Garton of Union Travel leads to a race to find the cause, but the convoy of ships is caught in a beam that pulls them to the edge of the galaxy, where they land on an alien planet. Another of the atrociously-written space operas by Hughes, essentially a transplanted western.

A255. *Hostile Worlds.* London: Curtis Warren, February 1951, 112 p., 1/6d. Cover by Ray Theobald.

Two "stars" are discovered heading for our "galaxy," causing earthquakes and storms on the inner worlds. Vaughan heads a group that escapes the destruction of Mars and heads for Celes and Phenae. They are met by a spaceship and receive a message from Earthmen who crashed on Celes many years ago. The group lands on the planet, hoping to find the Earth-men, but are captured by Celesians, who need their help in overthrowing the evil Pheneans. And all the while, the two worlds are drawing closer and closer together. An absolutely appalling Hughes space opera.

A256. *Planet X.* London: Curtis Warren, February 1951, 112 p., 1/6d. Cover by Ray Theobald.

A case of space piracy leads to a long chase through unexplored space for Crane, Spacial Police Patrol Captain. Eventually he reaches the Cradden-donck Galaxy, where Fragen, the pirate, lands on a planet four times the size of Jupiter. Crane follows him down and the situation seems dead-locked: Fragen's ship cannot escape the planet's gravitational pull; Crane cannot leave until he has rescued the hostages. Fragen captures Crane, but neither of the men has reckoned with the appearance of the planet's inhab-itants, nor the intervention of an even stranger life form controlling them. Rotten space opera.

A257. *Spaceflight.* London: Curtis Warren, August 1951, 111 p., 1/6d. Cover by Ray Theobald.

Kit Grierson is working on a stored energy space drive motor which he hopes will free Earth from reliance on Venurium, a mineral found only on Venus. Earthmen fear that the slave race used to mine the mineral on

Venus will overthrow their masters, leaving Earth's Space Navy grounded without fuel, and opening Earth to invasion. The plans are stolen by Dorice, Grierson's assistant, who is under the power of a Venusian, and he has to travel to Venus to catch her. A chance sighting of a derelict spaceship and the rescue of the crew's only survivor offers a solitary clue to where the plans may be hidden. Another shoddy space opera.

A258. *Spacial Ray.* London: Curtis Warren, September 1951, 111 p., 1/6d. Cover by Ray Theobald.

The prospecting ship *Deimos* picks up a distress signal and tracks it to an asteroid, where they rescue a girl whose story sends them to Tollaea 2. A strange molecular growth starts to form on their ship, and the crew discovers a beam emanating from deep space. With Earth's Space Navy a distant two-months flight away, they decide to track the beam to its source: Antar Vee, where alien vessels capture them. The aliens inform them that they are planning to evacuate their world—and make Earth their new home. Yet another appalling and meritless space opera.

as VON KELLAR, *house pseud.*

A259. *Ionic Barrier.* London: Curtis Warren, August 1953, 159 p., 1/6d. Cover by Gordon C. Davies.

Space travel is being impeded by the existence of a natural "ionic barrier" which is destroying space machines trying to reach beyond the atmosphere. Ertzan, a scientist who had previously forecast the existence of the barrier, is missing and believed dead. Actually, he is continuing his space research for a foreign power, an apparent traitor to the cause. One of Hughes's rare "straight" SF novels, this book is actually quite remarkable. Set in the near future, it describes how space travel would be so expensive and dangerous that only governments could attempt it, and with uncanny prescience, it delineates the international rivalry and intrigue that was mirrored in the American-Russian "Space Race" of the late 1950s through the 1970s. One of the author's best novels.

as BRAD KENT, *house pseud.*

A260. *Biology "A".* London: Curtis Warren, March 1952, 128 p., 1/6d. Cover by Gordon C. Davies.

"As far as Lieutenant Waldon was concerned, it began when he and his hard-pressed unit were rescued from certain death by a seeming miracle, to watch an enemy force march blindly to destruction in the frozen hills, victims of mass remote control. But that was only the beginning! When the girl with the red hair arrived, Waldron was to find himself embroiled in the most amazing experiment of all time...The Brain." A superior Hughes fantasy.

A261. *Catalyst.* London: Curtis Warren, January 1952, 112 p., 1/6d. Cover by Ray Theobald.

Michael Corrigan leases a cottage on Dartmoor, and on his first night there, meets a young girl walking alone on the moor at the height of a storm. Their story becomes more complex as they find themselves linked to the same future event: the coming of the blue lichen. Seegor, the leader of the Organized People, and Vana fight to save the underground dwellings and foodbeds from the ever-swelling growth of lichen. When no answer to the problem can be found, Seegor makes a brave decision to seek out Dirk, the outlaw scientist who killed his father and to ask his help. This story marked the start of Hughes's transformation from "straight-SF" hackery to intriguing science-fantasy.

A262. *The Fatal Law*. London: Curtis Warren, February 1952, 112 p., 1/6d. Cover by Ray Theobald.

Karen Maire discovers some strange side-effects to a duplicating ray invented by Professor Norrenson, when he uses her as a guinea pig. She finds that she can instantly travel any distance just by thinking about her destination. Her new boyfriend also falls foul of the ray, and together they try to find the professor, to return to their real bodies, and to stop a sudden and terrifying crime wave before the professor discovers another frightening aspect of their new powers which would make capture impossible. A weird and wonderful Hughes fantasy with a dreamlike atmosphere.

as JOHN LANE

A263. *Maid of Thuro*. London: Curtis Warren, November 1952, 128 p., 1/6d. Cover by Ray Theobald.

"The arrival of a party of aliens from a distant world would arouse mixed feelings in the mind of any human witness involved. But if the strangers prove to be the advance party of a gigantic global migration scheme, most human beings would almost certainly be afraid. Hardly surprising, therefore, that Mike and Jay, caught up in the mess of just such a situation, were two very frightened people...Borka, global ambassador from Thuro, selected them as assistants to aid his plan, and they were automatically blessed—or cursed—with the weird Thuron ability to move in Time. It was Borka's task to choose a suitable period in which to start his mass colonization of the world we know and love. Traveling ahead in time, he and his unwilling allies make their fateful choice." An extraordinary and compelling Hughes time-traveling fantasy.

A264. *Mammalia*. London: Curtis Warren, September 1953, 159 p., 1/6d. Cover by Gordon C. Davies.

"For space operators to find a derelict ship on one of the many dead worlds at the fringe of the galaxy was not unusual, but in this instance it led to one of the weirdest adventures ever experienced by mortal beings. From a salvage point of view it was a worthless find, but its log book—and the small but priceless cargo it carried—opened up a wide field of speculation, prompting the people who found it to penetrate deeper into space in search of the nameless world from which the wreck came." Typical Hughes fantasy, with the Spirit of Mammalia and a fight against the Seven, evil guardians of the darkness.

as RAND LE PAGE, *house pseud.*

A265. *Asteroid Forma.* London: Curtis Warren, February 1953, 159 p., 1/6d. Cover by Gordon C. Davies.

This interesting "straight" space opera tells of the introduction of a 5C drive which opens the way to travel throughout the whole galaxy. This enables thousands of worlds, many with their own particular humanoid races, to join together in a Galactic Federation. The only problem lies in communication, but when the secret of instantaneous communication is discovered, it is exploited by unscrupulous individuals in search of power.

as GRANT MALCOM

A266. *The Green Mandarin Mystery.* London: Curtis Warren, October 1950, 127 p., 1/6d. Cover by Ray Theobald.

Unlike the hackneyed space operas which comprised most of Hughes's work in 1950-51, *The Green Mandarin Mystery* is a scientific detective story. Ray Ellis is asked to discover why a number of top scientists have disappeared. He is contacted by a man dressed in black who hypnotizes him into joining the Green Mandarin, but the post-hypnotic suggestion is discovered by Gerald Baine, his assistant. Acting as if he is still under control, Ellis is taken to a castle where he discovers the identity of the Mandarin and a plot to take over the world to breed a more perfect race. A somewhat cliched but fast-moving story, superior to anything else that Hughes wrote during this period.

as G. R. MELDE

A267. *Pacific Adventure.* London: Curtis Warren Ltd., March 1954, 159 p., 1/6d. Cover by Gordon C. Davies.

"It was the beginning of a new and terrifying form of war that was launched among the nations of the world in a strange and bloodless way of conquest." An excellent "straight" future war story.

as VAN REED, *house pseud.*

A268. *House of Many Changes.* London: Curtis Warren, August 1952, 128 p., 1/6d. Cover by Gordon C. Davies.

"When creation, which is contrary to all the accepted Laws of Nature, springs directly from Genius in the grip of Evil, the results may well take a form so terrible as to be beyond human understanding. Philip Grayling did what he did when he turned his back on the beauty of Right, choosing instead the Paths of Darkness. He perished through the medium of his own foolhardiness, but even in death, his genius survived, an ally of Evil. To his sister, Veronique, to his friend, McGrath, and to his partner, Harman, he left a heritage of such awful malignancy that all three were engulfed in a sea of unspeakable peril." A charmingly bizarre mixture of mad scientist "laboratory horror" story and allegorical fantasy in the unique Hughes style.

as RUSSELL REY

A269. *The Queen People.* London: Curtis Warren, July 1952, 127 p., 1/6d. Cover by Ray Theobald.

"What human mind could conceive of a world in which one woman, dead for a thousand years or more, still rules and mothers an all-male race, alien to her own? Such were the Queen People, weird and uncanny in their strange existence. And what of the human beings who were tossed among them by the fickle hand of Fate...? You will walk beside them, feel the unearthly fascination of the lovely Pepicoona, share the fear of mortal beings confronted by the vast unknown of Metaphysical Change, men and women for whom the phrase 'there is no return,' has a terrible, significant meaning." An utterly fantastic, surreal, and erotic fantasy that shows Hughes's enigmatic talent at its best. As different from his earlier (1950) efforts as chalk from cheese!

A270. *Valley of Terror.* London: Curtis Warren, July 1953, 159 p., 1/6d. Cover by Gordon C. Davies.

"A base on 232 offered many advantages for the defence of the spaceways, as well as demanding occupation, lest rival races in the galaxy gained ahold of it first. But though successive ships blasted off with the avowed intent of landing on the cheerless gray satellite, none had ever been heard of again, save one that returned without landing—its crew reporting fantastic storms of unknown origin. It was not until Tony Wayne and John Reece surmounted the invisible Barrier of Time, and crash landed their ship on 232, that they learned its incredible secrets—and found there a fellow being whose story was akin to nightmare." Another charming fantasy, very similar to the same author's *Mammalia*, in a style unique to this author. LIke all later Hughes fantasies, it was written around a lurid, surreal Davies cover.

as WILLIAM ROGERSOIIN

A271. *Amiro.* London: Brown Watson, October 1954, 112 p., 1/6d. Cover by Leroi (Osborne).

The splendidly surreal cover painting suggested a superior Hughes fantasy, but unfortunately, this was one of his most pedestrian straight SF efforts. The crew of a spaceship accidently lands on an uncharted asteroid, Amiro. The tiny world has mysteriously been terraformed and given a breathable atmosphere. They find the skeleton of Jenks Illiar, an eccentric scientist reported missing decades earlier, whose diary and notes reveal that he had died in self-imposed exile on the asteroid. His automatic machinery to control the environment is still functioning, presided over by a gigantic automaton. The author deliberately throws away the intriguing potential of the opening for a quite banal sub-plot featuring Martian baddies seeking to annex Amiro before Earth does. It is written in such a way that it is completely free of any *real* science or imagination, as if it were set on a desert island. Obviously written to order, it remains an indictment of the mentality of British editors and publishers at this time. Because it was so bad, copies would be read and then thrown away, so that it has unjustly become an expensive collector's item today.

A272. *North Dimension.* London: Brown Watson, May 1954, 111 p., 1/6d. Cover by Gordon C. Davies.

Alvar Lazade is a veteran of the Korean War, which has left him crippled. When gazing at the plants in the house of his sister, he finds himself drawn into another dimension mentally, a fantastic green world peopled by alien flora and fauna. In this other world, he has full use of his body. Fascinated, he spends more and more time in a daily reverie bordering on self-hypnosis, having adventures in the green world, to be brought back to reality only when he relaxes his conscious control over his eyes and blinks. The story unfolds as a weird fairy tale, filled with green men, giant beetles, and a ravishing queen named Elvera who needs to be rescued from alien invasion.

as ARN ROMILUS, *house pseud.*

A273. *Brain Palaeo.* London: Curtis Warren, February 1953, 159 p., 1/6d. Cover by Gordon C. Davies.

Alex Larsen and his fellow scientists develop a system of telepathic communication. "They bridged the time-space gap between parallel planes of existence, aiding a race of slaves against their Masters, a group of evil, abnormally developed beings, half-brain, half-robot in form." A gorgeously screwy Hughes interdimensional space fantasy written around a way-out Davies cover depicting two spacemen on a Saturnian satellite, being pursued by dismebodied brains in transparent domes, atop fifty-foot high mechanical spider-like bodies!

A274. *Organic Destiny.* London: Curtis Warren, November 1953, 159 p., 1/6d. Cover by Gordon C. Davies.

A scientist, Herrick, perfects a three-dimensional color television receiver, and picks up what appear to be transmissions from an alien world. Eventually, his cousin Janet and her companion, Maclean, are transported to the alien realm, where they discover a dying race of ghostly Mystics, guardians of Mankind's destiny. Restrained Hughes fantasy, long on philosophy, short on action.

MAURICE G. HUGI, 1904-1947

Maurice G. Hugi made his first appearance in 1934, with a sale to *Scoops* called "Temple of Doom." He followed this with another *Scoops* story, and appearances in the other major British SF magazines such as *Tales of Wonder* and *New Worlds*. His last appearance was "Fantasia Dementia" in the third issue of *New Worlds*...his last because Hugi passed away at the age of 43. One pre-war story, "The Mechanical Mice," was reworked by his friend Eric Frank Russell and sold to *Astounding*, where it appeared under Hugi's name in January 1941. Hugi sold much of his work to Gerald G. Swan, Ltd., for whom he wrote a number of crime novels, and launched the juvenile detective series "Martin Speed" in the magazine *Scramble*. After his death, William F. Temple acted as literary executor for his unpublished stories, and a number were sold to Swan and Curtis, including the book listed below, which appeared five years later.

as BRAD KENT, *house pseud.*

A275.   *Out of the Silent Places.* London: Curtis Warren, April 1952, 127 p., 1/6d. Cover by Gordon C. Davies.

> An interesting story about post-Holocaust society. Superstition is rife: the gods have wiped out the cities and all scientific knowledge, and it is written in the holy books that Man should live by the sweat of his brow in small villages, and have no communication with each other, lest knowledge should be pooled and grow again. Only the priests can cross Nomunsland and communicate with the priests of other villages. And each and every priest is the king, judge, and law-giver to his village. One man, Weldon, sets out to challenge this rigid society. Superior to most of Hugi's work in the juvenile field, it was published five years after the author's untimely death.

LESLIE (George) HUMPHRYS, 1921-

Born on February 22, 1921 and educated at Camden College, Leslie George Humphrys became the headmaster at North Walsham County Primary School in Norfolk in 1959. He is the author of a number of textbooks aimed at younger readers of school age, including books on such subjects as science and space travel. His fiction output has been fairly limited; apart from the two books issued under the name BRUNO G. CONDRAY, he had called *Time To Live* published under the byline GEOFFREY HUMPHRYS, the same name under which he sold a short story to *Nebula SF*. It is interesting to note that CONDRAY is mentioned on his books as the "author of *Odyssey in Space* and *The Outer Beyond*." The former is probably the same book as the novel of that title published under the byline VEKTIS BRACK by Gannet Press; *The Outer Beyond* may have appeared under a different title.

as BRUNO G. CONDRAY

A276.   *The Dissentizens.* London: C. A. Pearson (TIT-BITS no #), October 1954, 64 p., 0/9d. Cover by Ronald Turner.

> Zana Dench was a dissentizen, an outlaw who fought against the rule of Earth regimentation to obtain freedom. Only ten dissentizens remained after the final purge of the security corps...and even less survived when a planetoid was found that could be used as a base for a new settlement away from the Earth Control Board.

A277.   *Exile from Jupiter.* London: C. A. Pearson (TIT-BITS no #), January 1955, 64 p., 0/9d. Cover by Ronald Turner.

A theatrical agent gets caught up in an interplanetary war when he unknowingly marries a mysterious woman from Jupiter. Competent and well-written, although highly implausible!

as VEKTIS BRACK, *house pseud.*

A20.   *Odyssey in Space.* London: Gannet Press, 1954, 127 p., 1/6d. Cover by Gerald Facey.

Space is finally conquered: a small rocket is launched and returns safely, and now top scientist Alva Maetrix makes plans to build a space platform. His ideas soon become reality, but there are others who want the platform for their own personal gain. The plot unfolds in a ludicrous fashion, with Alva deciding to play God—destroying all life on Earth in order to "save" humans from dictatorship!

GILL HUNT (House pseudonym)

A254.   *Elektron Union,* (by Dennis Talbot Hughes). London: Curtis Warren, June 1951, 112 p., 1/6d. Cover by Ray Theobald.

SEE: *Dennis Talbot Hughes* for synopsis.

A213.   *Fission,* (by David Griffiths). London: Curtis Warren, January 1952, 111 p., 1/6d. Cover by Ray Theobald.

SEE: *David Griffiths* for synopsis.

A23.   *Galactic Storm,* (by John Brunner). London: Curtis Warren, November 1951, 110 p., 1/6d. Cover by Ray Theobald.

SEE: *John Brunner* for synopsis.

A255.   *Hostile Worlds,* (by Dennis Talbot Hughes). London: Curtis Warren, February 1951, 112 p., 1/6d. Cover by Ray Theobald.

SEE: *Dennis Talbot Hughes* for synopsis.

A256.   *Planet X,* (by Dennis Talbot Hughes). London: Curtis Warren, February 1951, 112 p., 1/6d. Cover by Ray Theobald.

SEE: *Dennis Talbot Hughes* for synopsis.

A278.   *Planetfall,* (by E. C. Tubb). London: Curtis Warren, November 1951, 111 p., 1/6d. Cover by Ray Theobald.

SEE: *E. C. Tubb* for synopsis.

A257.   *Spaceflight,* (by Dennis Talbot Hughes). London: Curtis Warren, August 1951, 111 p., 1/6d. Cover by Ray Theobald.

SEE: *Dennis Talbot Hughes* for synopsis.

A258. *Spacial Ray,* (by Dennis Talbot Hughes). London: Curtis Warren, September 1951, 111 p., 1/6d. Cover by Ray Theobald.

SEE: *Dennis Talbot Hughes* for synopsis.

A279. *Station 7,* (by John Jennison). London: Curtis Warren, March 1952, 112 p., 1/6d. Cover by Ray Theobald.

SEE: *John Jennison* for synopsis.

A214. *Vega,* (by David Griffiths). London: Curtis Warren, October 1951, 111 p., 1/6d. Cover by Ray Theobald.

SEE: *David Griffiths* for synopsis.

A280. *Zero Field,* (by John Jennison). London: Curtis Warren, February 1952, 112 p., 1/6d. Cover by Ray Theobald.

SEE: *John Jennison* for synopsis.

PRESTON JAMES (Pseudonym?)

A281. *Secret of the Vase.* London: World Distributors, Ltd., June 1955, 128 p., 1/-. Cover uncredited.

A well-written mystery thriller, with borderline SF elements this book is listed here for completeness, and because *James* was once thought to be a pseudonym of *John Russell Fearn.* However, *Fearn*'s biographer, Philip Harbottle, is now inclined to discount this possibility. The story itself concerns a criminal scientist who seeks to overthrow society with the aid of an incredibly virulent poison known to the ancient Egyptians—the formula for which is inscribed on vase he has stolen from a museum. The byline JAMES PRESTON was later used on other mystery novels.

HANK JANSON (House pseudonym)

The name that started the boom in American gangster novels, JANSON was the creation of *Stephen D. Frances,* who wrote the first novel, *When Dames Get Tough* (Ward & Hitchon) in 1946. Two years later, *Frances* began to produce them for his own company and the series rapidly became a smash success. By the time the first science fiction title was published, Janson sales were topping eight million copies. At the same time, the books were being scrutinized by various Watch Committees for violence and pornography, and the fifty-two books published to that date had managed to collect 1,400 destruction orders! Seven books were taken to the Old Bailey, and the publishers (not *Frances* by that time) were jailed for publishing obscene literature. *Frances* himself was taken to court, but was released after it was shown that he did not write the books involved. Other authors of JANSON novels include *Harold Kelly* and *Victor Norwood,* both included in this volume. Eventually, sales were reported to be over 20,000,000, with some 250 different titles—only three of which are science fiction, all of them published as JANSON SPECIALS. *One Against Time* was published in May 1956 (Moring), and is outside the scope of this study. It was written by *Frances* himself, and reprinted in 1969 under the ASTRON DEL MARTIA byline.

A187. *Tomorrow and a Day*, (by Stephen D. Frances). London: Alexander Moring, 1955, 159 p., 2/6d. Cover by Reginald C. W. Heade.

> SEE: *Stephen D. Frances* for synopsis.

A188. *The Unseen Assassin*, (by Stephen D. Frances). London: Top Fiction Press, October 1953, 142 p., 2/-. Cover by Reginald C. W. Heade (girl's figure only) and Ronald Turner (background city).

> SEE: *Stephen D. Frances* for synopsis.

JOHN W(illiam) JENNISON, d.1969?

Jennison was the author of scores of SF and (mainly) western novels published by Curtis Warren, Dragon, and Edwin Self. Later, he is known to have penned the 1966 novel, *Lost World* (World Distributors, Ltd.), as "John Theydon," based on the Gerry Anderson animated puppet series, *Thunderbirds*. Jennison was talented writer who decided on quantity over quality (perhaps he needed the money!). Nothing is known about his personal life.

as MATTHEW C. BRADFORD

A282. *Invasion from Space.* London: Atlantic Book Company, May 1954, 128 p., 1/6d. Cover by Ray Theobald.

> An alien spaceship with a giant robot is discovered in the Sahara Desert. The robot heads straight for Cairo, where it is stopped by a force screen. Craig Wilson and Greta Farley of the International Television Service decide to explore the robot, but, along with other newspaper and security men, are caught inside the robot's own force field, and then dragged inside by an extendable claw to meet the alien occupants. This novel is similar in theme and characters to Jennison's *Para-Robot* (see #A77, below).

as GEORGE SHELDON BROWNE

A283. *The Yellow Planet.* London: Edwin Self, May 1954, 100 p., 1/-. Cover by Ronald Turner.

> The crew of the *Vulcan A.4* colonial space survey ship encounters a spatial warp and is flung across space to a strange solar system. Landing to explore a world they dub the Yellow Planet, they encounter various manifestations of alien life before discovering a wrecked Terran spaceship which had gone missing twenty years earlier. Complications with the crew's descendants ensue. A quite well written, if somewhat routine, space adventure.

as NEIL CHARLES, *house pseud.*

A77.   *Para-Robot.* London: Curtis Warren, February 1952, 112 p., 1/6d.
        Cover by Ray Theobald.

After a routine assignment in Japan, Jim Craig and Rita Farley were flying
back to America when they first see the Para-Robot, a monstrous construction that appears out of the sea and devastates a number of Pacific Islands. They fly to the Panama Canal to investigate a blockage they think is
somehow connected, but crash in the sea, only to be picked up by a giant
submarine controlled by Roger Vassar. Vassar is an ex-atomic scientist
who is trying to incite a world war so that he can become ruler of the devastated population. Very similar to Jennison's *Invasion from Space* (see
#A281).

as GILL HUNT, *house pseud.*

A279.   *Station 7.* London: Curtis Warren, March 1952, 112 p., 1/6d. Cover by
        Ray Theobald.

After a four-year voyage the relief crew for Station 7 is nearing its destination of Alpha Centauri. Three months out, the flight is interrupted by
the appearance of an FTL ship, which promptly vanishes again, to reappear
some months later to kidnap the crew. They awake after a drug-induced
sleep to learn the strange story of the planet Vla, where two hostile races
killed 90% of the population in an atomic war. The far-reaching con-
sequences mean that no males can be born, radiation having destroyed the
chromosomes, and the few remaining males were used as breeding
stock—which is also to be the fate of the captured Earthmen. A well-written and interesting study of a female-dominated world, with a surprisingly
downbeat ending.

A280.   *Zero Field.* London: Curtis Warren, February 1952, 112 p., 1/6d. Cover
        by Ray Theobald.

Captain Jim Duncan is called upon to help Professor Harlson set up an
atomic plant at the South Pole. A warning has been received to stop work,
and the mystery deepens when Duncan starts receiving strange dreams peopled by green-skinned aliens, and a security guard goes mad and tries to
kill Harlson. The plant is suddenly destroyed, and Duncan leads an expedition to the Pole, where the explosion has left a deep crater, revealing a
passageway into the earth. They are soon captured by telepathic Plutonians
who reveal their plans to breed a Human-Plutonian hybrid race capable
living on Earth, away from dying Pluto. A reasonably entertaining effort.

as EDGAR REES KENNEDY

A284.   *Conquerors of Venus.* London: Edwin Self, June 1953, 128 p., 1/6d.
        Cover by Ronald Turner.

In this routine space adventure set on Venus, explorers from Earth discover
two races of Venus: an ancient people now dying out, and a bestial, web-

PHILIP HARBOTTLE & STEPHEN HOLLAND

footed race now rapidly evolving in the Venusian swamps. The elders had initially enslaved the web-footed creatures, but had become effete, allowing their arts and sciences to fall into disuse. Finally, the slaves had turned on them and all but wiped them out.

A285. *The Mystery Planet.* London: Edwin Self, March 1952, 128 p., 1/6d. Cover by Terry Maloney.

The Solar Space Patrol spaceship under the command of Lafe Hansen is forced to crashland on Althan, one of the planets of Alpha Centauri. Exploring the frozen world in search of the crawler they jettisoned just before crashing, Hansen and his two colleagues discover another spaceship and its alien pilots. While hiding in a crevice, they also discover an ancient city. Captured by Siriuns descended from the dead city dwellers, Hansen has no way of warning the rest of his crew (or Earth) that the Siriuns may attack. A competent space opera.

as KING LANG, *house pseud.*

A286. *Space Line.* London: Curtis Warren, February 1952, 112 p., 1/6d. Cover by Ray Theobald.

In 2152, the moon begins to spiral away from Earth, and Mark Coppel, a Space Patrol operative, learns from Professor Hellstrom that an artificial planetoid is the source of a powerful electromagnetic force that is pulling the moon towards it. Coppel leads a team to the planetoid where they are captured by the Llanans, a dying race from Alpha Centauri. The use of an immortality drug has left them sterile and the remaining 200 need a source of vital organs for transplanting into their cybernetic bodies. An ambitious theme, but handled ineptly.

NAT KARTA (House pseudonym)

Launched in 1949, KARTA was a popular gangster house pseudonym originally used by Muir-Watson Ltd., before it was sold to Scion Ltd. The byline was used by a number of authors, including *Norman Lazenby* and *Victor Norwood*. The novel listed below is a scientific detective story.

A119. *Vision Sinister,* (by John Russell Fearn). London: Dragon Books, November 1954, 144 p., 2/-. Cover uncredited.

SEE: *John Russell Fearn* for synopsis.

VON KELLAR (House pseudonym)

A259. *Ionic Barrier,* (by Dennis Talbot Hughes). London: Curtis Warren, August 1953, 159 p., 1/6d. Cover by Gordon C. Davies.

SEE: *Dennis Talbot Hughes* for synopsis.

A287. *Tri-Planet,* (author unidentified). London: Curtis Warren, June 1953, 159 p., 1/6d. Cover by Gordon C. Davies.

91

A peculiar rash is the first evidence of invasion from space. Some intelligence is beaming radiation at Earth, killing thousands. World Leader Van Koff decides to evacuate the planet's population to Mars, but a spaceship is attacked by alien vessels. Earth then becomes the scene of great destruction as the ships devastate the cities, and disgorge their alien controllers: huge milky globes with twenty-foot tentacles. Captain Roc French, the newly appointed War Minister, and Leo Baun implement a daring plan to stop the invaders. An action-packed space opera.

HAROLD ERNEST KELLY, 1885?-1970?

Kelly was a prolific author of many kinds of books, including gangsters, westerns, and science fiction. Beginning in 1940 he wrote many novels under the byline DARCY GLINTO. Although this was his most popular pseudonym, he also used the names BUCK TOLER, LANCE CARSON, GORDON HOLT, CLINTON WAYNE, and later HANK JANSON. He wrote science fiction and weird tales under the name PRESTON YORKE, which he used in the early 1940s on short stories and some novels, including the novels *Death on Priority 1* (Mitre Press, 1945) and *The Gamma Ray Murders* (Everybody's Books, 1943), plus at least one weird story, "Strictly to Plan," which appeared in *Tales of Terror and Surprise* in 1942. The name was invented by his brother, Hector Kelly, who also published a later SF novel as YORKE. Harold Kelly died after moving to the Canary Islands for health reasons, aged about 85.

as PRESTON YORKE

A288.   *Space-Time Task Force.* London: Hector Kelly, April 1953, 192 p., 1/6d. Cover uncredited.

In the far distant future, the Earth is faced with alien invasion. The aliens have mastered the powers of time travel, and there seems to be no way to stop them from destroying the planet. The council of the syntho-selectives orders that contact should be made with the Primitives, living in what was once America, and the only true humans: years of selective breeding have made the syntho-selectives little more than robots, incapable of emotion or original thought. And these are the masters of the future, but they are powerless against the deadly rays of the aliens—so how can the Primitives help when their technology is thousands of years behind that of their enemies?

EDGAR REES KENNEDY—see: John Jennison

BRAD KENT (House pseudonym)

A260.   *Biology "A",* (by Dennis Talbot Hughes). London: Curtis Warren, March 1952, 128 p., 1/6d. Cover by Gordon C. Davies.

SEE: *Dennis Talbot Hughes* for synopsis.

A261.   *Catalyst,* (by Dennis Talbot Hughes). London: Curtis Warren, January 1952, 112 p., 1/6d. Cover by Ray Theobald.

SEE: *Dennis Talbot Hughes* for synopsis.

A262. *The Fatal Law,* (by Dennis Talbot Hughes). London: Curtis Warren, February 1952, 112 p., 1/6d. Cover by Ray Theobald.

SEE: *Dennis Talbot Hughes* for synopsis.

A275. *Out of the Silent Places,* (by Maurice G. Hugi). London: Curtis Warren, April 1952, 127 p., 1/6d. Cover by Gordon C. Davies.

SEE: *Maurice G. Hugi* for synopsis.

PHILIP KENT—see: H. Kenneth Bulmer

JOHN KING—see: Ernest Lionel McKeag

GEORGE KINLEY (Pseudonym?)

A289. *Ferry Rocket.* London: Curtis Warren, January 1954, 159 p., 1/6d. Cover by Gordon C. Davies.

"Philip Shane, journalist for the London *Sunday Sentinel* and undercover agent for the British government, sets out, at the Prime Minister's request, to investigate the deaths of key scientists on the moon. His fellow travelers are: Claire Scott, daughter of Fabian Scott, pioneer-planner of Lunar City; Professor Denis Quarles, a one-man Investigating Commission; Geoff Midly, a psychiatrist; the ferry rocket Commander, and his crew.   At Woomera, Shane is drugged and sabotage occurs. On the Commonwealth Space Station, the Commander is killed. Who is responsible...and why?" A low-key, near future space opera.

JOHN LANE—see: Dennis Hughes

KING LANG (House pseudonym)

A215. *Astro Race,* (by David Griffiths). London: Curtis Warren, February 1951, 112 p., 1/6d. Cover by Ray Theobald.

SEE: *David Griffiths* for synopsis.

A216. *Gyrator Control,* (by David Griffiths). London: Curtis Warren, January 1951, 112 p., 1/6d. Cover by Ray Theobald.

SEE: *David Griffiths* for synopsis.

A217. *Projectile War,* (by David Griffiths). London: Curtis Warren, September 1951, 111 p., 1/6d. Cover by Ray Theobald.

SEE: *David Griffiths* for synopsis.

A218. *Rocket Invasion,* (by David Griffiths). London: Curtis Warren, August 1951, 111 p., 1/6d. Cover by Ray Theobald.

SEE: *David Griffiths* for synopsis.

A290.   *Saturn Patrol,* (by E. C. Tubb). London: Curtis Warren, October 1951, 111 p., 1/6d. Cover by Ray Theobald.

   SEE: *E. C. Tubb* for synopsis.

A286.   *Space Line,* (by John Jennison). London: Curtis Warren, February 1952, 112 p., 1/6d. Cover by Ray Theobald.

   SEE: *John Jennison* for synopsis.

A219.   *Task Flight,* (by David Griffiths). London: Curtis Warren, February 1951, 112 p., 1/6d. Cover by Ray Theobald.

   SEE: *David Griffiths* for synopsis.

A228.   *Terra!* (by George Hay). London: Curtis Warren, January 1952, 112 p., 1/6d. Cover by Ray Theobald.

   SEE: *George Hay* for synopsis.

A230.   *Trans Mercurian,* (by Brian Holloway). London: Curtis Warren, February 1952, 112 p., 1/6d. Cover by Ray Theobald.

   SEE: *Brian Holloway* for synopsis.

VICTOR LA SALLE (House pseudonym)

A182.   *After the Atom,* (by Leonard Fish). London: John Spencer, April 1953, 108 p., 1/6d. Cover by Norman Light.

   SEE: *Leonard Fish* for synopsis.

A291.   *Assault from Infinity,* (by T. W. Wade). London: John Spencer, June 1953, 108 p., 1/6d. Cover by Norman Light.

   SEE: *T. W. Wade* for synopsis.

A97.   *The Black Sphere,* (by Gerald Evans). London: John Spencer, October 1952, 108 p., 1/6d. Cover by Norman Light.

   SEE: *Gerald Evans* for synopsis.

A199.   *Dawn of the Half Gods,* (by John Glasby). London: John Spencer, October 1953, 128 p., 1/6d. Cover by Ray Theobald.

   SEE: *John Glasby* for synopsis.

A98.   *Menace from Mercury,* (by R. Lionel Fanthorpe). London: John Spencer, March 1954, 128 p., 1/6d. Cover by Ray Theobald.

   SEE: *R. Lionel Fanthorpe* for synopsis.

A292. *Seventh Dimension,* (by T. W. Wade). London: John Spencer, July 1953, 124 p., 1/6d. Cover by Gordon C. Davies.

SEE: *T. W. Wade* for synopsis.

A293. *Suns in Duo,* (by T. W. Wade). London: John Spencer, January 1953, 108 p., 1/6d. Cover by Gordon C. Davies.

SEE: *T. W. Wade* for synopsis.

A200. *Twilight Zone,* (by John Glasby). London: John Spencer, February 1954, 130 p., 1/6d. Cover by Ray Theobald.

SEE: *John Glasby* for synopsis.

NORMAN (Austen) LAZENBY, 1914-

Norman Austen Lazenby was born in Gateshead, Tyne and Wear, on January 4, 1914. He started writing at the age of sixteen while an apprentice in a big electrical firm, but didn't make his first sale until 1941, with a number of short stories and a romance novel to Gerald G. Swan. He married in 1942 and stayed in reserved occupation during World War II. From 1941 he sold anything that he could quickly write, from confessional novels to westerns, sex-gangster works to fairy tales.

During the early 1950s he wrote many novels for the "mushroom" companies, including Scion Ltd., Curtis Warren, Muir-Watson, etc. Most appeared under house pseudonyms. He also sold numerous short stories. "A story a day was my motto at the time," he says, and has been a full-time writer ever since, although he has returned to electrical work when outlets have been slack. Between 1944-1945 he wrote nine SF stories for *Walter Gillings,* starting with "A Matter of Size" (*Fantasy,* December 1946), although only three were actually published. He also sold one tale to *New Worlds,* and thirteen stories to the John Spencer magazines. B. Z. Immanuel wanted him to write science fiction for both Scion Ltd. and Gannet Press, but he eventually only produced one novel, which appeared under the BENGO MISTRAL house name. Earlier, he had sold a collection of SF stories to another small publisher, listed below.

A294. *Terror Trap.* London: Shenstone Press, May 1949, 96 p., 9d. Cover uncredited.

A collection of four original stories: "The Coming of the Beetle Men," "The Designers," "Green Monsters," and "The Tunnel." An entertaining collection of stories, of which "The Designers" is outstanding.

as BENGO MISTRAL, *house pseud.*

A295. *The Brains of Helle.* London: Gannet Press, June 1953, 127 p., 1/6d. Cover by Gerald Facey.

The only thing that Chev Markham wanted was a bit of peace and a regular drink—his old man told him to "Go to Hell," so he had! A pleasant world, not that he really cared. Someone told him about the Gods, the owners of the Brains of Cireem. The Brains could do anything you asked—but the

Gods were bored with unlimited power, and just used them to play dirty tricks on people, like turning them into dwarfs, or dropping giant dung heaps in the city center. Chev wasn't bothered, but somehow got involved in a search for the Master Brain. Yet even after finding it, his problems weren't over. A combination of "Gods of Helle" (*Worlds of Fantasy 1*, June 1950) and "Plasma Men Bring Death" (*Futuristic Science Stories 2*, August 1950).

RAND LE PAGE (House pseudonym)

A231. *"A" Men,* (by Brian Holloway). London: Curtis Warren, March 1952, 127 p., 1/6d. Cover by Gordon C. Davies.

  SEE: *Brian Holloway* for synopsis.

A265. *Asteroid Forma,* (by Dennis Talbot Hughes). London: Curtis Warren, February 1953, 159 p., 1/6d. Cover by Gordon C. Davies.

  SEE: *Dennis Talbot Hughes* for synopsis.

A296. *Beyond These Suns,* (by Cyril Protheroe). London: Curtis Warren, August 1952, 128 p., 1/6d. Cover by Gordon C. Davies.

  SEE: *Cyril Protheroe* for synopsis.

A297. *Blue Asp,* (by David O'Brien). London: Curtis Warren, July 1952, 128 p., 1/6d. Cover by Gordon C. Davies.

  SEE: *David O'Brien* for synopsis.

A204. *Satellite B.C.,* (by John Glasby and Arthur Roberts). London: Curtis Warren, May 1952, 127 p., 1/6d. Cover by Gordon C. Davies.

  SEE: *John Glasby* for synopsis.

A205. *Time and Space,* (by John Glasby and Arthur Roberts). London: Curtis Warren, August 1952, 128 p., 1/6d. Cover by Gordon C. Davies.

  SEE: *John Glasby* for synopsis.

A15. *War of Argos,* (by William Bird). London: Curtis Warren, May 1952, 127 p., 1/6d. Cover by Gordon C. Davies.

  SEE: *William Bird* for synopsis.

A206. *Zero Point,* (by John Glasby and Arthur Roberts). London: Curtis Warren, October 1952, 128 p., 1/6d. Cover by Gordon C. Davies.

  SEE: *John Glasby* for synopsis.

FRANK LEDERMAN (Pseudonym?)

His style is similar to that of ALVIN WESTWOOD, and Lederman and Westward are possibly the same author.

A298. *Tremor.* London: Kaye Publications, 1952, 112 p., 1/6d. Cover by Ronald Turner.

"A nerve wrecking experience," reads the cover blurb. Indeed! In 2913 civilization survives in great space platforms ruled over by Stavius II. When his daughter, Zania, is kidnapped by green men, he sends a small group of adventurers, including Red, Lem, and the scientist Draker, to find her. They set off in pursuit, but are drawn to a strange planet that does not register on their charts. The ship is held by a living plant. While exploring the planet, Red and his friends are captured by a race of women also at war with the green men. Red is forced to agree to destroy the green men in return for the freedom of the spaceship, but he discovers later that the promise, and the war, are not all they seem to be. Distasteful clap-trap!

PAUL LORRAINE (House pseudonym)

A120. *Dark Boundaries,* (by John Russell Fearn). London: Curtis Warren, January 1953, 159 p., 1/6d. Cover by Gerald Facey.

SEE: *John Russell Fearn* for synopsis.

A16. *Two Worlds,* (by William Bird). London: Curtis Warren, October 1952, 128 p., 1/6d. Cover by Ray Theobald.

SEE: *William Bird* for synopsis.

A207. *Zenith-D,* (by John Glasby and Arthur Roberts). London: Curtis Warren, December 1952, 159 p., 1/6d. Cover by Gordon C. Davies.

SEE: *John Glasby* for synopsis.

KRIS LUNA (House pseudonym)

A17. *Operation Orbit,* (by William Bird). London: Curtis Warren, November 1953, 159 p., 1/6d. Cover by Gordon C. Davies.

SEE: *William Bird* for synopsis.

A299. *Stella Radium Discharge,* (by David O'Brien). London: Curtis Warren, November 1952, 128 p., 1/6d. Cover by Ray Theobald.

SEE: *David O'Brien* for synopsis.

CLEM MACARTNEY—see: B. Flackes

CARL MADDOX—see: E. C. Tubb

VECTOR MAGROON (Possible pseudonym of Julian Franklyn)

A300. *Burning Void.* London: Scion Ltd., December 1952, 128 p., 1/6d. Cover by George Ratcliffe.

Tom Pennant battles against the Viking of the Spaceways, Professor William Temple. Tom, a sub-reporter on the *Daily Courier*, seems to be the only person to note that Temple has made five trips into space and returned, while the 43 other spaceships attempting the journey have vanished! And why does the Professor only use long-term prisoners as his crew? With the aid of his editor, Tom infiltrates Temple's ship and is taken to Deimos, "primary" of Mars, where Temple has a base from which he intends to rule all of space. Tom's cover is blown and he and his friend, Prince Rudolph, are sentenced to be cast off. This story is so bad that it has a certain amusing charm. Incredibly, it was actually translated and published in French, strengthening the possibility that it was written by Franklyn, a Scion editor who would be in a position to do the necessary "string pulling," possibly by passing it off as a *Fearn* novel, since the French publishers (Fleuve Noir) had contracted to take a number of Fearn's Scion-published *Vargo Statten* novels. However—and bibliographers please note—this book was assuredly *not* written by Fearn!

GRANT MALCOM—see: Dennis Hughes

KARL MANNHEIM (Pseudonym?)

There is a chance that these books are reprints from Australia. Most SF books from W.D.L. were reprints from America in the WORLD FANTASY CLASSICS series, and a further two, under the byline of BELLI LUIGI, would appear to be Australian reprints from Transport Publications, Sydney. There are no further MANNHEIM books; if these are reprints, they must have appeared originally under some different byline.

A301. *Vampires of Venus.* London: World Distributors Ltd., 1950, 128 p., 1/6d. VENUS #2. Cover uncredited.

This sequel to *When the World Died* (see #A301) takes place twenty years after Lassiter arrives on Venus. Plato and Helen, king and queen of the Blackland, the last survivors of Earth, travel across the Flameless Fire in search of more of their kind. They find flying creatures similar to the Krebs of their homelands, but far advanced socially; plus another humanoid, a visitor from the red planet Ormandi, who shows Helen the vastness of space beyond the Sky Roof. While they are away, the king of the flying Tixtrils is killed by the Lukrils, giant vampiric birds, and Plato is made king on the promise that he will destroy the Lukrils. Yet Plato has a second battle with the Ormandian, whose motives may be more deadly than even those of the Vampires. Another tedious fairy story, no better than its predecessor.

A302. *When the World Died.* London: World Distributors Ltd., 1950, 128 p., 1/6d. VENUS #1. Cover uncredited.

Barry Lassiter had been on the run for seven days from the Empire Police. In the year 1998 there is no place to run for anyone who does not believe wholly in the justice of the Western Confederation—or the Eastern Empire, depending on where you live. And these two great blocks are poised on the brink of war when Lassiter is saved by a group of scientists with a crazy plan to set up a colony on Venus. Even as their spaceship leaves, the Earth is blown apart in the Final War. Only sixteen people remain of Humanity. This story was reprinted by Five Star Paperbacks in 1972 with the final page missing. Nobody seems to have minded, since they would have long since given up trying to finish this tedious tale.

KARL MARAS (House pseudonym)

A35.   *Peril from Space*, (by H. Kenneth Bulmer). London: Comyns (Publishers) Ltd., December 1954, 128 p., 1/6d.   Cover by Ronald Turner.

SEE: *Henry Kenneth Bulmer* for synopsis.

A224.   *The Plant from Infinity*, (by Peter Hawkins). London: Paladin Press, 1954, 128 p., 1/6d.   Cover by Ronald Turner.

SEE: *Peter Hawkins* for synopsis.

A36.   *Zhorani*, (by H. Kenneth Bulmer). London: Comyns (Publisher) Ltd., December 1953, 128 p., 1/6d.   Cover by Ronald Turner.

SEE: *Henry Kenneth Bulmer* for synopsis.

CLYDE MARFAX—see: Erroll Collins

ROY MARQUIS (Pseudonym?)

A303.   *The Moon Monsters*. Leigh-on-Sea, Essex: Barrington-Gray Ltd., August 1951, 128 p., 1/6d.   Cover uncredited.

A party of four Earth people are transported to the moon for a series of rapid adventures with its inhabitants who "lived below the surface. It was warm and sunny there and life of all kinds was abundant." They meet "the king of Moon Men" and have all sorts of ludicrous adventures in the unrealistic lunar world.

ERNEST (Lionel) McKEAG, 1896-1976

Born in Newcastle On Tyne and educated at South Shields Marine School, Armstrong College, and Durham University, Ernest Lionel McKeag began his sea career in the British Mercantile Marines (1913-1915). He returned to England in 1916 to join the Royal Navy as a midshipman, rising to the rank of Lieutenant Commander. In 1919 he became a newspaper reporter, and started to write stories for boys' magazines in 1921. In 1923 he joined the staff of Amalgamated Press, working on girls' story papers, and began writing freelance from 1928; he eventually retired in 1961 as editor of *The Schoolgirl's Picture Library*. During the 1940s and 1950s he wrote a great many stories for the original paperback market, his most popular pseudonym being "Roland Vane," which he used for "saucy" stories of Soho lowlife. Other McKeag pen names included: *Jacques Braza, Ramon Lacroix, Rene Laroche,* and *Griff,* all from *Modern Fiction,* plus two adventures as *John King.*

The books in the SHUNA series are lost-world adventures concerning an ancient Incan city situated in a volcanic crater on a sheer cliff-sided mountain thousands of feet above the Mato Grosso in South America. Shuna (or Esh'una) is the white queen of the Amazon-like black female tribe, where men are the workers, a situation brought about centuries ago when the Incas fled the invading Spaniards and cut themselves off from the outside world. The Reginald Heade covers have made this pair of books a prime target for collectors.

as JOHN KING

A304. *Shuna and the Lost Tribe.* Stoke-on-Trent: Harborough, November 1951, 128 p., 1/6d. SHUNA #2. Cover by Reginald C. W. Heade.

A huge asteroid sweeps down towards Earth and strikes it a glancing blow, lifting the Great Cliffs and the surrounding Mato Grosso bodily from South America. The ancient Incan city still stands, but the cliffs are split by great ravines. Esh'una and the three White men set out to explore the new world, and discover that it is inhabited by strange beetle-men who attack in vast numbers. It seems there is no escape from the tiny planet as it races on a collision course with the moon!...

A305. *Shuna, White Queen of the Jungle.* Stoke-on-Trent: Harborough, November 1951, 128 p., 1/6d. SHUNA #1. Cover by Reginald C. W. Heade.

Three adventurers search for the trail of an old friend who had sought the ancient Incan city. They are attacked by pygmy tribesmen who inhabit the lost land, but using modern weapons they escape.. They succeed in ascending the cliffs using an observation balloon (which is wrecked on landing), but are captured by the Amazons. Ta'feeta, the true leader of the tribe, wishes the white men dead, for the old stories of the coming of white men bringing destruction are still remembered. But Esh'una sees them as a way to find out about herself and how she came to be the only white among her people. She saves them from certain death, but finds herself fleeing with them from the anger of Ta'feeta.

G. R. MELDE—see: Dennis Hughes

A. J. MERAK—see: John Glasby

BENGO MISTRAL (House pseudonym)

A295. *The Brains of Helle,* (by Norman Lazenby). London: Gannet Press, June 1953, 127 p., 1/6d. Cover by Gerald Facey.

SEE: *Norman Lazenby* for synopsis.

A306. *Pirates of Cerebus*, (by B. Ward). London: Gannet Press, October 1953, 128 p., 1/6d. Cover by Ray Theobald.

SEE: *B. Ward* for synopsis.

A307. *Space Flight 139*, (author unidentified). London: Gannet Press, 1954, 128 p., 1/6d. Cover by "Ferrari" (Philip Mendoza).

An expeditionary spaceship sets out to try and find a "lost planet" on which the heroine's scientist father is presumed to be lost. While quite realistic and almost competently written, the author displays only the haziest knowledge of astronomy or SF conventions.

JOSEPH MOIS—see: Erroll Collins

DAN MORGAN, 1925-

Dan Morgan was born on December 24, 1925, and became interested in science fiction at an early age. He worked as a professional guitarist, being particularly interested in jazz, and wrote a manual about the instrument, *Guitar* (1965). He began publishing SF stories in 1952, and appeared in most of the major British magazines. His later work includes a number of series, the most popular being the "Ventura Twelve" space-opera series written in collaboration with "John Kippax" (John Hynam, whom he met while a guitarist) and the "Mind" series, about psi power.

A308. *Cee-Tee Man.* London: Hamilton & Co. ("Panther" #181), May 1955, 144 p., 1/6d. Cover by Josh Kirby.

"'Don't go back to Earth...They'll watch your every move,' warned the old spaceman.
"But Grant Shaw ignored the advice, he had been away for five long years and hoped that Janine would be waiting for him. She was, but there were others...Within a few hours of landing on Earth, Grant is struggling to escape from a Fed Pol murder charge, only to find himself becoming enmeshed in a web of intrigue and horror that threatens to enslave the entire planet. Every man's hand against him, he is told that upon him alone depends the fate of Earth. Behind these happenings lies the massive C.J.C. brain, whose powers are not even guessed by the men who were its builders. C.J.C. alone holds the key that will solve Grant's problem—the concept of Cee-Tee." An imaginative first novel by Morgan.

VICTOR (George Charles) NORWOOD, 1920-1983

Born in Sunthorpe on March 21, 1920, Norwood started a writing career in 1946 after being discharged from war service at sea (he was wounded seventeen times). During his long convalescence he wrote and sold a western. He left school at age fourteen, later studying for a diploma from Bennett's College, Sheffield by correspondence. His early jobs included: bank guard, heavyweight boxer, wrestler, head croupier for a gambling establishment, gold and diamond prospector, and private detective. He worked as a full-time writer from 1950, with over 330 books to his credit.

He traveled the world extensively, visiting Brazil, Africa, and Guyana, and led seven expeditions through little-known areas of the Amazon jungle, which provided backgrounds for the Jacare novels. He was one of the most prolific of the 1950s British paperback writers, writing a book a week, including many gangster stories and westerns under an army of different house names. He continued to write hardcovers well into the 1960s, but later turned to travel books, mainly on prospecting. During the early 1980s he suffered from heart problems; following major heart surgery, he was planning to return to SF, but his plans were interrupted by his sudden death in 1983. His fantastic fiction included *Night of the Black Horror* (Badger Books, 1962), and the Tarzanesque "Jacare" series listed below. The novel *Drums Along the Amazon* (Scion, 1953) is usually listed as part of the JACARE series, but it is not, although it *is* part of the Scion JUNGLE series.

A309. *The Caves of Death.* London: Scion Ltd., September 1951, 112 p., 1/6d. JACARE #2. Cover by Ronald Turner.

Featuring two of the most disgusting villains imaginable. Karl Borg is "a typical[!] Hun," with close-cropped head, bulging neck, beetling brows, piggy eyes, scarred, bearded, and filthy. Bull Corbo, on the other hand, was born of a Negro father and a half-caste mother; his skin is mottled with leprous patches of pinky-brown and sooty-black, and he has no eyebrows, hideous pink eyes, scarred cheek, broken nose and teeth. "His brain was that of a beast, cunning, depraved, utterly without morals or scruples," the whole topped off with a "festering rash that covered his chest and stomach." Escaping from a prison camp in Peru, this charming couple flees to the Amazonian jungle where they abduct the lovely Helen, Jacare's Jane-like mate. Jacare tracks them to "the Caves of Death," a kind of prehistoric grotto, where Jacare dispatches a pterodactyl and assorted horrors before disposing of the rascally pair. All a bit much...but the Turner cover is superb!

A310. *Cry of the Beast.* London: Scion Ltd., 1953, 128 p., 1/6d. JACARE #6. Cover by John Richards.

An earthquake releases a pack of strange creatures—werewolves. Jacare is bitten by one while saving the life of Helen, and the curse of the werewolf means that he becomes one of the beasts when the moon is full. To save him, Helen asks the help of two tough oilmen and two doctors, but all four are greedy for the rewards they have been offered, and Helen cannot be certain whether they will wait and help, or simply kill Jacare and take what they want.

A311. *The Island of Creeping Death.* London: Scion Ltd., March 1952, 112 p., 1/6d. JACARE #5. Cover by G. P. Micklewright.

A diamond prospector returns from the Amazon babbling about a great White Ape that attacked his expedition. Circus owner Steve Brody hears the story while his troupe is stuck in the area, and sets out to capture the "ape" for his circus. Eventually they capture, not an ape, but Jacare!

A312. *The Skull of Kanaima.* London: Scion Ltd., December 1951, 112 p., 1/6d. JACARE #4. Cover by Ronald Turner.

A prospector discovers uranium in the Brazilian interior, and the American and English governments reach a secret agreement with the Brazilian government to find and develop the ore (ahead of the inevitable Russians). The ore deposits are situated in dense, unexplored jungle in an area populated by a savage tribe of primitive Indians. They will kill all strangers, unless they are carrying a special talisman, a shrunken human skull, revered by the Indians across countless generations, and imagined to bring them prosperity and avert catastrophes: the skull of Kanaima. Jacare and Helen become involved, and Jacare eventually dispatches the Russian villains in his inimitable ruthless fashion.

A313. *The Temple of the Dead.* London: Scion Ltd., November 1951, 112 p., 1/6d. JACARE #3. Cover by Ronald Turner.

The mixture is very much as before, with Norwood's stock characters (the American geologist, beautiful girl, English agent, Russian agent, ex-Gestapo Hun, and assorted escaped convicts) encountering an ancient temple inhabited by cannibalistic subhuman apemen, effectively depicted in a stunning Turner cover painting, which one suspects is the main reason why these books are collected.

A314. *The Untamed.* London: Scion Ltd., August 1951, 112 p., 1/6d. JACARE #1. Cover by Ronald Turner.

The first novel to introduce Jacare, jungle lord of the Amazon, "a man monster born of a mad mother in a den beneath a hollow tree, delivered like a beast while outraged Nature lashed the elements to howling fury, bowing the great trees like reeds before the savagery of their onslaught! Jacare! The mighty—the invincible!—before whose giant strength and savage cunning the wild creatures of the jungle fled in terror...Jacare the beast god, able to assume at will either human or animal form, and when his terrible cry arose above the jungle fastness, terror gripped the primitive savages." A fast-moving, savage, and sadistic Burroughs pastiche.

DAVID O'BRIEN

David O'Brien wrote a number of SF novels for Curtis Warren that rank among the worst ever published. Three novels fall into a loose series based around the International Research Council, published under the pseudonyms BERL CAMERON and KRIS LUNA. His other pseudonyms include RAND LE PAGE and BRIAN SHAW.

as BERL CAMERON, *house pseud.*

A45. *Black Infinity.* London: Curtis Warren, June 1952, 127 p., 1/6d. I.R.C. #2. Cover by Ray Theobald.

"A spaceship crippled by a blowout on the starboard cruising-tube, helplessly adrift in the uncharted regions of the Outer Galaxy...That was the position in which Nick Warren, Spacescout, and Tom Greer, his astrograd, found themselves!...A planetary war for control of the Universe, involving the clash of thousands of spaceships...The transformation of a planet into red-hot molten lava...All these ingredients, involving the usage of scientific wonders belonging to an age yet to come..." This second book in the "I.R.C. Future History" series is fully as bad as it sounds.

A49. *Photomesis.* London: Curtis Warren, May 1952, 127 p., 1/6d. I.R.C. #1. Cover by Gordon C. Davies.

A dark cloud begins to envelop the world, cutting off the sunlight that is vital to life. Vebber, leader of the I.R.C., suspects that it is the prelude to an invasion from Mars, and selects forty men to form an attacking unit, the Space Commandos. Using a new form of matter-transportation, "Photomesis," they beam themselves to Mars, only to lose half their numbers when attacked by a Martian spaceship. Messy and confused, this first book in the "I.R.C." series reads like a bad fairy tale.

as RAND LE PAGE, *house pseud.*

A297. *Blue Asp.* London: Curtis Warren, July 1952, 128 p., 1/6d. Cover by Gordon C. Davies.

"When two American scientists, Gorse Bush and Charles Cobus, were commissioned to investigate overfrequent visits of those supersonic discs—known to the public as 'flying saucers'—little did they imagine the series of sensational adventures which would follow...thousands of enemy spaceships ejecting lethal rays upon the Earth, temperatures rising to abnormal heights, bringing about a plague of giant insects..." A shockingly badly written would-be epic filled with torturous prose and scientific gobbledygook, typical of this author.

as KRIS LUNA, *house pseud.*

A299. *Stella Radium Discharge.* London: Curtis Warren, November 1952, 128 p., 1/6d. I.R.C. #3. Cover by Ray Theobald.

"When many areas of the Earth suddenly become radioactive, and those areas rapidly increased in size and number, something had to be done about it...and quickly!" The responsibility is handed to Visor, head of the I.R.C., who "has many strange but fascinating experiences," among them planets that can move under their own power at will, bringing disaster to the solar system; and the kidnapping of Queen Helenus, of a "mystery planet, Zeba." Absolute rubbish from start to finish. See also the first two books in this stories (#A49 and #A45).

as BRIAN SHAW, *house pseud.*

A315. *Ships of Vero.* London: Curtis Warren, October 1952, 128 p., 1/6d. Cover by Ray Theobald.

"The sun, provider of heat, light, and power for the whole galaxy [sic], dying! Dying so fast that within a matter of months, the known Universe would be plunged into icy blackness...The design and building of a super-spaceship to be used in an exploratory expedition through the dreaded 'space-warp' and far into the Outer Spaces, and, despite attempts at sabotage, how the expedition fared under the leadership of Weir, the ace physicist...The threatened invasion of our galaxy by thousands of supersonic discs under the command of the dreaded Vero..." Badly-written hodgepodge!

JOHN T(homas) PHILLIFENT, 1916-1976

Phillifent was born on November 10, 1916, and was better known under his pen name, JOHN RACKHAM, under which he wrote four novels for the TIT-BITS series—his first published SF. He became a regular contributor to all the British SF magazines, and wrote many original novels for Ace Books in the United States, publishing some twenty-five SF adventures before his death on December 16, 1976. He also contributed three novels under his own name to THE MAN FROM U.N.C.L.E. series.

The editor of *Operation Fantast*, Kenneth F. Slater, often acted as an unpaid authors' agent, putting other writers in touch with many publishers, including John Spencer and TIT-BITS, and he claims credit for launching the career of Phillifent/Rackham.

as JOHN RACKHAM

A316. *Alien Virus.* London: C. A. Pearson (TIT-BITS no #), February 1955, 64 p., 9d. SPACE PUPPET #4. Cover by Ronald Turner.

The radar beacon at Canal City on Mars stops working, the first clue that something is wrong there. The Nordens and the Chief of the Space Service travel to Mars and discover that the whole population, including Frank Fairless, has been paralyzed.

A317. *Jupiter Equilateral.* London: C. A. Pearson (TIT-BITS no #), September 1954, 64 p., 9d. SPACE PUPPET #3. Cover by Ronald Turner.

Asteroid miner Joe Ganley discovers a derelict spaceship in the Trojan asteroids of Jupiter, and accidentally sets in motion a new plan to destroy the Space Service when he saves the frozen body of Nina Orloff, and gives her information about a new and deadly weapon he has discovered.

A318. *The Master Weed.* London: C. A. Pearson (TIT-BITS no #), August 1954, 64 p., 9d. SPACE PUPPET #2. Cover by Ronald Turner.

With Nina Orloff and Marvin Lacey out of the way, the Nordens and Frank Fairless try to find out who is the controller of the organization that is trying to take over Mars. Dr. Floyd Rask is their only clue—and the mysterious botanist has an even more sinister plan as to how he can achieve supremacy—by using a mind-controlling plant!

A319. *Space Puppet.* London: C. A. Pearson (TIT-BITS no #), June 1954, 64 p., 9d. SPACE PUPPET #1. Cover by Ronald Turner.

After yet another accident, this time on the mail ferry, Frank Fairless, space pilot for the Space Service, is transferred by request to the command of Dr. Sven Norden. Valuable ores are being stolen by space pirates, and

Fairless is put aboard one of the ore carriers. He captures the pirates, discovers that the crews are being gassed, and uses that discovery to track down Marvin Lacey and Nina Orloff, who have plans to take over Mars.

CYRIL PROTHEROE

Cyril Protheroe is known to have contributed one SF novel under the byline of RAND LE PAGE. He also wrote and illustrated several humorous cartoon strip pages for Gerald G. Swan comics. Nothing else is known about his personal life.

as RAND LE PAGE, *house pseud.*

A296. *Beyond These Suns.* London: Curtis Warren, August 1952, 128 p., 1/6d. Cover by Gordon C. Davies.

Gavin Kale, a British test pilot, is given the hazardous task of piloting a rocketship from Earth to the Moon, investigating the surface, and getting back to Earth. This story represented an attempt at a peculiar sub-genre of British SF, the first lunar expedition, no doubt inspired by the film *Destination Moon*, based on Robert A. Heinlein's novel (see also *Lee Stanton's Seven to the Moon*). The usual faults abound: an ill-assorted crew (which would never have been chosen in the first place), and extremely shaky science (the space helmets of the explorers have a unique feature: "below the visor and in front of the mouth was a shutter which could be lowered to allow speech for short periods"). After striving vainly for realism, the novel ends in a barrage of nonsense about "Earthians," Martians, and Asteroid X70 ("the most beautiful orb in the whole universe").

SIMON QUERRY—see: Erroll Collins

JOHN RACKHAM—see: John T. Phillifent

FRANCIS G(eorge) RAYER, 1921-1981

Born on June 6, 1921 in Worcestershire, Rayer became interested in science fiction at an early age. His first story, "Juggernaut," was published in 1944 in a Link House publication. His later stories appeared mostly in the Nova magazines, and he wrote a number of novels, starting with *Realm of the Alien* (Grafton, 1947). He also worked as a technical journalist, designer, and engineer, and wrote many articles on electronics and radio. His nonfiction projects included *Electrical Projects in Hobbies* and *How to Build Your Own Solid State Electroscope*, both published in 1979. He died on July 11, 1981.

A320. *Coming of the Darakua.* London: Hamilton & Co. ("Authentic" #17), January 1952, 109 p., 1/6d. Cover by George Ratcliffe.

The Darakua of the title is a huge, gaseous intelligence which has drifted through space for centuries—the ultimate adaptable life form. Drifting to the Earth, it finds the remnants of Mankind waging a desperate, losing battle against alien oppressors who have brought civilization to its knees by inhibiting all electricity. Mentally evaluating humanity, the Darakua intervenes to preserve Mankind and routs the invaders. A well-written adventure story, with emphasis on human interest despite the storyline.

A321. *Earth—Our New Eden.* London: Hamilton & Co. ("Authentic" #20), April 1952, 109 p., 1/6d. Cover by George Ratcliffe.

War, and the threat of more wars, has divided Mankind into more than two factions. Apart from the opposing forces, there is a semi-slave culture of workers in "protected" underground cities, with a supervisory "Boss" grade who live on, or have access to, the world's surface. Against this backdrop, a shower of seeds from space settle on the Earth, grow with enormous vigor, and completely destroy this civlilization. A handful of people survive by hibernation until the botanical extravaganza has matured, seeded, and departed.

A322. *The Star Seekers.* London: C. A. Pearson (Tit-Bits no #), December 1953, 64 p., 1/6d. Cover by Ronald Turner.

It was a natural step that Man should build ships to reach other planets—other stars. Project 13 was such a rocket—a spaceship efficient, self-contained, and larger than any built before. Nick Riordan was a man to whom the ship meant much—it was Mankind's expansion to the stars. Space and Time can be strange factors, as Nick soon found. Einstein's theory that no object can exceed the speed of light was right...yet wrong in an astonishing way, which made Project 13 a hulk that must never reach space. Based on the stories "Time Was" (*New Worlds*, Winter 1952) and "...Man's Questing Ended" (*New Worlds*, July 1952).

A323. *We Cast No Shadow.* London: Hamilton & Co. ("Authentic" #28), December 1952, 108 p., 1/6d. Cover by George Ratcliffe.

An electronic experiment opens up a gateway to another dimension, leading to an invasion by entities able to imitate the appearance of human beings. A drawn-out and disappointingly dull novel.

A324. *Worlds at War.* Bolton, Lancs.: Tempest Publications, October 1949, 128 p., 1/6d. Cover by Holden.

This anthology, anonymously edited by Rayer, contains five original stories: "Fearful Barrier," by F. G. Rayer; "Masque," by Somerset Draco; "Dodie Slammed the Door," by E. R. James; "Scapegoat," by Edward Hannah; and "The Cleverjacks and the Moonstalks," by E. R. James. The Draco and Hannah stories were probably written either by Rayer or his cousin, E. R. James.

JOHN RAYMOND—see: Leonard G. Fish

VAN REED (House pseudonym)

A325. *Dwellers in Space,* (author unidentified). London: Curtis Warren, July 1953, 159 p., 1/6d. Cover by Gordon C. Davies.

"The *Atlantis* is no ordinary spaceship. Armed with the most deadly weapons that science can provide; faster and more powerful than any other spaceship in the universe, she is crewed by an army of picked men from Earth, Venus, Jupiter, and Mercury. Her task—to keep peace between the inhabitants of those planets. By force, if necessary. For years, she has flown unceasingly in space—watching and waiting, ever alert for the first threat of another interplanetary war. An Earthman, Kark Fenton, is taking his turn as captain. Reports of strange activities on Mercury make him direct the huge ship to that planet—the age-old enemy of Earth." Fast-paced thriller of conflict between genetically-adapted descendants of Earth colonies.

A268. *House of Many Changes*, (by Dennis Talbot Hughes). London: Curtis Warren, August 1952, 128 p., 1/6d. Cover by Gordon C. Davies.

SEE: *Dennis Talbot Hughes* for synopsis.

MARX REISEN (Pseudonym)

A326. *Before the Beginning.* London: C. A. Pearson (TIT-BITS no #), January 1954, 64 p., 9d. Cover by Ronald Turner.

After 500 trouble-free phases on the planet Beatus, there is sudden unrest among the workers. DON 5/A, an ex-member of the Security Brigade, is recalled to do some undercover checking on the Economic Re-allocation Association, and into the possible invasion from a neighboring planet, Actomdor, a strange world where even the air must be imported. DON meets Professor Carodoran, who is attacked by one of his own creations—a humanoid named Mijn—whom DON tracks down to the Mottica, a vast tract of unhoused land where he is also attacked. He awakes to find himself mysteriously transported to Actomdor where he is hailed as the new Messiah. An imaginative story, but marred by an "Adam and Eve" ending that spoils it completely.

RUSSELL REY—see: Dennis Hughes

JOHN ROBB—see: Norman Robson

ARTHUR ROBERTS

Nothing is known about this writer, except that he collaborated with *John Glasby* under various house names.

with John Glasby as BERL CAMERON, *house pseud.*

A46. *Cosmic Echelon.* London: Curtis Warren (TERRAN EMPIRE series), August 1952, 128 p., 1/6d. Cover by Gordon C. Davies.

SEE: *John Glasby* for synopsis.

A51. *Sphero Nova.* London: Curtis Warren, 1953, 159 p., 1/6d. Cover by Ray Theobald.

SEE: *John Glasby* for synopsis.

with John Glasby as RAND LE PAGE, *house pseud.*

A204. *Satellite B.C.* London: Curtis Warren, May 1952, 127 p., 1/6d. Cover by Gordon C. Davies.

SEE: *John Glasby* for synopsis.

A205. *Time and Space.* London: Curtis Warren, August 1952, 128 p., 1/6d. Cover by Gordon C. Davies.

SEE: *John Glasby* for synopsis.

A206. *Zero Point.* London: Curtis Warren, October 1952, 128 p., 1/6d. Cover by Gordon C. Davies.

SEE: *John Glasby* for synopsis.

with John Glasby as PAUL LORRAINE, *house pseud.*

A207. *Zenith-D.* London: Curtis Warren, December 1952, 159 p., 1/6d. Cover by Gordon C. Davies.

SEE: *John Glasby* for synopsis.

NORMAN ROBSON

Norman Robson is known to have used the pen name JOHN ROBB, which appeared on a number of foreign legion books and one SF adventure from Hamilton & Co. between 1951-1954, and later on a number of children's books into the 1960s.

as JOHN ROBB

A327. *Space Beam.* London: Hamilton & Co., September 1951, 111 p., 1/6d. Cover by George Ratcliffe.

A somewhat dated story, its opening is highly derivative of the film *Destination Moon*, by Robert A. Heinlein, with a privately constructed first moon rocket, the *Grainger One*. A note of originality is injected after the takeoff for the moon, when a member of the crew turns out to be a Venusian, and the ship is diverted to that planet. Once Venus is reached, the story degenerates into a routine Flash Gordon-type juvenile adventure.

WILLIAM ROGERSOHN—see: Dennis Hughes

ARN ROMILUS (House pseudonym)

A232. *Beyond Geo,* (by Brian Holloway). London: Curtis Warren, March 1953, 159 p., 1/6d. Cover by Gerald Facey.

SEE: *Brian Holloway* for synopsis.

A273. *Brain Palaeo,* (by Dennis Talbot Hughes). London: Curtis Warren, February 1953, 159 p., 1/6d. Cover by Gordon C. Davies.

SEE: *Dennis Talbot Hughes* for synopsis.

A274. *Organic Destiny,* (by Dennis Talbot Hughes). London: Curtis Warren, November 1953, 159 p., 1/6d. Cover by Gordon C. Davies.

SEE: *Dennis Talbot Hughes* for synopsis.

LAWRENCE F. ROSE—see: John Russell Fearn

E. R. ROYCE (Pseudonym?)

A328. *Experiment in Telepathy.* London: Curtis Warren, October 1954, 159 p., 1/6d. Cover uncredited.

"In medical science, it is an accepted fact that sudden and violent shock can affect the delicate mechanism of the human brain, despite there being no physical damage to the organ. The nerve-shattering shock that Diana Graham sustained reacted in a remarkable manner; she developed the power of receiving messages telepathically. Stranger still, these messages always came out of the Past, delaying in transit for periods varying from a few days to as many months." Low-key, nicely understated human interest drama, centered around a peculiar form of telepathy. Well-written and interesting.

JOHN RUSSELL—see: John Russell Fearn

DAVID (William Hardy) SCOTT MONCRIEFF, 1907-1987

David Scott Moncrieff (his double surname was unhyphenated) had a previous collection, *Not for the Squeamish,* published in 1948 by Background Books.

A329. *The Vaivasukko's Bride.* Glasgow, Scotland: Scots Digest (HORROR CLUB), 1949, 63 p., 1/-d. Cover uncredited.

This collection contains ten original stories, mostly weird tales, including: "The Vaivasukko's Bride," "An Unimaginative Man," "Strange Shelter," "Not Forty Months Ago" [love story], "She'll Never Leave You," "They Kept Their Bargain" [love story], "Diamond Cut Diamond," "The Agnostic Chess Player," "The Man With Flaxen Hair," and "Mind Over Matter."

ROBERT (George) SHARP

Robert George Sharp is something of a surprise in this volume. With no previous track record known in the SF field, he was recently identified as being JON J. DEEGAN, author of the OLD GROWLER stories, which ranks as one of the best series to be produced during the 1950s' paperback days. Many critics had thought that the OLD GROWLER books were really the work of *H. J. Campbell,* who probably had a strong editorial hand in shaping the OLD GROWLER stories and in editing the COR-

RIDORS OF TIME fantasy series, which was copyrighted in *Sharp*'s name when the titles were imported into America.

Sharp did write for Hamilton & Co. during this period, and his work dates back to the mid-1930s, starting with *In the Hands of the Enemy* (PICADILLY NOVELS #15, 1935). He contributed a number of novels to the PICADILLY NOVELS series, and had a fantasy novel, *Horror Castle*, published by Arthur Gray in 1936. He later graduated to hardcovers from Hutchinson, then to Hamilton & Co., where his own name was used on foreign legion titles.

The Deegan pseudonym was used on a number of novels from Hamilton & Co. A strip cartoon, "Old Growler—Spaceship No. 2213," in *The Authentic Book of Space*, edited by *H. J. Campbell* (Hamilton & Co., 1954), bylined by DEEGAN, was loosely based on *Old Growler—Spaceship No. 2213*. In SF *Sharp* is only definitely known to have penned the three TIME-TRAVEL novels (1953-1954), during which period he also wrote foreign legion novels for Panther. However, recent research has unearthed the interesting fact that *Sharp* had written a thriller called *The Cry from the Ether* (1934) in the PICADILLY NOVELS series. The first chapter of *Old Growler and Orbis* was entitled "The Cry from the Ether," which points to *Sharp* as the author of this series.

The nine novels in the "Old Growler" series concern the adventures of a three-man survey team attached to the Interplanetary Exploration Bureau, which was responsible for exploring newly discovered planets and star systems within a few light years of Earth. The series was far superior to many of the books appearing at the time, the characterization less cardboardish, the plots a little more credible. The scientific background was considerably sounder than the norm, based on then-current knowledge, and no alien lifeforms were killed unless hostility was established beyond a doubt, which marked a refreshing change from the xenophobic shoot-'em-ups so frequently employed by the other writers of this period.

as JON J. DEEGAN

A330. *Amateurs in Alchemy.* London: Hamilton & Co. ("Panther" #32), December 1952, 128 p., 1/6d. OLD GROWLER #7. Cover by Gordon C. Davies.

The survey team from *Old Growler* are the first to land on unexplored planets, but this time their task is set on Hamman, a world already civilized by Man—a planet where revolt flares up as a threat against Man's civilization.

A331. *Antro, the Life Giver.* London: Hamilton & Co. ("Panther" #39), February 1953, 144 p., 1/6d. OLD GROWLER #8. Cover by George Ratcliffe.

The survey team from *Old Growler* crash lands in the crater of an extinct volcano on Antro. Their adventures on the dead planet reveal the secrets that gave birth to the population of the Universe.

A332. *Beyond the Fourth Door.* London: Hamilton & Co. ("Panther" #96), January 1954, 159 p., 1/6d. TIME-TRAVEL #2. Cover by John Richards.

A thief has fled into the time web with priceless symbolic jewels, leaving only a tenuous trail of radioactivity to mark the portal through which he escaped. Dysart and Magda set out on his trail through the widely diverse webs of time...past, present, and future. An interesting saga, with detective fiction overtones.

A333. *Corridors of Time.* London: Hamilton & Co. ("Panther" #85), November 1953, 159 p., 1/6d. TIME-TRAVEL #1. Cover by John Richards.

Janquo, the beloved ruler of Londonin-la, the greatest city-state of 39th Century Earth, is doomed. For it has been written that the fabulous warrior, Kazan, will soon emerge from the portals of time to slay Janquo and claim the throne. Dysart and Magda plunge into the time web to seek and destroy Kazan, drawing ever closer to their quarry, and to the ultimate fate that awaits them in the Corridors of Time.

A334. *Exiles in Time.* London: Hamilton & Co. ("Panther" #117), April 1954, 159 p., 1/6d. TIME-TRAVEL #3. Cover by John Richards.

Illegal excavations to discover the secrets buried beneath the fabulous portals of time misfire, trapping a thousand men in the time web. Dysart and Magda must once again brave the fates that guard the time web in an attempt to rescue them.

A335. *The Great Ones.* London: Hamilton & Co. ("Panther" #58), May 1953, 158 p., 1/6d. OLD GROWLER #9. Cover by Ronald Turner.

Bent on conquest, they sprang from the mists of legend into terrifying reality—the Great Ones from the Andromeda Galaxy were to return. Yet, despite their cold logic, something happens that the Great Ones could not foresee, something that sows a tiny seed of doubt in their minds. This novel ostensibly kills off the characters of the *Old Growler*, but a further story in the series, "The Lights of Anker-Mo," later appeared in *Authentic* (October 1957).

A336. *Old Growler and Orbis.* London: Hamilton & Co. ("Authentic" #9), May 1951, 104 p., 1/6d. OLD GROWLER #3. Cover by D.L.W.

Orbis, another planet of Vega, is devoid of all but plant life. So what is killing members of the landing party by draining them of blood, even when they are in guarded buildings?

A337. *Old Growler—Spaceship No. 2213.* London: Hamilton & Co. ("Authentic" #4), February 1951, 124 p., 1/6d. OLD GROWLER #2. Cover by D.L.W.

Landing on Fellik, the fourth of Vega's planets, the team encounters an underground-dwelling humanoid race which, they are amazed to discover, originated on Earth two million years ago. They escaped from the cataclysm of the Deluge, carrying with them Mankton, the Oracle of the Great Ones, a vastly superior race from the Andromeda Galaxy, who decrees that the team should be destroyed.

A338. *Planet of Power.* London: Hamilton & Co. ("Authentic" #14), October 1951, 110 p., 1/6d. OLD GROWLER #4. Cover by George Ratcliffe.

Old Growler concludes its survey of Vega's planets with a trip to the enigmatic planet Zeton. The planet is totally impervious to telescopic and radar survey due to its thick, ionized atmosphere. Upon landing, the team witnesses a ghastly execution and becomes embroiled in a civil war between Zeton's strange inhabitants.

A339. *Reconnoitre Krellig II.* London: Hamilton & Co. ("Authentic" #2), January 1951, 126 p., 1/6d. OLD GROWLER #1. Cover by D.L.W.

Krellig, one of the planets of Vega, has an unusual property...it has no red in its spectrum! Sent to investigate, Tubby, Hartnell, and Pop encounter two similar races: the benign cave-dwelling Shakkies, and the Holons who, with the aid of science left by a long-dead culture, dwell in the malevolent city of Kor, the City of Light.

A340. *The Singing Spheres.* London: Hamilton & Co. ("Authentic" #23), July 1952, 109 p., 1/6d. OLD GROWLER #5. Cover by Gordon C. Davies.

The planet Kardoon is the home of a weird alien race of glowing spheres. Tubby, Hartnell, and Pop become entangled in the struggles of the dying species and their egotistical ruler. Held prisoners, they watch the Machine of Revelations as it predicts their deaths.

A341. *Underworld of Zello.* London: Hamilton & Co. ("Panther" #17), August 1952, 128 p., 1/6d. OLD GROWLER #6. Cover by Gordon C. Davies.

What is the strange menace that lures spacemen to their doom in Zello's mysterious waters? The Inter X team investigates and finds itself facing great danger, caught in the middle of a conflict between amphibian civilizations.

BRIAN SHAW (House pseudonym)

A342. *Argentis,* (by E. C. Tubb). London: Curtis Warren, February 1952, 112 p., 1/6d. Cover by Ray Theobald.

SEE: *E. C. Tubb* for synopsis.

A233. *Lost World,* (by Brian Holloway). London: Curtis Warren, July 1953, 159 p., 1/6d. Cover by Gordon C. Davies.

SEE: *Brian Holloway* for synopsis.

A315. *Ships of Vero,* (by David O'Brien). London: Curtis Warren, October 1952, 128 p., 1/6d. Cover by Ray Theobald.

SEE: *David O'Brien* for synopsis.

A123. *Z Formations,* (by John Russell Fearn). London: Curtis Warren, March 1953, 159 p., 1/6d. Cover by Gerald Facey.

SEE: *John Russell Fearn* for synopsis.

DAVID SHAW—see: David Griffiths

ROY SHELDON (House pseudonym)

The SHINY SPEAR series and the PREHISTORIC series were both written by *H. J. Campbell* under the *Sheldon* pen name.

The first novel of the PREHISTORIC series has been wrongly credited to *George Hay*, who says of the story: "Harry Assael persuaded me to embark on a prehistory novel. I was very dubious, but agreed. When the novel—or a considerable part thereof—was presented, he was furious, refusing to make any payment. The work may have been, probably was, in fact, inferior, and I must accept responsibility for having allowed myself to be talked into doing it. All the same, the thing put me off fiction for decades." The novel and a sequel were quickly passed on to H. J. Campbell. The series is fairly rare, and much sought-after by collectors.

A62.   *Atoms in Action,* (by H. J. Campbell).   London: Hamilton & Co. ("Panther" #47), March 1953, 159 p., 1/6d.   SHINY SPEAR #6. Cover by Gordon C. Davies.

SEE: **H. J. CAMPBELL** for synopsis.

A63.   *Beam of Terror,* (by H. J. Campbell).   London: Hamilton & Co. ("Authentic" #13), September 1951, 110 p., 1/6d.   SHINY SPEAR #3. Cover by George Ratcliffe.

SEE: **H. J. CAMPBELL** for synopsis.

A64.   *Energy Alive,* (by H. J. Campbell).   London: Hamilton & Co. ("Authentic" #7), April 1951, 101 p., 1/6d.   SHINY SPEAR #2. Cover by D.L.W.

SEE: **H. J. CAMPBELL** for synopsis.

A343.   *Gold Men of Aureus,* (author unidentified).   London: Hamilton & Co. ("Authentic" #3), February 1951, 124 p., 1/6d.   Cover by D.L.W.

An awful story about a space voyage to Mars that goes wrong when the deceleration tubes fail, and the ship heads off into outer space. Eventually, it lands on a previously unknown planet, inhabited by three-foot-high golden-colored humanoids. No explanation is offered for the existence of a new planet in the solar system. The plot and writing are banal.

A65.   *House of Entropy,* (by H. J. Campbell).   London: Hamilton & Co. ("Panther" #59), June 1953, 160 p., 1/6d.   SHINY SPEAR #7. Cover by John Richards.

SEE: **H. J. CAMPBELL** for synopsis.

A66.   *Mammoth Man,* (by H. J. Campbell).   London: Hamilton & Co., February 1952, 110 p., 1/6d.   PREHISTORIC #1. Cover by George Ratcliffe.

SEE: H. J. CAMPBELL for synopsis.

A67. *The Menacing Sleep*, (by H. J. Campbell). London: Hamilton & Co. ("Authentic" #16), August 1952, 126 p., 1/6d. Cover by Gordon C. Davies.

SEE: H. J. CAMPBELL for synopsis.

A344. *The Metal Eater*, (by E. C. Tubb). London: Hamilton & Co. ("Panther" #109), March 1954, 158 p., 1/6d. Cover by John Richards.

SEE: *E. C. Tubb* for synopsis.

A68. *Moment out of Time*, (by H. J. Campbell). London: Hamilton & Co., 1951, 111 p., 1/6d. Cover by J. Pollack.

SEE: H. J. CAMPBELL for synopsis.

A69. *Phantom Moon*, (by H. J. Campbell). London: Hamilton & Co. ("Authentic" #6), March 1951, 117 p., 1/6d. SHINY SPEAR #1. Cover by D.L.W.

SEE: H. J. CAMPBELL for synopsis.

A70. *The Plastic Peril*, (by H. J. Campbell). London: Hamilton & Co. ("Authentic" #25), September 1952, 109 p., 1/6d. SHINY SPEAR #4. Cover by J. Pollack.

SEE: H. J. CAMPBELL for synopsis.

A345. *Space Warp*, (author unidentified). London: Hamilton & Co. ("Authentic" #19), March 1952, 109 p., 1/6d. Cover by George Ratcliffe.

A scientific expedition into the interior of Brazil discovers aliens from another dimension, creatures whose planet inhabits the same position in space, but with a different vibrationary phase that puts it on a different plane. The aliens take the expedition members to Alimonde to be used as specimens for study.

A71. *Star of Death*, (by H. J. Campbell). London: Hamilton & Co. ("Authentic" #27), November 1952, 108 p., 1/6d. SHINY SPEAR #5. Cover by Gordon C. Davies.

SEE: H. J. CAMPBELL for synopsis.

A72. *Two Days of Terror*, (by H. J. Campbell), London: Hamilton & Co. ("Panther" nn), May 1952, 112 p., 1/6d. PREHISTORIC #2. Cover by Ronald Turner.

SEE: H. J. CAMPBELL for synopsis.

LEE STANTON (Pseudonym?)

His style is similar to that of RICK CONROY (q.v.), and STANTON and CONROY are probably pseudonyms of the same author.

A346. *Mushroom Men from Mars.* London: Hamilton & Co. ("Authentic" #1), January 1951, 127 p., 1/6d. Cover by D.L.W.

"The sight which met Neron's eye was something he would never forget as long as he lived. The thing which emerged from the machine was like nothing so much as a huge purple-green mushroom, about five feet in height. The creature had a short, stubby stalk, topped by a thick, fleshy cap or dome. The dome was covered with green fibrous threads and round the edge ran a sort of fringe of tentacles about an inch thick. The thing leapt from the door to the ground and stood poised on the base of its stalk." A notoriously bad story which the "Authentic" series never quite managed to live down. The terrible cover and title all combined to make this one of the all-time stinkeroos. Mercifully, *Stanton* improved mightily in his later works.

A347. *Report from Mandazo.* London: Hamilton & Co. ("Authentic" #15), November 1951, 110 p., 1/6d. Cover by George Ratcliffe.

An amusing black satire of present-day Humanity as seen through the eyes of a group of humanoid interstellar visitors from the planet Mandazo, who land on Earth in a satellite plane, and take Leroy Flack back to their mother ship in space. They become entangled in a gang war when they try to impose peace on a gangster-terrorized American town, and then precipitate the Third World War.

A348. *Seven to the Moon.* London: Hamilton & Co. ("Authentic" #5), March 1951, 125 p., 1/6d. Cover by George Ratcliffe.

One of the then-fashionable variants on the film, *Destination Moon*, but still of some interest because of some quite good characterization: the moon crew are made up of well-delineated individuals, rather than the usual cardboard type, particularly K. Arthur Kimpie. Kimpie, an introverted intellectual with delusions of grandeur, is originally employed on the moon project as a lowly technician, but manages to stow away on the rocket. Unfortunately, the story is marred by some visible scientific derelictions.

VARGO STATTEN—see: John Russell Fearn

MARK STEEL (Pseudonym?)

He may also be the author of *Space Flight 139*, by BENGO MISTRAL, and *Worlds Away!*, by CRAGG BEEMISH.

A349. *Trouble Planet.* London: Gannet Press, May 1954, 127 p., 1/6d. Cover uncredited.

A low-key interplanetary novel in which Justin Kent, Universal Research Control operative, is sent on an undercover assignment to the Martian colony. He uncovers various political intrigues involving an intelligent race living on an asteroid called Coletos. The SF props are few and far between, and totally unconvincing, although the writing is fairly competent. The cover (by an unidentifiable artist) shows a dinosaur wrestling with a spaceship, and has no connection whatsoever with the story.

BRIAN STORM—see: Brian Holloway

EARL TITAN—see: John Russell Fearn

E(dwin) C(harles) TUBB, 1919-

Born in London on October 15, 1919, Ted Tubb was one of the most prolific authors of SF during the early 1950s. A one-time printing machine salesman, he had read SF since his teens, first contacting other fans in 1938, and subsequently becoming a regular part of the London fan scene. He sold his first story in June 1950, and launched himself on a writing career. Tubb's prolific output meant that, by 1956, he had already published forty novels and 100 short stories, including westerns, detective thrillers, and foreign legion novels. In 1955, he assumed editorship of *Authentic Science Fiction*, guiding it through twenty issues before its demise in 1957. After 1960 his output diminished greatly as he concentrated on picture scripts for Fleetway, although he returned to the field a couple of years later, finding success in 1967 with the first novel of the DUMAREST series. Since then he has concentrated on novels, chalking up number 100 in 1979, and has earned himself a vast following and a solid reputation with fans and professionals for his colorful adventure stories.

A350. *Alien Impact.* London: Hamilton & Co. ("Authentic" #21), May 1952, 109 p., 1/6d. Cover by Gordon C. Davies.

Jim Warren discovers the secret of the planet Venus—that it is inhabited by an ancient alien race who came from the Earth 20,000 years earlier in an attempt to build a great new civilization devoted to mental processes. To consummate their civilization, it is necessary for them to remain withdrawn from the disruptive influence of latter-day terrestrial colonists—to which end the "Watchers" are appointed—and Warren is faced with a dilemma.

A351. *Alien Life.* London: Paladin Press, January 1954, 128 p., 1/6d. Cover by Ronald Turner.

Only one man, Carmodine, returns alive from the first expedition to the planet Pluto. He has taken refuge in madness and is unable and unwilling to speak of his experience on the outermost planet. Given therapy, Carmodine is forced, against his will, to go on a second expedition led by Brensco, a scientist-adventurer who hates Carmodine, to face again the terrors of an incredible alien life. A masterful suspense novel.

A352. *Atom War on Mars.* London: Hamilton & Co. ("Panther" no #), December 1952, 112 p., 1/6d. Cover by Gordon C. Davies.

This book tells of the invention of an incredible new system of space travel—the Merrill tube. Using the invention, the Martian colony declares its independence, and overthrows the dictatorship of Earth. An early Tubb exploration of one of his favorite themes: a fresh start for humanity.

A353. **City of No Return.** London: Scion Ltd., April 1954, 140 p., 1/6d. Cover by Ronald Turner.

For countless years, the enigmatic city of Klaglan has rested beneath the racing moons of ancient Mars. Forbidden, guarded, sheltered in the cup of the Blue Mountains, and surrounded by the waterless deserts, it has rested there, a place of a thousand rumors and whispered fantasies, and has given birth to muttered tales of incredible wealth and riches. To this city comes Halmar the guide, Lorna the dancer from Venus, and the man called Smith. Defying the ban by the Terran authorities, the fanatical Drylanders, and the harsh deserts, they reach the crystal walls of the strange city. There, they discover a tremendous mystery, the deserted artifacts of a vanished civilization—and find themselves snared in an incredible trap. For Klaglan was more than a city.

A354. **The Hell Planet.** London: Scion Ltd., May 1954, 144 p., 1/6d. Cover by Ronald Turner (reprint of the cover on *City of No Return*).

Between the frozen wastes of the night-side and the searing inferno of the day-side, the Twilight Belt held all that was human of the tiny world of Mercury, Hell Planet of the Solar System. A strange world, airless, subject to the alien distortions of Einsteinian mathematics, Mercury was both a promise and a challenge, for here could be found torrents of cheap power essential to the ships and men of space. Lee Correy, commander of the Station, plunges into the frigid wastes in a desperate race against time to rescue his brother and find the essential component of the beam control. Fighting impossible conditions and incredible alien life, he is up against the enigmatic mysteries of the sand devils, a dead man who walked, and a machine that could not fail—but did.

A355. **Journey to Mars.** London: Scion Ltd., March 1954, 144 p., 1/6d. Cover by John Richards.

All Verrill wanted to do was to get to Mars, to Port Mersham, where a ship was getting ready to make the Big Jump to the stars. But he was stranded on Venus without money, papers, or weapons, with nothing but a keepsake between him and starvation and the revengeful fury of the powerful Brotherhoods—and charity was a forgotten word.

A356. **The Mutants Rebel.** London: Hamilton & Co. ("Panther" #38), May 1953, 144 p., 1/6d. Cover by Gordon C. Davies.

"Earth was a matriarchy, with women in command and pledged to thwart the men. And Earth, which had barely survived the results of atomic war, was taking too long to regain its feet. Other processes were acting against success, dragging the world into famine and rioting, bloodshed, and murder. The women could not see this—at least some of them couldn't. But there were others—those who were not quite human, whose mothers had been in radiation during the war—who did see. They saw more than the human eye could possibly see. With that mutant vision, that mutant telepathy, and the mutant power of teleportation, they began a rebellion." A complete and ambitious early novel by Tubb.

A357. *The Resurrected Man.* London: Scion Ltd., May 1954, 120 p., 1/6d. Cover by Ronald Turner.

Baron is killed in space in an interplanetary war and is set adrift, frozen solid, protected from all decay and cellular breakdown. Five years later, he is found and revived by the perfection of a new medical technique of resurrection—is revived to become an inhuman freak, and to be hounded in a corrupt Earth society to a shocking, final death. A superb novel later reprinted in the American magazine *Satellite SF* (December 1958).

A358. *The Stellar Legion.* London: Scion Ltd., May 1954, 144 p., 2/-d. Cover by John Richards.

Born in the midst of pain and terror, Wilson, an unwanted waif of a generation-long war of unity, grows up to spend his boyhood in forced labor and intense persecution. Rebelling, he is sent as a convicted murderer to the newly-formed penal world, and to the harsh, incredible logic of the Stellar Legion. There, where life is measured by the ability to think fast and act faster, he survives, to win promotion in the most brutal military system ever founded. Here also comes Laurence, Director of the Federation of Man, afraid of the things he has helped create, and using every means of guile and intelligence to undo what has been done. Laurence pits his wits against Hogarth, Commander of the Stellar Legion, in a tense, two-sided battle, with the entire Federation as the prize, terrified lest the human wolves trained and hardened in blood and terror should range the defenseless galaxy. A fascinating precursor to Robert A. Heinlein's *Starship Troopers*.

A359. *Venusian Adventure.* London: Comyns (Publisher) Ltd., December 1953, 128 p., 1/6d. Cover uncredited.

Another Tubb story of a supposed Elder Race who withdrew and vanished from the Earth four thousand years ago, but who left their traces throughout the worlds of the solar system. A party of Earthmen initiate an expedition through the jungles of Venus in an attempt to discover a fabled Venusian "El Dorado."

A360. *World at Bay.* London: Hamilton & Co. ("Panther" #110), March 1954, 158 p., 1/6d. Cover by John Richards.

Earth was starving when cheap power could have saved her—power that would have been available if the atomic research had not been forbidden by the watchful League of Peace. But two scientists choose to ignore this ban and launch an experiment, which succeeds too well, spreading a tide of black death across the country and threatening the whole planet. A fast-paced thriller.

as CHARLES GREY

A361. *Dynasty of Doom.* London: Milestone Publications, May 1953, 126 p., 1/6d. Cover by Ronald Turner.

"Wilner pointed, his finger trembling as he stared at the screen. 'There, ships, hundreds of them! A space fleet!' These were the vessels which had vanished in space over many years. This was the center of hyperspace, the resting place of derelict starships, the Sargasso of Space...' The amazing happenings following this momentous discovery of a fabulous starship graveyard, of human life preserved over centuries, lead to an exciting climax.

A362. *Enterprise 2115.* London: Merit Books, September 1954, 160 p., 1/6d. Cover by Ronald Turner.

"There were two, Rosslyn the pilot, and Comain the dreamer. Rosslyn died in space, frozen, preserved for two centuries until found and resurrected by a miracle of future surgery. Comain remained on Earth, and crystallized his dreams, and when Rosslyn returned, he found a civilization beyond his wildest imagination. Women ruled the planet, guided solely by automatic predictions of a relentless, tremendous, and frightening machine...a machine that foretold the future and determined the actions of the entire world with devastating accuracy. And the presence of Rosslyn brought near chaos. He had to be assimilated—or eliminated!" One of Tubb's best early works, this novel was later published in the United States as *The Mechanical Monarch* (Ace, 1958). Another point, persistently overlooked by careless bibliographers is that the correct title of this work, *The Extra Man*, was transposed with the novel immediately below, by a mistake of the printer.

A363. *The Extra Man.* London: Milestone Publications, February 1954, 128 p., 1/6d. Cover by Ronald Turner.

"The Galaxy is at war; a war between the oxygen-breathing Terrans and the chlorine-breathing Ginzoes. Neither side dare attack the habitable worlds for fear of reprisals, and so the war became a matter of spaceships firing on each other as they emerge from hyperspace. But now, the Ginzoes possess a catalyst which can break down sodium chloride into its basic elements, and if dropped in the oceans of the oxygen world, Mankind would become a dying memory. Lasser has lived with a dream too long. He has fifty days to decide. Fifty days to death. Fifty days to save a planet." This title of this book was supposed to have been *Enterprise 2115*, but was accidentally transposed with the above work by the printer.

A364. *The Hand of Havoc.* London: Merit Books, July 1954, 128 p., 1/6d. Cover by Ronald Turner.

From the coffin ship of Terran control, five Venusians, carriers of the dreaded rhylla disease, escape to continue the hopeless war against Earth. Armed with a ship and with terse orders to end the potential rhylla menace, Ron Prentice sets out into space to track the escaped Venusian fanatics, who refuse to admit that the interplanetary war is over. Prentice must make a final nerve-stopping decision that may mean the safety or the awful plague-death of Earth. One of Tubb's best early novels, which formed the basis for his later novel, *C.O.D. Mars* (Ace Books, 1968).

A365. *I Fight for Mars.* London: Milestone Publications, October 1953, 128 p., 1/6d. Cover by Ronald Turner.

"Fighting for Mars means a battle with the Lobants, a formidable enemy, robot yet human, whose origins are shrouded in a terrifying Martian mystery. Ace rocketship pilot John Delmar, on a dangerous and unlicensed space flight to the fabulous planet, solves the answer to the swarming scourge of Mars." A colorful, superior adventure novel.

A366. *Space Hunger.* London: Milestone Publications, August 1953, 128 p., 1/6d. Cover by Ronald Turner.

"Earth possessed weapons capable of turning small planets into dust—rocket planes, guided missiles, and much more to kill any alien coming from outer space. Yet the Arbitrators came. From orbiting vessels in space, they sprayed the Earth with an alien form of radiation. A microwave pattern of incredible complexity flooded the planet, and the Arbitrators were masters. The populace, glazed with drug-induced euphoria, are scraps of human debris hovering on the thin edge of annihilation. Chaos is truly come again." Just one atomic warhead would liberate Earth—or so the Antis thought... One of Tubb's best early novels, with dystopian overtones.

A367. *The Tormented City.* London: Milestone Publications, July 1953, 126 p., 1/6d. Cover by Ronald Turner.

"The highest paid troops in history are deployed in a tremendous gamble with Earth as the prize. The lethal towers of an alien world are generating disintegration beams which can raze a city in a few seconds and produce malign effects on all humanity." A gripping thriller.

A368. *The Wall.* London: Milestone Publications, April 1953, 128 p., 1/6d. Cover by Ronald Turner.

"Immortality is a myth, a fable, a legend extant on a thousand worlds," Brett said.
The old man nodded, "But behind all legend there must exist a grain of truth; distorted, perhaps, but there."
"Ages ago," Brett said, "other races ruled the stars and their ships spread knowledge among the people of the Universe. Somewhere there is a fountain of youth. Somewhere—but where?"
"Beyond the Wall?" the old man said.
A fast-paced adventure, redolent with a sense of wonder.

as VOLSTED GRIDBAN, *house pseud.*

A208. *Alien Universe.* London: Scion Ltd., November 1952, 94 p., 1/6d. Cover by George Ratcliffe.

An exciting space opera in which Tubb introduced many of the plot elements that he used in later books: hyperspace, flareguns, urillium, etc. It also set the pattern for monstrous forms of alien life existing in other universes. Outrageous action adventure.

A209. *De Bracy's Drug.* London: Scion Ltd., February 1953, 1/6d. Cover by John Richards.

De Bracy's drug destroys all disease, but causes spiritual death as a side effect by eliminating most emotions. A minority group—the Freedom Army—refuses to take the drug, and civil war ensues. A small group of the Freedom Army are cornered, but escape into another probability world. Here, Earth is under the domination of the hideous Star People and an alien race called the Zytlen. Lanson, the leader of the transported group, uses his knowledge of spaceflight—a lost art in this new world—to destroy the alien oppressors.

A210. *Fugitive of Time.* London: Milestone Publications, February 1953, 112 p., 1/6d. Cover by Ronald Turner.

The future world faces a dilemma: replete with every possible scientific advancement, but impotent because of the exhaustion of essential fuels. Starships are grounded, interrupting vital interstellar commerce, and all the highly developed industries have stopped. Man turns to primitive sources of fuels—animal fats and wood for light and heat. With civilization waning, the young scientist Kleon, sentenced to death for using precious conserves of power in an attempt to generate vast energy from dead matter, makes a spectacular bid for the freedom of the whole universe.

A211. *Planetoid Disposals Ltd.* London: Milestone Publications, January 1953, 112 p., 1/6d. Cover by Ronald Turner.

"Volsted Gridban's concept of the space-time continuum is thrilling in its suggestive possibilities. In this story, which is fascinatingly interesting from the science angle, as well as breathtaking in its excitement and suspense, he conceives of speeds superior to that of light, transport by dematerialization and re-assembly of atoms in a remote sector of space-time. This story bridges the gap between physics and metaphysics. It is practical, possible, occult, mysterious. It is the finest piece of SF published for a number of years." Warning: don't believe everything blurb writers tell you!

A212. *Reverse Universe.* London: Scion Ltd., December 1952, 128 p., 1/6d. Cover by John Richards.

An expeditionary ship equipped with a new type of force screen is sent closer to the sun than ever before in an attempt to solve the riddle of perfect atomic energy and anti-gravity. The ship is warped into another universe by seetee matter—whereupon Tubb gives full reign to his hyperspace ideas in another action-packed space opera.

as GILL HUNT, *house pseud.*

A278. *Planetfall.* London: Curtis Warren, November 1951, 111 p., 1/6d. Cover by Ray Theobald.

Somewhere on Venus lies the wreck of Space Patrol Vessel XX15, which holds a secret vital to Earth's security. Only one man knows where the wreck lies: Rex Carson. But he has been unjustly banished to a terrible Jovian penal colony, where he organizes a revolt of the prisoners and the overthrowing of a corrupt regime. A colorful action story, handled with some panache.

as KING LANG, *house pseud.*

A290. *Saturn Patrol.* London: Curtis Warren, October 1951, 111 p., 1/6d. Cover by Ray Theobald.

A galactic civilization of the far future is plundered by a loosely-knit group of outlaws known as the Warbirds. The hero, Gregg Hammond, becomes involved with them as a mercenary. After many adventures (including a memorable battle with a giant insect), he obtains command and reunites the inhabited worlds of the galaxy under a Galactic Patrol. An extraordinarily accomplished first novel by Tubb which laid the foundations for many of his later themes. Now a collector's item, this book is fetching (deservedly) high prices, despite its rotten cover.

as CARL MADDOX

A369. *The Living World.* London: C. A. Pearson (TIT-BITS no #), February 1954, 64 p., 9d. Cover by Ronald Turner.

A standard Tubb novel from his early period featuring all of his stock characters: Tendris, "the tall adventurer," Carl, "the big engineer," an ancient alien race, hyperspace, and the wonder metal, "urillium." Excellent escapist reading provided you haven't already read the same thing in a dozen or so other Tubb novels. This one is a pure parallel of his *The Metal Eater*, as ROY SHELDON.

A370. *Menace from the Past.* London: C. A. Pearson (TIT-BITS no #), March 1954, 64 p., 9d. Cover by Ronald Turner.

An ancient race marooned in our solar system for several thousand years enlists the aid of a group of desperate criminals and adventurers to help them return to their own world in another dimension. An action-packed space opera, reminiscent of the best of the pulps, with more than a touch of Leigh Brackett in the Martian locale. The better of Tubb's two stories for Pearson.

as BRIAN SHAW, *house pseud.*

A342. *Argentis.* London: Curtis Warren, February 1952, 112 p., 1/6d. Cover by Ray Theobald.

This colorful, action-packed space opera tells of rival factions, including Earthmen and an enigmatic and fanatical Venusian, who voyage through space in a race to find the derelict ship of an ancient civilization, a Venusian Elder Race. *Argentis* contains many of the plot elements typical of Tubb's early novels. The book was copyrighted to David Griffiths, who commissioned it, but actually written by Tubb.

as ROY SHELDON, *house pseud.*

A344. *The Metal Eater.* London: Hamilton & Co. ("Panther" #109), March 1954, 158 p., 1/6d. Cover by John Richards.

"It was the last planet left for Man to conquer—a planet rich in priceless urillium ore, yet no man laid a finger on this wealth that was there for the taking. For the planet Vendor could not be conquered. Spacemen tried time and time again, but always, Voices drove them mad and destroyed them. Some intangible power kept men away from that taunting prize—until a scientist on Deneb IV perfected a blanketing device to protect his ship through the barrier. It took him twenty years to do it, and every penny he possessed, but at last, his voyage to Vendor began. It was the voyage of a gambler who knew that only two alternatives faced him—unlimited wealth and glory...or failure and death. But the journey to Vendor brought hazards that neither he nor his crew had foreseen, and before its conclusion, a force was unwittingly released that could have swept human life from the universe—the indestructible and horrifying force of the Metal Eater." An entertaining space opera, Tubb's homage to Jack Williamson's LEGION OF SPACE series.

KARL VALLANCE (Pseudonym)

A371. *Global Blackout.* London: Gannet Press, May 1954, 126 p., 1/6d. Cover by Ray Theobald.

On Saturday, April 25, 2058, the world is suddenly plunged into total darkness by some unknown cause. So begins a nightmare struggle for survival, the search for food and water and shelter. It is the survival of the fittest as bands of men move from house to house, looting and killing; there is no place for the sick and the weak, and only a faint hope that light will ever return. A well-written story and a pleasant surprise after the rubbish that comprises most of Gannet's output.

ERLE VAN LODEN—see: Lisle Willis

T(homas) W. WADE

A prolific writer of SF for John Spencer & Co., Thomas W. Wade wrote under his own name and several pseudonyms. He also had connections with artist Norman

Light, for whom he wrote stories for the magazine, *Worlds of the Universe*. Wade later penned plot continuities for Light's *Captain Future* strip (not connected with Edmond Hamilton's hero of the same name), and had two novels from Digit Books under his own name, *The World of Theda* (1962) and *The Voice from Baru* (1962). Nothing else is known of his personal life.

as VICTOR LA SALLE, *house pseud.*

A291. *Assault from Infinity.* London: John Spencer, June 1953, 108 p., 1/6d. Cover by Norman Light.

> While searching deep space via radar, Dr. Phyllis Busby discovers that something is moving towards Earth at a very high speed. Using a new radar on Mars, the object proves to be a fleet of spaceships. Busby's warnings are ignored by Earth and the Outer Planets, but Martian leader Roon Darvat believes, and Mars is prepared when the Outer Planets fall—soon though, Martian forces are depleted in battle, and with Earth forces only now beginning to prepare, a retreat to Earth may not save the solar system from the Denebian invaders, especially if they are joined by the warlike Sirians. A badly-written and quite absurd space opera.

A292. *Seventh Dimension.* London: John Spencer, July 1953, 124 p., 1/6d. Cover by Gordon C. Davies.

> While on holiday on the Devon moors, Rol, Fran, Paula, and Avis discover a doorway into another dimension. They find that this new land is inhabited by a strange variety of flora and fauna, including huge, six-legged beasts and crawling white maggot-people, the dominant species. Their actions and high technology seem to indicate an invasion force will be going through the doorway soon. The four try to return to their dimension to warn others, but they are chased and Paula is captured. Fully as bad as it sounds!

A293. *Suns in Duo.* London: John Spencer, January 1953, 108 p., 1/6d. Cover by Gordon C. Davies.

> A revolutionary new space fuel takes a spaceship far into space to the planet Lorania, where the crew meet friendly inhabitants. But Lorania has two suns, and every seventy-two years they combine to cause huge tides which all but destroy the Loranians. The normally placid men are not immune from the chaos and a savage battle for survival takes place each time. And there is little time before the strange storms are due to gather.

as KARL ZEIGFRIED, *house pseud.*

A372. *Chariot into Time.* London: John Spencer, May 1953, 128 p., 1/6d. Cover by Ray Theobald.

> During an evening's conversation with friends, John and Grace Wilson are presented with a challenge—Time Travel, which their friends claim is impossible. John thinks otherwise and after many months of work, he creates a machine, the "Fluxon." The husband-and-wife team then launch them-

selves into the year 10,000 A.D. for a series of routine adventures. First, they are captured by giant robots, then held as "guests" in the great city of Dedra, which is maintained by human slaves. Repulsed, the Wilsons lead the inevitable revolt against tyranny.

B(arney?) WARD

B. Ward is believed to be a real name. Two stories appeared under this name in the John Spencer magazines, and a Gannet Press western originally published under the name M. FINGAL was reprinted in 1957 as by BARNEY WARD. One further "Ward"-suspect story appeared from Spencer, published anonymously as "Space Adventurer". While biographical information is sparse, one fact remains extremely plain: *Ward must rate as the all-time worst-ever SF author!* His stories are pure rubbish, and display no writing ability whatsoever. This may seem a rather strong claim, but one reading of his novel, *Pirates of Cerebus* (as by BENGO MISTRAL), will show that Ward's version of the English language is not the normally accepted one. He displays a stunning lack of astronomical knowledge that makes the book compulsive reading—in the hope that it can't get any worse! But it does...

as BENGO MISTRAL, *house pseud.*

A306.   *Pirates of Cerebus.* London: Gannet Press, October 1953, 128 p., 1/6d. Cover by Ray Theobald.

The escape of Magoth from the penal colony on Halma plunges the Dominion into the worst danger it has ever faced. Magoth has discovered how to speed up the evolutionary process, and plans to use his knowledge to take over the Four Planets. Casper Carlyon discovers his hiding place beyond the Atmosphere and rescues the kidnapped Regina Zelda, but escape seems impossible in the face of Nature's revolt, and their spaceship is attacked by walking trees! Possibly the worst SF novel ever published. For a lengthier discussion of this dreadful book, see the companion volume, *Vultures of the Void* (Borgo Press, 1992), p. 92-94.

ELTON WESTWARD (Pseudonym)

Elton Westward is "credited" with a number of novels from Brown Watson published in 1953-1954, but no further science fiction.

A373.   *Return to Mars.* London: Brown Watson, April 1954, 111 p., 1/6d. Cover by Gordon C. Davies.

Mars has hidden behind a barrier of silence for many years before Brant Sellers and Lars Denmon decide to find out why. They discover that the Martians have evacuated their homeworld, leaving a small population of degenerate slaves and the Yisti—terrifying monsters, the results of strange biological experimentation. Sellers soon finds himself alone when traitors steal his spaceship, but with the aid of a Martian female, he discovers the reason for the Martian evacuation and of their plans to return to Mars. The high-speed ending, no doubt generated as the author realized he was over his word quota, leaves the reader (and probably the author) dizzy and confused. An awful story.

ALVIN WESTWOOD (Pseudonym)

His style is similar to that of FRANK LEDERMAN, and it's possible both are the same author.

A374. *Sinister Forces.* London: Brown Watson, February 1953, 111 p., 1/6d. Cover by Ronald Turner.

On a routine patrol flight Steve Norman discovers an unknown planet which has drifted into the controlled space of Ortimo III. An exploratory expedition to the planet reveals that it is dead, but the population could only have vanished hours beforehand. An exploration force on Ortimo is mysteriously destroyed before launch, and Steve suspects it to be the work of a traitor. Suspicion falls on Professor Danstay, who has vanished, and who is later found to be starting a war between Ortimo and the alien Bridians, after which he hopes to take over both planets. Confused? You will be, after reading this mediocre story from another author obviously unversed in SF.

LISLE WILLIS, 1919-

Lisle Willis was a highly prolific author during the late 1940s and early 1950s, writing for most of the paperback markets, penning primarily westerns and gangster stories. His work ran the full gamut from spicy confessions to fairy tales, plus a few science fiction stories in the John Spencer magazines, and two novels under the ERLE VAN LODEN byline from Edwin Self. For Self, he also wrote a sexy French-style series for which he was threatened with prosecution (and for which, partly, Self himself was jailed). He most recently worked as a producer for Tyne Tees Television until his retirement.

as ERLE VAN LODEN

A375. *Curse of Planet Kuz.* London: Edwin Self., June 1953, 128 p., 1/6d. Cover by Terry Maloney.

This atrocious space opera is reminiscent of the early *Dennis Talbot Hughes*, but remains oddly appealing, in that the author seems to have been unaware of his deficiencies and scientific derelictions (bird-men of Jupiter, indeed!) The story develops as a mishmash of Flash Gordon, sword-and-sorcery, and fairy tale: an unknown planet, hostile life forms, and the rescue of a beautiful princess.

A376. *Voyage into Space.* London: Edwin Self, May 1954, 100 p., 1/-d. Cover by Ronald Turner.

Routine space opera, only slightly better written than *Curse of the Planet Kuz* (see #A375). Willis was actually a very talented journeyman writer of sex/thrillers and simon-pure schoolgirl fiction, who happened to wander into science fiction via the Spencer crudzines, and then was detailed to try writing SF by his gangster publisher. He was probably capable of much better work, if he had been sufficiently grounded in science, astronomy, and SF tradition.

G(ranville) L(eslie) WILSON, 1912-

Wilson worked as a scientific and industrial journalist, and authored several other books, including *Gateway to Journalism* (nonfiction) and *The Silver Ring* (1946). A later, more smoothly-written thriller was *Formula for Death* (1960).

A377. *Murder Goes Underground.* London: Fiction House (PICADILLY NOVELS #281), June 1949, 96 p., 9d. Cover uncredited.

Ostensibly a detective story, but included here for completeness, because one chapter of the story contains bona fide SF elements: several crooks involved in a high-speed car chase are incinerated by a death-ray military device which explodes their car engine, projected from an "atom-ray car." One of the minor characters is called "Herbert Gillings," and the story is written in a smooth style uncannily similar to that of *John Russell Fearn.*

ARTHUR (Lennard) WOOLF, 1911-1994?

Woolf was once President of the National Poetry Circle, and editor of their official magazine, *The Melody.* He wrote several books about poetry, and contributed many columns to writers' magazines in the 1930s. He later compiled *Pressman's Holiday*, a prose anthology for journalists, filled with anecdotes and tips on writing from such authors as Edgar Rice Burroughs, published by Matson's Publications in 1948. His other work included a hobby book and official town guides. He began writing for Curtis Warren in 1953, and he known to have penned two non-SF books for them, as well as the lost race novel listed below, under the house name Adam Dale (which was also used for non-fantastic foreign legion novels by Brian Holloway).

as ADAM DALE, *house pseud.*

A378. *Southern Exploration.* London: Curtis Warren, November 1953, 160 p., 1/6d. Cover uncredited.

Professor Gregg, an internationally famous naturalist, leads an expedition to South America in search of a specimen of flower known as the Divine Sceptre of the Incas, an orchid which was reputed to banish all diseases. With the other members of the expedition, he stumbles upon an ancient obelisk which opens, becoming the entrance to an underground passage leading to the lost Kingdom of Primo. A ploddingly dull narrative.

PRESTON YORKE—see: Harold Ernest Kelly

KARL ZEIGFRIED (House pseudonym)

ZIEGFRIED continued to be used as a house name by Spencers until 1965 under the variation, KARL ZEIGFREID, with eighteen novels appearing under that byline altogether. All of the Zeigfreid books were the work of *R. Lionel Fanthorpe.*

A379. *Beyond the Galaxy,* (author unidentified, but possibly T. W. Wade). London: John Spencer, March 1953, 112 p., 1/6d. Cover by Norman Light.

Reckless scientists experimenting with an "Infinitely Powerful Drive" hurl a spaceliner out of the solar system and into deep space. The crew of the ship (plus two convenient female stowaways) become involved in a space war between the amiable Vril and the nasty Tor Scruti, which they eventually settle by blowing up the home planet of the latter. Many copies were printed with *Victor la Salle*'s name on the title page, superimposed with *Zeigfried*'s byline label.

A380. *Chaos in Arcturus,* (author unidentified, but possibly T. W. Wade). London: John Spencer, October 1953, 128 p., 1/6d. Cover by Ron Embleton.

Spaceship *Galaxy X,* en route to Regulus, is caught by a galactic storm. Hurled far off course, it crashlands on a planet of Acturus. There, the crew find that the humanoid Bendags have been ousted from the supremacy by the fox-like Vikens. Captured and ill-used by the Vikens, a few humans escape and lead the Bendags in a successful revolt. A routine story, outrageously "xenocentric" towards humans, and full of pseudo-rhapsodic comments about the vastness of the universe.

A372. *Chariot into Time,* (by T. W. Wade). London: John Spencer, May 1953, 128 p., 1/6d. Cover by Ray Theobald.

SEE: *T. W. Wade* for synopsis.

A202. *Dark Centauri,* (by John Glasby). London: John Spencer, April 1954, 130 p., 1/6d. Cover by Ron Embleton.

SEE: *John Glasby* for synopsis.

A203. *The Uranium Seekers,* (by John Glasby). London: John Spencer, December 1953, 128 p., 1/6d. Cover by Ray Theobald.

SEE: *John Glasby* for synopsis.

B.

PAPERBACK BOOKS FROM ESTABLISHED HOUSES, 1949-1956

This section contains a checklist of other science fiction paperback books issued between 1949 and 1955, published by (mostly) the more respectable publishers of the period. They are, for the most part, reprints of previously issued hardcover novels from the same publisher, although some appear for the first time in book form. The original source is given with each title, and in the case of reprints of books, the original publisher as well. This list is presented alphabetically by publishing house with imprints indicated where necessary, then listed chronologically within the house.

ARROW BOOKS—see HUTCHINSON & CO.

T. V. BOARDMAN & CO. LTD.

B1. *No Place Like Earth,* edited by E. J. Carnell, 1954, 192 p., 2/-d. Cover by Denis McLouglin.

House number 140. Original source: T. V. Boardman, 1952; contains seven reprinted stories—the original hardcover contained ten.

B2. *The Big Eye,* by Max Ehrlich, 1954, 192 p., 2/-d. Cover by Pagram.

House number 149. Original source: Doubleday & Co. (USA), 1949.

B3. *What Mad Universe,* by Fredric Brown, 1954, 192 p., 2/-d. Cover by Pagram.

House number 154. Original source: *Startling Stories* (September 1948). Enlarged for first book publication by E. P. Dutton (USA), 1949.

B4. *Wrong Side of the Moon,* by Francis Ashton and Stephen Ashton, 1955, 190 p., 2/-d. Cover by Pagram.

House number 159. Original source: T. V. Boardman, 1951.

B5. *Best from New Worlds SF,* edited by E. J. Carnell, 1955, 190 p., 2/-d. Cover by Gerard Quinn.

House number 163. First edition. Contains eight reprinted stories.

BRITISH PUBLISHERS GUILD

B6. *Green Mansions*, by William H. Hudson, 1950, 216 p., 1/6d. Cover uncredited.

Original source: G. P. Putnam's Sons (US), 1904).

B7. *The Burning Court*, by John Dickson Carr, 1952, 192 p., 2/-d. Cover uncredited.

Original source: Hamish Hamilton, 1932.

B8. *Life Comes to Seathorpe*, by Neil Bell (aka Stephen Southwold), 1953, 192 p., 2/-d. Cover uncredited.

Original source: Eyre & Spottiswoode, 1946.

B9. *The Long, Loud Silence*, by Wilson Tucker, 1953, 191 p., 2/-d. Cover uncredited.

Original source: Rinehart & Co. (US), 1952.

CHERRY TREE BOOKS—see: KEMSLEY NEWSPAPERS

WILLIAM COLLINS SONS & CO. LTD.

B10. *Death of a World*, by J. Jefferson Farjeon, 1952, 192 p., 1/6d. Cover uncredited.

House number 205c. Original source: Collins, 1948.

B11. *The Screwtape Letters*, by C. S. Lewis, 1955, 160 p., 2/-d. Cover uncredited.

Under Fontana Books imprint. House number 49B. Original source: Geoffrey Bles, 1942.

B12. *Twenty Thousand Leagues Under the Sea*, by Jules Verne, 1955, 116 p., 3/6d. Cover by John Rose.

Under Fontana Books imprint. Original source: as *Vingt Milles Sous les Mers*, published by Hetzel (France), 1870.

CORGI BOOKS—see: TRANSWORLD PUBLISHERS

FONTANA BOOKS—see: WILLIAM COLLINS, SONS & CO. LTD.

W. FOULSHAM & CO.

B13. *The Lair of the White Worm*, by Bram Stoker, 1950, 188 p., 1/6d. Cover uncredited.

Original source: William Rider, 1911.

GERALD G. SWAN LTD.—see: SWAN LTD.

MARK GOULDEN LTD.
(First printings only)

B14. *Tarzan and the Lost Empire*, by Edgar Rice Burroughs, 1949, 128 p., 1/6d. Cover by John Coleman Burroughs, same as U.S. edition dustjacket, 1929.

House number 1. Original source: serial in *Blue Book*, five parts from October 1928; book published by Metropolitan Books (US), 1929.

B15. *Tarzan, Lord of the Jungle*, by Edgar Rice Burroughs, 1949, 136 p., 1/6d. Cover by G. R. Ratcliffe?

House number 2. Original source: serial in *Blue Book*, six parts from December 1927; book published by A. C. McClurg (US), 1928.

B16. *Tarzan the Invincible*, by Edgar Rice Burroughs, 1949, 127 p., 1/6d. Cover from U.S. edition dustjacket, 1931.

House number 3. Original source: serial in *Blue Book*, seven parts from October 1930 and called "Tarzan, Guard of the Jungle"; book published by Edgar Rice Burroughs Inc. (US), 1931.

B17. *Tarzan at the Earth's Core*, by Edgar Rice Burroughs, 1949, 128 p., 1/6d. Cover by M. A. Donohue, same as U.S. edition dustjacket, 1930.

House number 4. Original source: serial in *Blue Book*, seven parts from September 1929; book published by Metropolitan Books (US), 1930.

B18. *Tarzan's Quest*, by Edgar Rice Burroughs, 1949, 127 p., 1/6d. Cover by J. Allen St. John, same as U.S. edition dustjacket, 1936.

House number 5. Original source: serial in *Blue Book*, six parts from October 1935; book published by Edgar Rice Burroughs Inc. (US), 1936.

B19. *A Princess of Mars*, by Edgar Rice Burroughs, 1949, 127 p., 1/6d. Cover by Schoonover, same as U.S. edition dustjacket, 1917.

House number 6. Original source: serial in *All Story Magazine*, six parts from February 1912 and called "Under the Moons of Mars," as by Norman Bean; book published by A. C. McClurg (US), 1917.

B20. *Tarzan and the Lion Man*, by Edgar Rice Burroughs, 1950, 136 p., 1/6d. Cover by J. Allen St. John, same as U.S. edition dustjacket, 1934.

House number 7. Original source: serial in *Liberty*, nine parts from 11 November 1933; book published by Edgar Rice Burroughs Inc. (US), 1934.

B21. *Tarzan and the Forbidden City,* by Edgar Rice Burroughs, 1950, 136 p., 1/6d. Cover by John Coleman Burroughs, same as U.S. edition dustjacket, 1938.

House number 8. Original source: serial in *Argosy,* six parts from 19 March 1938 and called "The Red Star of Tarzan"; book published by Edgar Rice Burroughs Inc. (US), 1938.

B22. *Carson of Venus,* by Edgar Rice Burroughs, 1950, 240 p., 1/6d. Cover by John Coleman Burroughs, same as U.S. edition dustjacket, 1939.

House number 9. Original source: serial in *Argosy,* six parts from 8 January 1938; book published by Edgar Rice Burroughs Inc. (US), 1939.

B23. *Tarzan and the Leopard Men,* by Edgar Rice Burroughs, 1950, 136 p., 1/6d. Cover by J. Allen St. John, same as U.S. edition dustjacket, 1935.

House number 10. Original source: serial in *Blue Book,* six parts from August 1932; book published by Edgar Rice Burroughs Inc. (US), 1935.

B24. *Tarzan and the City of Gold,* by Edgar Rice Burroughs, 1950, 136 p., 1/6d. Cover by J. Allen St. John, same as U.S. edition dustjacket, 1933.

House number 11. Original source: serial in *Argosy,* six parts from 12 March 1932; book published by Edgar Rice Burroughs Inc. (US), 1933.

B25. *Tarzan Triumphant,* by Edgar Rice Burroughs, 1950, 128 p., 1/6d. Cover by Terry Maloney?

House number 12. Original source: serial in *Blue Book,* six parts from October 1931 and called "The Triumph of Tarzan"; book published by Edgar Rice Burroughs Inc. (US), 1932.

B26. *Tarzan and the Foreign Legion,* by Edgar Rice Burroughs, 1950, 128 p., 1/6d. Cover by John Coleman Burroughs, same as U.S. edition dustjacket, 1947.

House number 13. Original source: Edgar Rice Burroughs Inc. (US), 1947.

B27. *Tarzan the Magnificent,* by Edgar Rice Burroughs, 1950, 128 p., 1/6d. Cover by John Coleman Burroughs, same as U.S. edition dustjacket, 1939.

House number 14. Original source: Edgar Rice Burroughs Inc. (US), 1939. Collection of two stories.

B28. *Tarzan of the Apes,* by Edgar Rice Burroughs, 1951, 136 p., 2/-d. Cover by M. A. Donohue, same as U.S. edition frontispiece, *Tarzan at the Earth's Core,* 1930.

House number 15. Original source: story in *All Story Magazine*, October 1912; book published by A. C. McClurg (US), 1914.

B29.   *Tarzan the Untamed,* by Edgar Rice Burroughs, 1951, 136 p., 2/-d. Cover by G. R. Ratcliffe?

House number 16. Original source: A. C. McClurg (US), 1920. Collection of two stories.

B30.   *Tarzan and the Jewels of Opar,* by Edgar Rice Burroughs, 1951, 136 p., 2/-d. Cover by G. R. Ratcliffe?

House number 17. Original source: serial in *All Story Magazine*, five parts from 18 November 1916; book published by A. C. McClurg (US), 1918.

B31.   *The Beasts of Tarzan,* by Edgar Rice Burroughs, 1951, 136 p., 2/-d. Cover by Studley Burroughs, same as U.S. edition dustjacket, *Tarzan Triumphant.*

House number 18. Original source: serial in *All Story Cavalier*, five parts from 16 May 1914; book published by A. C. McClurg (US), 1916.

B32.   *The Return of Tarzan,* by Edgar Rice Burroughs, 1951, 136 p., 2/-d. Cover by John Coleman Burroughs, same as U.S. edition dustjacket, *Land of Terror*, 1944.

House number 19. Original source: serial in *New Story Magazine*, seven parts from June 1913; book published by A. C. McClurg (US), 1915.

B33.   *Tarzan and the Golden Lion,* by Edgar Rice Burroughs, 1952, 136 p., 2/-d. Cover by James E. McConnell.

Under Pinnacle Books imprint. House number 20. Original source: serial in *Argosy All Story*, seven parts from 9 December 1922; book published by A. C. McClurg (US), 1923.

B34.   *The Son of Tarzan,* by Edgar Rice Burroughs, 1953, 136 p., 2/-d. Cover by James E. McConnell.

Under Pinnacle Books imprint. House number 21. Original source: serial in *All Story Magazine*, six parts from 4 December 1915; book published by A. C. McClurg (US), 1917.

B35.   *Tarzan the Terrible,* by Edgar Rice Burroughs, 1953, 136 p., 2/-d. Cover by James E. McConnell.

Under Pinnacle Books imprint. House number 22. Original source: serial in *Argosy All Story*, seven parts from 12 February 1921; book published by A. C. McClurg (US), 1921.

B36. *Lost on Venus,* by Edgar Rice Burroughs, 1953, 136 p., 2/-d. Cover by James E. McConnell.

Under Pinnacle Books imprint. House number 23. Original source: serial in *Argosy,* seven parts from 4 March 1933; book published by Edgar Rice Burroughs Inc. (US), 1935.

B37. *Tarzan and the Ant Men,* by Edgar Rice Burroughs, 1953, 136 p., 2/-d. Cover by James E. McConnell.

Under Pinnacle Books imprint. House number 24. Original source: serial in *Argosy All Story,* seven parts from 2 February 1924; book published by A. C. McClurg (US), 1924.

B38. *Thuvia, Maid of Mars,* by Edgar Rice Burroughs, 1953, 136 p., 2/-d. Cover by James E. McConnell.

Under Pinnacle Books imprint. House number 25. Original source: serial in *All Story,* three parts from 8 April 1916; book published by A. C. McClurg (US), 1920.

B39. *Warlord of Mars,* by Edgar Rice Burroughs, 1953, 152 p., 2/-d. Cover by James E. McConnell.

Under Pinnacle Books imprint. House number 26. Original source: serial in *All Story,* four parts from December 1913; book published by A. C. McClurg (US), 1919.

B40. *The Eternal Lover,* by Edgar Rice Burroughs, 1953, 152 p., 2/-d. Cover by James E. McConnell.

Under Pinnacle Books imprint. House number 28. Original source: A. C. McClurg (US), 1925. Collection of two short novels.

B41. *Tanar of Pellucidar,* by Edgar Rice Burroughs, 1953, 154 p., 2/-d. Cover by James E. McConnell.

Under Pinnacle Books imprint. House number 29. Original source: serial in *Blue Book,* six parts from March 1929; book published by Metropolitan Books (US), 1930.

B42. *The Gods of Mars,* by Edgar Rice Burroughs, 1953, 160 p., 2/-d. Cover by James E. McConnell.

Under Pinnacle Books imprint. House number 30. Original source: serial in *All Story,* five parts from January 1913; book published by A. C. McClurg (US), 1918.

B43. *Jungle Tales of Tarzan,* by Edgar Rice Burroughs, 1954, 190 p., 2/-d. Cover by James E. McConnell.

Under Pinnacle Books imprint. House number 32. Original source: serial in *Blue Book*, twelve parts from September 1916 and called "New Tales of Tarzan"; book published by A. C. McClurg (US), 1919.

B44. *Fighting Man of Mars*, by Edgar Rice Burroughs, 1954, 154 p., 2/-d. Cover by James E. McConnell.

Under Pinnacle Books imprint. House number 33. Original source: serial in *Blue Book*, six parts from April 1930; book published by Metropolitan Books (US), 1932.

B45. *Pirates of Venus*, by Edgar Rice Burroughs, 1954, 153 p., 2/-d. Cover by James E. McConnell.

Under Pinnacle Books imprint. House number 34. Original source: serial in *Argosy*, six parts from 17 September 1932; book published by Edgar Rice Burroughs Inc. (US), 1934.

B46. *Cave Girl*, by Edgar Rice Burroughs, 1954, 153 p., 2/-d. Cover by James E. McConnell.

Under Pinnacle Books imprint. House number 35. Original source: A C. McClurg (US), 1925.

B47. *Chessmen of Mars*, by Edgar Rice Burroughs, 1954, 151 p., 2/-d. Cover by James E. McConnell.

Under Pinnacle Books imprint. House number 36. Original source: serial in *Argosy*, seven parts from 18 February 1922; book published by A. C. McClurg (US), 1922.

B48. *Rogue Queen*, by L. Sprague de Camp, 1954, 160 p., 2/-d. Cover by James E. McConnell.

Under Pinnacle Books imprint. Original source: Doubleday & Co. (US), 1951.

B49. *Mastermind of Mars*, by Edgar Rice Burroughs, 1955, 158 p., 2/-d. Cover by James E. McConnell.

Under Pinnacle Books imprint. House number 38. Original source: *Amazing Stories Annual*, 1927; book published by A. C. McClurg (US), 1928.

B50. *Pellucidar*, by Edgar Rice Burroughs, 1955, 159 p., 2/-d. Cover by James E. McConnell.

Under Pinnacle Books imprint. House number 39. Original source: serial in *All Story Cavalier*, five parts from 1 May 1915; book published by A. C. McClurg (US), 1923.

ROBERT HALE LTD.

B51. *Atom At Spithead*, by David Divine (aka Arthur Durham Divine), 1955 160 p., 2/-d. Cover uncredited.

Original source: Robert Hale, 1953.

HAMILTON & CO. (STAFFORD) LTD.

B52. *The World Below*, by S. Fowler Wright, 1953, 160 p., 1/6d. Cover by John Richards.

Under Panther Books imprint. House number 44. Original source: Merton Press, 1924, as "The Amphibians."

B53. *Sprague de Camp's New Anthology*, edited by H. J. Campbell, 1953, 159 p., 1/6d. Cover by John Richards.

Under Panther Books imprint. House number 92. First edition. Six reprinted stories by L. Sprague de Camp.

B54. *The Dwellers*, by S. Fowler Wright, 1954, 127 p., 1/6d. Cover by John Richards.

Under Panther Books imprint. Original Source: William Collins, 1929 as *The World Below*.

HECTOR KELLY LTD.—see: KELLY LTD.

HODDER AND STOUGHTON LTD.

B55. *She: A History of Adventure*, by H. Rider Haggard, 1949, 255 p., 2/-. Cover uncredited.

House number 119. Original source: serial in *The Graphic*, between 2 October 1886 and 8 January 1887; book published by Lovell, 1887.

B56. *The Avenging Ray*, by Seamark (aka Austin J. Small), 1952, 191 p., 2/-d. Cover uncredited.

Original source: Hodder & Stoughton, 1930.

B57. *The Prisoner in the Opal*, by A. E. W. Mason, 1953, 191 p., 2/-d. Cover uncredited.

Original source: Doubleday, Doran & Co. (US), 1928.

HUTCHINSON & CO. (PUBLISHERS) LTD.

B58. *The Fabulous Valley*, by Dennis Wheatley, 1953, 286 p., 2/-d. Cover uncredited.

Under Arrow Books imprint. House number 284H. Original source: Hutchinson, 1935.

B59. *They Found Atlantis,* by Dennis Wheatley, 1953, 256 p., 2/-d. Cover uncredited.

Under Arrow Books imprint. House number 335H. Original source: Hutchinson, 1936.

B60. *The Secret War,* by Dennis Wheatley, 1953, 288 p., 3/6d. Cover uncredited.

Under Arrow Books imprint. House number 336H. Original source: Hutchinson, 1937.

B61. *The Devil Rides Out,* by Dennis Wheatley, 1954, 245 p., 2/-d. Cover uncredited.

Under Arrow Books imprint. House number 345H. Original source: Hutchinson, 1935.

B62. *Star of Ill Omen,* by Dennis Wheatley, 1954, 288 p., 2/-d. Cover uncredited.

Under Arrow Books imprint. House number 378H. Original source: Hutchinson, 1952.

HECTOR KELLY LTD.

B63. *Enemy Beyond Pluto,* by Jean Gaston Vandel, 1954, 192 p. 2/-d. Cover by R. Brantonne.

Originally published as *Attendant Cosmique* by Fleuve Noir (France), #21 in the "Anticipation" series, 1953.

KEMSLEY NEWSPAPERS LTD.

B64. *John Carstairs: Space Detective,* by Frank Belknap Long, 1951, 192 p. 1/6d. Cover by Ron Embleton.

Under Cherry Tree Novels imprint. House number 400. Original source: Frederick Fell (US), 1949. Collection of six stories.

B65. *The Kid from Mars,* by Oscar J. Friend, 1951, 190 p., 1/6d. Cover by Terry Maloney.

Under Cherry Tree Novels imprint. House number 401. Original source: *Startling Stories,* September 1940; book published by Frederick Fell (US), 1949.

B66. *The Sunken World,* by Stanton A. Coblentz, 1951, 190 p., 1/6d. Cover by Terry Maloney.

Under Cherry Tree Novels imprint. House number 402. Original source: *Amazing Stories Quarterly*, Summer 1928; book published by Fantasy Publishing Co. Inc. (US), 1949.

B67. *Flight Into Space*, edited by Donald A. Wollheim, 1951, 190 p., 1/6d. Cover by Terry Maloney.

Under Cherry Tree Novels imprint. House number 403. Original source: Frederick Fell (US), 1949. Collection of twelve stories; omits one from original version.

B68. *The Last Spaceship*, by Murray Leinster (aka Will F. Jenkins), 1952, 190 p., 1/6d. Cover by Terry Maloney.

Under Cherry Tree Novels imprint. House number 404. Original source: Frederick Fell (US), 1949.

B69. *Gabriel Over the White House*, by Thomas F. Tweed, 1952, 190 p., 1/6d. Cover uncredited.

Under Cherry Tree Novels imprint. House number 405. Original source: Arthur Barker, 1933, as *Rinehard*.

B70. *Ralph 124C41+*, by Hugo Gernsback, 1952, 190 p., 1/6d. Cover by Terry Maloney.

Under Cherry Tree Novels imprint. House number 406. Original source: serial in *Modern Electronics*, twelve parts from April 1911; book published by Stratford Co. (US), 1925.

B71. *Sinister Barrier*, by Eric Frank Russell, 1952, 190 p., 1/6d. Cover by Terry Maloney.

Under Cherry Tree Novels imprint. House number 407. Original source: *Unknown*, March 1939; book published by World's Work, 1943.

B72. *The Thing and Other Stories*, by John W. Campbell, Jr., 1952, 190 p., 1/6d. Cover by Terry Maloney.

Under Cherry Tree Novels imprint. House number 408. Original source: as *Who Goes There?*, Shasta Press (US), 1948. Collection of seven stories.

B73. *Typewriter in the Sky* and *Fear*, by L. Ron Hubbard, 1952, 190 p., 1/6d. Cover by Ron Embleton.

Under Cherry Tree Novels imprint. House number 409. Original source: Gnome Press (US), 1950. Both novels had appeared previously: *Fear* in *Unknown*, July 1940; *Typewriter in the Sky*, serial in *Unknown*, two parts from November 1940.

B74. *Vanguard to Neptune*, by J. M. Walsh, 1952, 190 p., 1/6d. Cover by Ronald Turner.

Under Cherry Tree Novels imprint. House number 410. Original source: novel serialization in *Wonder Stories Quarterly*, Spring 1932; first book edition.

B75.   *Solution T-25,* by Theodora DuBois, 1952, 190 p., 1/6d. Cover by Ron Embleton.

Under Cherry Tree Novels imprint. House number 411. Original source: Doubleday & Co. (US), 1951.

MARK GOULDEN LTD.—see: GOULDEN LTD.

NOVA PUBLICATIONS

B76.   *Stowaway to Mars,* by John Beynon (pseudonym of John Beynon Harris), 1953, 128 p., 1/6d. Cover by Gordon Hutchings.

Original source: serial in *Passing Show*, three parts from May 1936; book published as *Planet Plane*, by George Newnes (UK), 1936. This is an abridged version.

B77.   *The Weapon Shops of Isher,* by A. E. van Vogt, 1954, 159 p., 2/-d. Cover by Gerard Quinn.

House number NS1. Original source: *Thrilling Wonder Stories*, February 1949; book published by Greenberg: Publisher (US), 1951. The book includes not only the above story, but also "The Weapon Shops," (*Astounding*, December 1942) and "The Seesaw," (*Astounding*, July 1941).

B78.   *City in the Sea,* by Wilson Tucker, 1954, 154 p., 2/-d. Cover by Gerard Quinn.

House number NS2. Original source: Rinehart & Co. (US), 1951.

B79.   *The Dreaming Jewels,* by Theodore Sturgeon, 1955, 156 p., 2/-d. Cover by Gerard Quinn.

House number NS3. Original source: *Fantastic Adventures*, February 1950; book published by Greenberg: Publisher (US), 1950. The book is an expanded version of the story.

B80.   *Jack of Eagles,* by James Blish, 1955, 159 p., 2/-d. Cover by Gerard Quinn.

House number NS4. Original source: as "Let the Finder Beware," in *Thrilling Wonder Stories*, December 1949; book published by Greenberg: Publisher (US), 1952. The book is an expanded version of the story.

PAN BOOKS LTD.

B81.   *The Lost World,* by Sir Arthur Conan Doyle, 1949, 224 p., 2/-d. Cover uncredited.

House number 100. Original source: Hodder & Stoughton (UK), 1912.

B82. *The Doomsday Men*, by J. B. Priestley, 1949, 256 p., 2/-d. Cover by Stiein.

House number 109. Original source: William Heinemann (UK), 1938.

B83. *Told in the Dark*, edited by Herbert van Thal, 1950, 256 p., 2/-d. Cover by Val Biro.

House number 152. First edition. Anthology of eleven stories. A second edition published in 1952 omits two of the stories in this volume.

B84. *King Solomon's Mines*, by H. Rider Haggard, 1951, 191 p., 1/6d. Cover by Philip Mendoza.

House number 163. Original source: Cassell (UK), 1885.

B85. *Father Malachy's Miracle*, by Bruce Marshall, 1952, 191 p., 1/6d. Cover by Val Biro.

House number 207. Original source: William Heinemann, 1931.

B86. *The Stone of Chastity*, by Margery Sharp, 1953, 192 p., 1/6d. Cover by Carl Wilton.

House number 246. Original source: Collins, 1940.

B87. *The Time Machine* and *The Man Who Could Work Miracles*, by H. G. Wells, 1953, 157 p., 2/-d. Cover by George Woodman.

House number 251. Original source: *The Time Machine*, published by Heinemann (UK), 1895; *The Man Who Could Work Miracles*, published by Cresset Press (UK), 1936.

B88. *Voyage to Venus*, by C. S. Lewis, 1953, 190 p., 2/-d. Cover by Carl Wilton.

House number 253. Original source: as *Perelandra*, published by John Lane (UK), 1943.

B89. *Ghost Stories of an Antiquary*, by M. R. James, 1953, 159 p., 2/-d. Cover by Carl Wilton.

House number 266. Original source: Edward Arnold (UK), 1904. Collection of eight stories.

B90. *The Return*, by Walter de la Mare, 1954, 221 p., 2/-d. Cover by Carl Wilton.

House number 270. Original source: Edward Arnold, 1910.

B91. *Spaceways,* by Eric Charles Maine (aka David McIlwain), 1954, 190 p., 2/-d. Cover by Gerard Quinn.

House number 297. Original source: Hodder & Stoughton (UK), 1953.

B92. *Prelude to Space,* by Arthur C. Clarke, 1954, 156 p., 2/-d. Cover by Gerard Quinn.

House number 301. Original source: Galaxy Science Fiction Novel (US), 1951.

B93. *Night in Babylon,* by James Wellard, 1954, 220 p., 2/-d. Cover uncredited.

House number 313. Original source: Macmillan (UK), 1953.

B94. *A Book of Strange Stories,* edited by Herbert van Thal, 1954, 188 p., 2/-d. Cover by Sax.

House number 315. First edition. Collection of thirteen reprinted stories.

B95. *That Hideous Strength,* by C. S. Lewis, 1955, 252 p., 2/-d. Cover by Sax.

House number 321. Original source: John Lane (UK), 1945.

B96. *The Man Who Sold the Moon,* by Robert Heinlein, 1955, 252 p., 2/-d. Cover by Gerard Quinn.

House number 327. Original source: Shasta Press (US), 1950. Collection of six reprinted stories.

B97. *More Ghost Stories of an Antiquary,* by M. R. James, 1955, 160 p., 2/-d. Cover by Carl Wilton.

House number 359. Original source: Edward Arnold (UK), 1911. Collection of seven stories.

PENGUIN BOOKS LTD.

B98. *The Picture of Dorian Gray,* by Oscar Wilde, 1949, 256 p., 2/-d. Cover uncredited.

House number 616. Original source: Ward Lock (UK), 1891.

B99. *Fairy Tales from the Isle of Man,* edited by D. Broome, 1951, 156 p., 1/6d. Cover uncredited.

House number PS59.

B100. *Animal Farm,* by George Orwell (aka Eric Arthur Blair), 1951, 120 p., 1/6d. Cover uncredited.

House number 838. Original source: Secker & Warburg (UK), 1945.

B101. *Many Dimensions*, by Charles Williams, 1951, 254 p., 2/-d. Cover uncredited.

House number 884. Original source: Victor Gollancz (UK), 1932.

B102. *Men and Gods*, by Rex Warner, 1952, 207 p., 2/-d. Cover uncredited.

B103. *Voyage to Purilia*, by Elmer L. Rice, 1954, 185 p., 2/-d. Cover uncredited.

House number 901. Original source: Cosmopolitan Book Corp. (US), 1930.

B104. *1984*, by George Orwell (aka Eric Arthur Blair), 1954, 256 p., 2/-d. Cover uncredited.

House number 972. Original source: Secker & Warburg, 1949.

B105. *The Day of the Triffids*, by John Wyndham (aka John Beynon Harris), 1954, 272 p., 2/6d. Cover uncredited.

House number 993. Original source: serial in *Collier's Magazine*, five parts from 6 January 1951; book published by Michael Joseph, 1951.

B106. *Seven Men and Two Others*, by Max Beerbohm, 1954, 185 p., 2/-d. Cover uncredited.

House number 1010. Original source: William Heinemann (UK), 1949. Collection of six stories. Earlier Heinemann edition contained five stories, and called *Seven Men*.

B107. *Collected Short Stories*, by E. M. Foster, 1954, 222 p., 2/-d. Cover uncredited.

House number 1031. Original source: as *Collected Tales*, by Alfred A. Knopf (US), 1947. Collection of twelve stories.

B108. *After Many a Summer Dies the Swan*, by Aldous Huxley, 1955, 251 p., 2/6d. Cover uncredited.

House number 1049. Original source: as "After Many a Sunset," serial in *Harper's Magazine*, from 1938; book published by Chatto & Windus (UK), 1939.

B109. *Brave New World*, by Aldous Huxley, 1955, 201 p., 4/-d. Cover uncredited.

House number 1052. Original source: Chatto & Windus (UK), 1932.

B110. *The Kraken Wakes,* by John Wyndham (aka John Beynon Harris), 1955, 240 p., 2/-d. Cover uncredited.

House number 1075. Original source: Michael Joseph (UK), 1953.

PINNACLE BOOKS—see: MARK GOULDEN LTD.

REGAL BOOKS

B111 *The Island of Captain Sparrow,* by S. Fowler Wright, 1953, 174 p., 2/-d. Cover by Norman Light.

House number 101. Original source: Victor Gollancz (UK), 1928.

B112. *The Screaming Lake,* by S. Fowler Wright, 1953, 175 p., 2/-d. Cover by Norman Light.

House number 102. Original source: Robert Hale (UK), 1937.

REGULAR PUBLICATIONS

B113. *Threatened People,* by George Borodin (aka George Sava), 1954, 160 p., 2/-d. Cover uncredited.

Original source: As *Spurious Sun,* T. Werner Laurie, 1948.

RIDER & CO.

B114. *Dracula,* by Bram Stoker, 1954, 335 p., 2/-d. Cover uncredited.

Original source: Archibald Constable (UK), 1897.

ROBERT HALE LTD.—see: HALE LTD.

SCOTTIE BOOKS—see: TRANSWORLD PUBLISHERS

GERALD G. SWAN LTD.

B115. *The Great Mirror,* by Arthur J. Burks, 1952, 128 p., 1/-d. Cover uncredited.

Original source: in *Science Fiction Quarterly,* Summer 1942. First edition.

B116. *The Man on the Meteor,* by Ray Cummings, 1952, 125 p., 1/-d. Cover uncredited.

Original source: serial in *Science and Invention,* nine parts from January 1924. First edition.

TRANSWORLD PUBLISHERS

B117. *Castaway,* by James Gould Cozzens, 1952, 121 p., 2/-d. Cover uncredited.

Under Corgi Books imprint. House number 1007. Original source: Random House (US), 1934.

B118. *Donovan's Brain,* by Curt Siodmak, 1952, 181 p., 2/-d. Cover uncredited.

Under Corgi Books imprint. House number 819. Original source: *Black Mask Magazine,* 1942; book published by Alfred A. Knopf (US), 1943.

B119. *The Silver Locusts,* by Ray Bradbury, 1952, 256 p., 2/-d. Cover by John Richards.

Under Corgi Books imprint. House number 886. Original source: Doubleday & Co. (US), 1951.

B120. *Space on My Hands,* by Fredric Brown, 1953, 239 p., 2/-d. Cover uncredited.

Under Corgi Books imprint. House number 1077. Original source: Shasta Press (US), 1951. Collection of nine stories.

B121. *The Witching Night,* by C. S. Cody (aka Leslie Waller), 1953, 280 p., 2/-d. Cover uncredited.

Under Corgi Books imprint. House number T27. Original source: World Publishing Co. (US), 1952.

B122. *The Sands of Mars,* by Arthur C. Clarke, 1954, 251 p., 2/-d. Cover by John Richards.

Under Corgi Books imprint. House number T43. Original source: Sidgwick & Jackson (UK), 1951.

B123. *City at Worlds End,* by Edmond Hamilton, 1954, 221 p., 2/-d. Cover by John Richards.

Under Corgi Books imprint. House number T58. Original source: in *Startling Stories,* July 1950; book published by Frederick Fell (US), 1951. Expanded version of the above story.

B124. *The Illustrated Man,* by Ray Bradbury, 1955, 246 p., 2/-d. Cover by John Richards.

Under Corgi Books imprint. House number 1282. Original source: Doubleday & Co. (US), 1951. This is a differing edition containing sixteen stories, omitting four and replacing them with two others.

B125. *The Star Raiders*, by Donald Suddaby, 1955, 188 p., 2/-d. Cover by John Richards.

Under Scottie Books imprint. House number J7. Original source: Oxford University Press (UK), 1950.

T. V. BOARDMAN & CO. LTD.—see: BOARDMAN & CO. LTD.

W. FOULSHAM & CO.—see: FOULSHAM & CO.

WARD, LOCK LTD.

B126. *Colonists of Space*, by Charles Carr (aka S. C. Mason), 1955, 192 p., 2/-d. Cover by Harold Johns?

House number 25. Original source: Ward, Lock (UK), 1954.

B127. *Wheel in the Sky*, by Rafe Bernard, 1955, 193 p., 2/-d. Cover by Harold Johns?

House number 26. Original source: Ward, Lock (UK), 1954.

WORLD DISTRIBUTORS (MANCHESTER) LTD.

B128. *The Beasts from Beyond*, by Manly Wade Wellman, 1950, 160 p., 1/6d. Cover by Leroi Osborne?

"World Fantasy Classics" series. Previously published as *Strangers on the Heights* in *Startling Stories*, Summer 1944. Author's byline on book reads "Manley" Wade Wellman. First book edition.

B129. *Tharkol, Lord of the Unknown*, by Edmond Hamilton, 1950, 160 p., 1/6d. Cover by Leroi Osborne?

"World Fantasy Classics" series. Previously published as *The Prisoner of Mars* in *Startling Stories*, May 1939. First book edition.

B130. *The Whispering Gorilla*, by David V. Reed (aka David Vern), 1950, 160 p., 1/6d. Cover by Robert Gibson Jones (copied from the magazine publication).

"World Fantasy Classics" series. Previously published as *The Return of the Whispering Gorilla*, in *Fantastic Adventures*, February 1943, as by DAVID VERN. The R. G. Jones cover was also used. First book edition.

B131. *The Monsters of Juntonheim*, by Edmond Hamilton, 1950, 160 p., 1/6d. Cover by Leroi Osborne?

"World Fantasy Classics" series. Previously published as *A Yank in Valhalla* in *Startling Stories*, January 1941. First book edition.

B132. *Devil's Planet,* by Manly Wade Wellman, 1951, 128 p., 1/6d. Cover by Leroi Osborne?

"World Fantasy Classics" series. Previously published in *Startling Stories,* January 1942. Author's byline on book reads "Manley" Wade Wellman. First book edition.

B133. *Shadow Over Mars,* by Leigh Brackett, 1951, 128 p., 1/6d. Cover by Leroi Osborne?

"World Fantasy Classics" series. Previously published in *Startling Stories,* Fall 1944. First book edition.

B134. *Master Mind Menace,* by Belli Luigi, 1951, 128 p., 1/6d. Cover by Leroi Osborne?

"World Fantasy Classics" series. Original source: Transport Publications (Sydney, Australia), 1950.

B135. *The Metal Monster,* by Belli Luigi, 1951, 128 p., 1/6d. Cover by Leroi Osborne?

"World Fantasy Classics" series. Original source: Transport Publications (Sydney, Australia), 1950/51 under a different unidentified title.

C.

A CHECKLIST OF BRITISH SCIENCE FICTION MAGAZINES, 1949-1956

The following checklist lists each issue of original British science fiction magazines published betweeen 1949 and February 1956 (the cut-off date of this volume). The first column is a code which relates to the magazine index which follows this list; the second column is the date the issue was published (or, where the magazine has no date, the approximate date of issue); the third and fourth give the volume and whole issue number; the fifth column gives the page count of each issue; the final column indicates the cover artist. Interior black-and-white illustrators are listed for each magazine, with the issues they appeared in shown in parentheses.

AUTHENTIC SCIENCE FICTION SERIES
Editors; G(ordon) H(olmes) Landsborough, 1-10; Herbert J. Campbell, 11-48

Abbr.	Date	Vol.	Iss.	Pages	Cover artist
AUT 1	Jan 1951		1	128	D.L.W.
AUT 2	Jan 1951		2	128	D.L.W.

SCIENCE FICTION FORTNIGHTLY

AUT 3	Feb 1951		3	112	D.L.W.
AUT 4	Feb 1951		4	112	D.L.W.
AUT 5	Mar 1951		5	112	D.L.W.
AUT 6	Mar 1951		6	112	D.L.W.
AUT 7	Apr 1951		7	112	D.L.W.
AUT 8	Apr 1951		8	112	D.L.W.

SCIENCE FICTION MONTHLY

AUT 9	May 1951		9	112	George Ratcliffe
AUT 10	Jun 1951		10	112	George Ratcliffe
AUT 11	Jul 1951		11	112	George Ratcliffe
AUT 12	Aug 1951		12	112	George Ratcliffe

AUTHENTIC SCIENCE FICTION

AUT 13	Sep 1951		13	112	D.L.W.
AUT 14	Oct 1951		14	112	D.L.W.
AUT 15	Nov 1951		15	112	D.L.W.
AUT 16	Dec 1951		16	112	D.L.W.
AUT 17	Jan 1952		17	112	D.L.W.

AUT 18	Feb 1952	18	112	D.L.W.
AUT 19	Mar 1952	19	112	D.L.W.
AUT 20	Apr 1952	20	112	Vann
AUT 21	May 1952	21	112	Gordon C. Davies
AUT 22	Jun 1952	22	112	Gordon C. Davies
AUT 23	Jul 1952	23	112	Gordon C. Davies
AUT 24	Aug 1952	24	112	Gordon C. Davies
AUT 25	Sep 1952	25	128	J. Pollack
AUT 26	Oct 1952	26	128	J. Pollack
AUT 27	Nov 1952	27	128	Gordon C. Davies
AUT 28	Dec 1952	28	128	Vann
AUT 29	Jan 1953	29	144	Vann
AUT 30	Feb 1953	30	144	John Richards
AUT 31	Mar 1953	31	144	John Richards
AUT 32	Apr 1953	32	144	DAVIS
AUT 33	May 1953	33	144	DAVIS
AUT 34	Jun 1953	34	144	DAVIS
AUT 35	Jul 1953	35	144	DAVIS
AUT 36	Aug 1953	36	144	DAVIS
AUT 37	Sep 1953	37	144	DAVIS
AUT 38	Oct 1953	38	144	DAVIS
AUT 39	Nov 1953	39	144	DAVIS
AUT 40	Dec 1953	40	144	DAVIS
AUT 41	Jan 1954	41	144	DAVIS
AUT 42	Feb 1954	42	160	DAVIS
AUT 43	Mar 1954	43	160	DAVIS
AUT 44	Apr 1954	44	160	DAVIS
AUT 45	May 1954	45	160	DAVIS
AUT 46	Jun 1954	46	160	DAVIS
AUT 47	Jul 1954	47	160	DAVIS
AUT 48	Aug 1954	48	160	DAVIS
AUT 49	Sep 1954	49	160	DAVIS
AUT 50	Oct 1954	50	160	DAVIS
AUT 51	Nov 1954	51	160	DAVIS
AUT 52	Dec 1954	52	160	DAVIS
AUT 53	Jan 1955	53	160	DAVIS
AUT 54	Feb 1955	54	160	DAVIS
AUT 55	Mar 1955	55	160	John Richards
AUT 56	Apr 1955	56	160	John Stewart
AUT 57	May 1955	57	160	John Richards
AUT 58	Jun 1955	58	160	John Stewart
AUT 59	Jul 1955	59	160	John Stewart
AUT 60	Aug 1955	60	160	Slater
AUT 61	Sep 1955	61	160	Josh Kirby
AUT 62	Oct 1955	62	160	D. A. Stowe
AUT 63	Nov 1955	63	160	D. A. Stowe
AUT 64	Dec 1955	64	160	D. A. Stowe
AUT 65	Jan 1956	65	160	Ken Woodward
AUT 66	Feb 1956	66	160	Ken Woodward

INTERIOR ILLUSTRATORS: Fischer (29-36); Patrick Kemmish (65); Philip Mendoza (49-50); John Mortimer (51-64, 66), James Rattigan (55); John Richards (29, 36);

John Richards as DAVIS (29-48); John Richards as GERALD (38-39); John Richards as MALLORY (33-35); John Richards as MULLER (40-42).

FUTURISTIC SCIENCE STORIES
Editors: Michael Nahum and Sol Assael (anonymous)

FSS 1	Apr 1950	1	128	Gerald Facey
FSS 2	Aug 1950	2	128	Gerald Facey
FSS 3	Dec 1950	3	128	Gerald Facey
FSS 4	Feb 1951	4	128	Gerald Facey
FSS 5	Dec 1951	5	112	Gerald Facey
FSS 6	Apr 1952	6	112	Gerald Facey
FSS 7	Jul 1952	7	112	Ronald Turner
FSS 8	Oct 1952	8	112	Norman Light
FSS 9	Jan 1953	9	112	Gordon C. Davies
FSS 10	Apr 1953	10	112	Norman Light
FSS 11	May 1953	11	128	Norman Light
FSS 12	Aug 1953	12	128	Gordon C. Davies
FSS 13	Oct 1953	13	128	Ray Theobald
FSS 14	Jan 1954	14	128	Ray Theobald
FSS 15	Apr 1954	15	128	Ron Embleton

INTERIOR ILLUSTRATORS: Norman Light (8-15), Philip Mendoza (7); Artwork was decorative/representative, but did not illustrate individual stories.

GRIPPING TERROR

GT1	Jun 1949		64	unidentified

NEBULA SCIENCE FICTION
Editor: Peter Hamilton

NEB 1	Aut 1952 1	1	120	Alan Hunter
NEB 2	Spr 1953 1	2	120	Alan Hunter
NEB 3	Sum 1953 1	3	120	Bob Clothier
NEB 4	Sep 1953 1	4	128	Bob Clothier
NEB 5	Aut 1953 2	1	128	Ken McIntyre
NEB 6	Dec 1953 2	2	128	G. H. IRWIN*
NEB 7	Feb 1954 2	3	130	Bob Clothier
NEB 8	Apr 1954 2	4	136	Ken McIntyre
NEB 9	Aug 1954	9	136	Bob Clothier
NEB 10	Oct 1954	10	128	Bob Clothier
NEB 11	Dec 1954	11	128	James Rattigan
NEB 12	Apr 1955	12	128	Bob Clothier
NEB 13	Sep 1955	13	112	James Rattigan
NEB 14	Nov 1955	14	112	Ken McIntyre
NEB 15	Jan 1956	15	112	James Stark

*This magazine credit is clearly an error since G. H. IRWIN was a house pseudonym invented by American editor and writer, Ray Palmer, for use in his various magazines. The style of this *Nebula* cover is identical to some of the back cover experiments on *Other Worlds*. It is very similar to the November 1955 issue, which was painted by Robert Gibson Jones and achieved "by letting daubs of paint run on the board, haphazardly. When one suggests a scene, it is filled in with detail and human figures."

INTERIOR ILLUSTRATORS: Bob Clothier (3-9, 11); Martin Frew (7, 9-13, 15); Jon J. Greengrass (9, 12-15); Alan Hunter (2-6, 8-12, 15); Terry Jeeves (4); JORDAN (10); Ken McIntyre (15); Brian Miller (6); Bill Price (2, 5, 7, 12); Gerard Quinn (3); Tony Steele (7); Arthur "ATom" Thompson (13-14); Harry Turner (8, 10-15); Pat Wake (4); Jack Wilson (3, 5-11).

NEW WORLDS
Editor: E(dward) J(ohn) Carnell

NW 4	Jun 1949	2	4	88	Dennis (Slack)
NW 5	Sep 1949	2	5	96	Bob Clothier
NW 6	Spr 1950	2	6	96	Bob Clothier
NW 7	Sum 1950	3	7	96	Bob Clothier
NW 8	Win 1950	3	8	96	Bob Clothier
NW 9	Spr 1951	3	9	96	Bob Clothier
NW 10	Sum 1951	3	10	96	Bob Clothier
NW 11	Aut 1951	4	11	96	Reina Bull
NW 12	Win 1951	4	12	96	Bob Clothier
NW 13	Jan 1952	5	13	96	Gerard Quinn
NW 14	Mar 1952	5	14	96	Bob Clothier
NW 15	May 1952	5	15	96	Gerard Quinn
NW 16	Jul 1952	6	16	96	Bob Clothier
NW 17	Sep 1952	6	17	96	Gerard Quinn
NW 18	Nov 1952	6	18	96	Reina Bull
NW 19	Jan 1953	7	19	96	Gerard Quinn
NW 20	Mar 1953	7	20	96	Bob Clothier
NW 21	Jun 1953	7	21	128	Gerard Quinn
NW 22	Apr 1954	8	22	128	J. Kinnear
NW 23	May 1954	8	23	128	Gerard Quinn
NW 24	Jun 1954	8	24	128	Gerard Quinn
NW 25	Jul 1954	9	25	128	Gerard Quinn
NW 26	Aug 1954	9	26	128	Gerard Quinn
NW 27	Sep 1954	9	27	128	Gerard Quinn
NW 28	Oct 1954	10	28	128	Gerard Quinn
NW 29	Nov 1954	10	29	128	Gerard Quinn
NW 30	Dec 1954	10	30	128	Gerard Quinn
NW 31	Jan 1955	11	31	128	Gerard Quinn
NW 32	Feb 1955	11	32	128	Gerard Quinn
NW 33	Mar 1955	11	33	128	Gerard Quinn
NW 34	Apr 1955	12	34	128	M. Bradshaw
NW 35	May 1955	12	35	128	Gerard Quinn
NW 36	Jun 1955	12	36	128	Gerard Quinn
NW 37	Jul 1955	13	37	128	Gerard Quinn
NW 38	Aug 1955	13	38	128	M. Bradshaw
NW 39	Sep 1955	13	39	128	Gerard Quinn
NW 40	Oct 1955	14	40	128	M. Bradshaw
NW 41	Nov 1955	14	41	128	M. Bradshaw
NW 42	Dec 1955	14	42	128	Gerard Quinn
NW 43	Jan 1956	15	43	128	Gerard Quinn

NW 44	Feb 1956 15	44	128	M. Bradshaw

INTERIOR ILLUSTRATORS: M. Bradshaw (34); Reina Bull (11, 18); Bob Clothier (5-21, 25); DENNIS (Slack) (4); Alan Hunter (7-24); Gordon Hutchings (21, 24, 28, 32, 33, 37, 39, 41); Brian Lewis (26, 29-30, 34, 42); (Leroi) OSBORNE (33, 35); Gerard Quinn (9-36); SMITH (23); Harry Turner (5-6); H. White (4, 43).

OUT OF THIS WORLD
Editors: Michael Nahum and Sol Assael (anonymous)

OTW 1	Oct 1954	1	128	Ray Theobald
OTW 2	Win 1954/5	2	128	Ronald Turner

SCIENCE-FANTASY
Editors: Walter H(erbert) Gillings, 1-2; E(dward) J(ohn) Carnell, 3-64

SF 1	Sum 1950 1	1	96	Frederic Powell
SF 2	Win 1950 1	2	96	Harry Turner
SF 3	Win 1951 1	3	96	Reina Bull
SF 4	Spr 1952 2	4	96	Reina Bull
SF 5	Aut 1952 2	5	96	Gerard Quinn
SF 6	Spr 1953 2	6	96	Gerard Quinn
SF 7	Mar 1954 3	7	128	Gerard Quinn
SF 8	May 1954 3	8	128	Gerard Quinn
SF 9	Ju 1954 3	9	128	Gerard Quinn
SF 10	Sep 1954 4	10	128	Norman Partridge
SF 11	Dec 1954 4	11	128	Gerard Quinn
SF 12	Feb 1955 4	12	128	Gerard Quinn
SF 13	Apr 1955 5	13	128	Gerard Quinn
SF 14	Jun 1955 5	14	128	Gerard Quinn
SF 15	Sep 1955 5	15	128	Gerard Quinn
SF 16	Nov 1955 6	16	128	Gerard Quinn
SF 17	Feb 1956 6	17	128	Gerard Quinn

INTERIOR ILLUSTRATORS: John Ashcroft (10); M. Bradshaw (13); Reina Bull (4); Bob Clothier (3-7); ERNST (2); Bruce Gaffron (1); Alan Hunter (3-8); Gordon Hutchings (7-9, 15); Brian Lewis (11-12); (Leroi) OSBORNE (14); POWELL (1-2); Gerard Quinn (3-17); ROWLAND (14); SMITH (8); Harry Turner (1-2); Ken Woodward (14).

SPACE FACT AND FICTION
Editor: Gerald G. Swan (anonymous)

SFF 1	Mar 1954	1	32	David Williams
SFF 2	Apr 1954	2	32	David Williams
SFF 3	May 1954	3	32	David Williams
SFF 4	Jun 1954	4	32	David Williams
SFF 5	Jul 1954	5	32	David Williams
SFF 6	Aug 1954	6	32	David Williams
SFF 7	Sep 1954	7	32	David Williams
SFF 8	Oct 1954	8	32	David Williams

INTERIOR ILLUSTRATORS: Hannes Bok (8); Boris Dolgov (7-8); John Forte (8); Ron McCail (1, 5, 7); A. P. (5-6).

SUPERNATURAL STORIES
Editors: Michael Nahum and Sol Assael as "John S. Manning"

SN 1	May 1954	1	128	Ray Theobald
SN 2	Jul 1954	2	128	Ray Theobald
SN 3	Sep 1954	3	128	Gerald Facey
SN 4	Nov 1954	4	128	Gerald Facey
SN 5	Jan 1955	5	128	Gerald Facey
SN 6	Mar 1955	6	128	Ronald Turner
SN 7	May 1955	7	128	Gerald Facey
SN 8	Aut 1955	8	128	Ray Theobald

INTERIOR ILLUSTRATOR: Norman Light (1-8).

SUSPENSE STORIES

SUS 1	Jul 1954	96	unidentified
SUS 2	Sep 1954	96	unidentified
SUS 3	Nov 1954	96	unidentified

INTERIOR ILLUSTRATOR: unidentified.

TALES OF TOMORROW
Editors: Michael Nahum and Sol Assael (anonymous)

TOT 1	Sep 1950	1	128	Gerald Facey
TOT 2	Jan 1951	2	128	Gerald Facey
TOT 3	Mar 1951	3	128	Ronald Turner
TOT 4	Jul 1952	4	112	Ronald Turner
TOT 5	Sep 1952	5	112	Norman Light
TOT 6	Jan 1953	6	112	Ronald Turner
TOT 7	May 1953	7	112	Norman Light
TOT 8	Aug 1953	8	128	Gordon C. Davies
TOT 9	Oct 1953	9	132	Gordon C. Davies
TOT 10	Apr 1954	10	128	Gordon C. Davies
TOT 11	Jun 1954	11	132	Gordon C. Davies

INTERIOR ILLUSTRATORS: Norman Light (5-11); Philip Mendoza (4); Artwork was decorative/representative, but did not illustrate individual stories.

VARGO STATTEN SCIENCE FICTION MAGAZINE
Editors: Alistair Blair Johns Paterson, 1-6; John Russell Fearn, 7-19

VSS 1	Jan 1954	1	1	64	Ronald Turner
VSS 2	Feb 1954	1	2	64	John Richards
VSS 3	Apr 1954	1	3	64	John Richards

INTERIOR ILLUSTRATORS: Jim Holdaway (3); Philip Mendoza (3); John Richards (1-2); Ray Theobald (3).

VARGO STATTEN BRITISH SCIENCE FICTION MAGAZINE

VSS 4	May 1954 1		4	128	Ronald Turner
VSS 5	Jul 1954 1		5	128	Ronald Turner

INTERIOR ILLUSTRATORS: From fourth issue, only small stock filler plates were used, mainly by James Rattigan.

BRITISH SCIENCE FICTION MAGAZINE

VSS 6	Sep 1954 1		6	128	John Richards
VSS 7	Nov 1954 1		7	128	John Richards
VSS 8	Dec 1954 1		8	128	John Richards (reprint of 7)
VSS 9	Jan 1955 1		9	128	John Richards (reprint of 6)
VSS 10	Feb 1955 1		10	128	Ronald Turner
VSS 11	Mar 1955 1		11	128	Ronald Turner
VSS 12	Apr 1955 1		12	128	Ronald Turner

BRITISH SPACE FICTION MAGAZINE

VSS 13	Jun 1955	2	1	128	Ronald Turner (contents panel)
VSS 14	Jul 1955	2	2	128	Ronald Turner (standardized)
VSS 15	Aug 1955	2	3	128	Ronald Turner (standardized)
VSS 16	Sep 1955	2	4	128	Ronald Turner (standardized)
VSS 17	Oct 1955	2	5	128	Ronald Turner (standardized)
VSS 18	Dec 1955	2	6	128	Ronald Turner (standardized)
VSS 19	Feb 1956	2	7	128	Ronald Turner (standardized)

WEIRD WORLD

WWD 1	1955	1	1	48	Roger Davis
WWD 2	Feb 1956	1	2	48	Roger Davis

INTERIOR ILLUSTRATOR: Roger Davis (1-2).

WONDERS OF THE SPACEWAYS
Editors: Michael Nahum and Sol Assael (anonymous)

WOS 1	Feb 1951		128	Gerald Facey
WOS 2	Jan 1952	2	96	Gerald Facey
WOS 3	May 1952	3	112	Ronald Turner
WOS 4	Sep 1952	4	112	Gordon C. Davies
WOS 5	Nov 1952	5	112	Gordon C. Davies
WOS 6	Jan 1953	6	112	Norman Light
WOS 7	Jul 1953	7	128	Norman Light
WOS 8	Oct 1953	8	128	Ray Theobald
WOS 9	Jan 1954	9	128	Ray Theobald
WOS 10	Apr 1954	10	128	Ray Theobald

INTERIOR ILLUSTRATORS: Norman Light (4-10); Artwork was decorative/representative, but did not illustrate particular stories.

WORLDS OF FANTASY
Editors: Michael Nahum and Sol Assael (anonymous)

WOF 1	Jun 1950	1	128	Gerald Facey
WOF 2	Nov 1950	2	128	Gerald Facey
WOF 3	Jan 1951	3	128	Gerald Facey
WOF 4	Nov 1951	4	96	Gerald Facey
WOF 5	Apr 1952	5	112	Gerald Facey
WOF 6	Aug 1952	6	112	Norman Light
WOF 7	Sep 1952	7	112	Ronald Turner
WOF 8	Dec 1952	8	112	Norman Light
WOF 9	Apr 1953	9	112	Norman Light
WOF 10	Jun 1953	10	112	Gordon C. Davies
WOF 11	Sep 1953	11	128	Ray Theobald
WOF 12	Feb 1954	12	128	Ron Embleton
WOF 13	Apr 1954	13	128	Gordon C. Davies
WOF 14	Jun 1954	14	128	Ray Theobald

INTERIOR ILLUSTRATORS: Norman Light (7-14); Ron Turner (6); Artwork was decorative/representative, but did not illustrate particular stories.

WORLDS OF THE UNIVERSE
Editor: Norman Light (anonymous)

WOU 1	Nov 1953	1	102	MARCUS (aka Norman Light)

INTERIOR ILLUSTRATORS: MARCUS (aka Norman Light)

D.

A COMPLETE AUTHOR INDEX TO THE STORIES IN THE BRITISH SCIENCE FICTION MAGAZINES, JUNE 1949-FEBRUARY 1956

Below is a complete index, alphabetical by author, then by title. The first column indicates the title of the work; (nf) indicates a nonfiction article. The second column is the date, and the third is the magazine abbreviation, which can be checked against section C of this volume for complete details. The index commences with the Nova relaunch of *New World*, and ends with the demise of *The British Space Fiction Magazine*.

FORREST J(ames) ACKERMAN, 1916- (USA)

Atoms and Stars	Spr 1953	NEB 2
The Mute Question	Jan 1955	AUT 53
	Reprint of *Other Worlds* (Sep 1950)	
Sabina	Sep 1953	NEB 5
What an Idea!	Feb 1953	AUT 30

RONALD ADISON (UK)

Revolt!	Jan 1951	WOF 3

NIGEL AHERNE (UK)

Pharaoh Lives Forever	Sep 1954	VSS 6

JOHN (Kempton) AIKEN, 1913-1990 (UK)

Cassandra	Sep 1949	NW 5
Edge of Night	Jun 1949	NW 4
Performance Test	May 1952	NW 15
Phoenix Nest	Spr 1950	NW 6

BRIAN W(ilson) ALDISS, 1925- (UK)

Breathing Space	Feb 1955	SF 12
Criminal Record	Jul 1954	SF 9
The Great Time Hiccup	Apr 1955	NEB 12
Non-Stop	Feb 1956	SF 17
On Writing Science Fiction	May 1954	AUT 45 (nf)

156

Our Kind of Knowledge	Jun 1955	NW 36
Outside	Jan 1955	NW 31
Panel Game	Dec 1955	NW 42
Pogsmith	May 1955	AUT 57
There Is a Tide	Feb 1956	NW 44

ARMSTRONG ALEXANDER—see: Alistair Paterson

POUL (William) ANDERSON, 1926- (USA)

Butch	Jul 1955	NW 37

Reprint from *Time to Come*, August Derleth, ed.

ANTHONY ARMSTRONG—see: George Willis

FRANK (i.e., Francis Edward) ARNOLD, 1914-1987 (UK)

The Circle of the White Horse	Mar 1952	NW 14 (nf)

ROY ARNOLD (UK)

Cano Sapiens	Jul 1952	FSS 7

ROBERT R. ARTHUR (UK)

Space-Script Stunts	Jun 1954	SFF 4

JOHN ASHCROFT, 1936- (UK)

Dawn of Peace Eternal	May 1954	SF 8
Otherwise	May 1955	AUT 57
Silk Petals Gone	Jul 1955	AUT 59
Stone and Crystal	Sep 1954	SF 10

FRANCIS (Leslie) ASHTON, 1914- (UK)

Jet Landing	Spr 1950	NW 6

PETER BAILLIE (UK)

The Deadly City (w/Ron Deacon)	Nov 1954	VSS 7
The Fishers (w/Ron Deacon)	Mar 1955	VSS 11
Nova (w/Ron Deacon)	Jul 1955	VSS 14
Time, Please! (w/Ron Deacon)	Feb 1956	VSS 19

MARTIN L. BAKER—see: Sydney J. Bounds

R. W. BALDERSTONE (UK)

Time and Timothy	Jun 1955	AUT 58

ALAN BARCLAY—see: George B. Tait

MICHAEL BARNES, 1926-1982 (UK)

as RICKY DRAYTON

White Zombie   1955   WWD 1

L(awrence) E(dward) BARTLE, 1911- (UK)

as RICHARD LAWRENCE

One in Every Port   Spr 1953   SF 6

with Francis Parnell, as FRANCIS RICHARDSON

The Trojan Way   Mar 1954   SF 7

FRANK BASSEY (UK)

The Days of the Dogs	Feb 1956	VSS 19
Leander's Oracle	Jul 1955	VSS 14
Registered Client	Jan 1955	VSS 9

BARRINGTON J(ohn) BAYLEY, 1937- (UK)

The Bargain	Sep 1955	VSS 16
Combat's End	May 1954	VSS 4
Fugitive	Feb 1956	VSS 19
Kindly Travelers	Jul 1955	AUT 59
Last Post	Apr 1955	VSS 12
Martyrs Appointed	Oct 1955	VSS 17
The Reluctant Death	Jan 1956	AUT 65

CHARLES BEAUMONT (legalized from Charles Leroy Nutt), 1929-1967 (USA)

The Beautiful Woman   Sum 1953   NEB 3
            Reprint of "The Beautiful People" from *Worlds of If* (Sep 1952)

ALICE BEECHAM—see: E. C. Tubb

ERIC BENTCLIFFE, 1927?-1992 (UK)

Who's Who in Fandom   Feb 1954   VSS 2 (nf)

WILLIAM E. BENTLEY (UK)

The Black Occupier   Apr 1955   VSS 12

BRYAN BERRY, 1930-1955 (UK)

The Adaptable Man	Sep 1953	AUT 37
Aftermath	Aug 1952	AUT 24

Ancient City	May 1953	AUT 33
Hidden Shepherds	Feb 1954	AUT 42
Savious	Jun 1954	AUT 46
Strange Suicide	Apr 1955	AUT 56
The Tree	Aug 1953	AUT 36
Widening Gulf	Jul 1953	AUT 35

ALFRED BESTER, 1913-1987 (USA)

Disappearing Act	Nov 1954	NW 29

Reprint from *Star SF Stories 2*, Frederik Pohl, ed.

What's the Difference?	Feb 1955	SF 12 (nf)

JOHN BEYNON—see: John Beynon Harris

WILLIAM (Henry Fleming) BIRD, 1896-1971 (UK)

Critical Age	Aug 1953	FSS 12

as JOHN TOUCAN

Genesis	Apr 1954	WOF 13
Point in Time	Nov 1952	WOS 5
Repercussion	Aug 1953	TOT 8
War Potential	Sep 1952	TOT 5

MORRIS BISHOP, 1893-1973 (USA)

as W. BOLLINGBROKE JOHNSON

Tryst	Jul 1954	AUT 47

(Drexel) JEROME (Lewis) BIXBY, 1923- (USA)

It's a *Good* Life	Nov 1955	SF 16

Reprint from *Star SF Stories 2*, Frederik Pohl, ed.

ANTHONY BLAKE—see: E. C. Tubb

JOHN BODY—see: John Brody

THOMAS BOND (UK)

The Botanist	Jul 1955	AUT 59 (nf)

W. H. BOORE (UK)

Playing with Time	Jan 1955	AUT 53

S(ydney) J(ames) BOUNDS, 1920- (UK)

The Active Man	Mar 1955	NW 33

The Adaptable Planet	Aut 1953	NEB 5
The Beautiful Martian	Nov 1955	NEB 14
First Trip	Dec 1954	SF 11
The Flame Gods	Mar 1952	NW 14
Frontier Legion	From Oct 1952	AUT 26 (six part serial)
It's Dark Out There	Nov 1954	AUT 51
John Brown's Body	Dec 1954	AUT 52
Leave	Jan 1956	AUT 65
Liaison Service	Win 1951	NW 12
A Matter of Salvage	Jan 1952	NW 13
Portrait of a Spaceman	Oct 1954	NW 28
Project Starship	Oct 1954	NEB 10
Sole Survivor	Feb 1955	NW 32
The Spirit of Earth	Win 1950	NW 8
Time for Murder	Oct 1955	AUT 62
Too Efficient	Sep 1949	NW 5
The Treasure of Tagor	Spr 1951	SF 4
Weather Station	Apr 1954	NEB 8

as MARTIN L. BAKER

The Planeteer	Nov 1950	WOF 2

as ROGER CARNE

Prison Planet	Dec 1950	FSS 3

as W. E. CLARKSON

Martian Ape Men	Dec 1950	FSS 3
Menace from the Atom	Dec 1950	FSS 3

as GEORGE DUNCAN

Galactic Quest	Jan 1953	NW 19

as PAUL HAMMOND

Exiles of Time	Sep 1950	TOT 1

as JAMES ROSS

Invaders from the Stars	Sep 1950	TOT 1

as LAWRENCE SMITH

The Outlaw of Space	Nov 1950	WOF 2

as CLIFFORD WALLACE

Terror Stalks the Seance Room	Sep 1954	SUS 2
Vultures of the Void	Aug 1950	FSS 2

KENNETH BOYCE—see: Kenneth Boyea

MORTON BOYCE—see: John Russell Fearn

KENNETH BOYEA (UK)

Kenneth Boyea was a cartoonist who worked with Scottish writer *John F. Watt*, who was a prolific contributor to the Spencer magazines. All these stories may be collaborations with *Watt*.

The Lethal Mist	Jun 1954	TOT 11
No Tomorrows	Jan 1954	FSS 14
Project Survival	Aug 1953	TOT 8
Renegades of the Void	Apr 1954	WOS 10
Riddle of the Robots	Feb 1954	WOF 12

as KENNETH BOYCE

Robot Threat	Jan 1953	WOS 6

with John F. Watt?, as IAN BRUCE

Death from the Swamps	Jan 1954	FSS 14

with John F. Watt?, as JOHN ELLIS

Forgotten World	Mar 1951	TOT 3

with John F. Watt?, as BRUCE FENTON

The Fugitive	Apr 1954	TOT 10
Marooned on Venus	Sep 1953	WOF 11
Robot Rebels	Feb 1954	WOF 12
Satellite Peril	Aug 1953	TOT 8
Slaves of Space	Jan 1953	FSS 9
Space Menace	Apr 1954	WOF 13
Threat from Space	Jul 1952	TOT 4

with John F. Watt?, as MACK JAMES

Suicide Mission	Jul 1952	TOT 4
Wreckers of Space	Aug 1952	WOF 6

with John F. Watt?, as MACK JONES

Alien Threat	Apr 1954	TOT 10

with John F. Watt?, as FRANK C. KNELLER

Danger Out of Space	Oct 1953	TOT 9
Death Ships	Aug 1950	FSS 2
Journey into Tomorrow	Jan 1953	FSS 9

The Last Chance	Jun 1954	TOT 11
Lunar Revolt	Nov 1950	WOF 2
Lust for Conquest	Feb 1951	WOS 1
Rebels of Venus	Jul 1952	FSS 7
Sillisian Menace	Jul 1953	WOS 7
Spaceman's Luck	Aug 1953	FSS 12
Threat from Mars	Aug 1952	WOF 6
Vandal of the Void	Jun 1950	WOF 1
The World Beyond	Sep 1953	WOF 11
World of Dread	Jan 1954	FSS 14

with **John F. Watt?,** *as* RAY MASON

Captives of Vesta	Apr 1954	WOS 10
Death from the Swamps	Aug 1952	WOF 6
The Devil's Weed	Oct 1953	FSS 13
Doomed World	Nov 1951	WOF 4
The Green Ray	Apr 1950	FSS 1
Martian Terror	Dec 1952	WOF 8
Slave Ships	Jul 1952	TOT 4
Spawn of Space	Jul 1953	WOS 7
The Thought Machine	Jan 1953	TOT 6

with **John F. Watt?,** *as* D. R. MENCER/D. J. MENCER/D. R. MENCET/D. J. MENCET

Convoy to the Unknown	Feb 1951	WOS 1
The Death Planet	Nov 1951	WOF 4
The Fire Goddess	Aug 1950	FSS 2
Lost in Space	Oct 1953	FSS 13
Plan for Conquest	Nov 1950	WOF 2
Prisoners of Mars	Jan 1953	WOS 6
Scarlet Invaders	Jun 1950	WOF 1
Scourge of Space	May 1952	WOS 3
Traitor of the Void	Jan 1954	FSS 14
World of Fear	Aug 1953	FSS 12

with **John F. Watt?,** *as* ROD PATTERSON

Crimson Terror	Apr 1953	FSS 10
Destination—Infinity	Apr 1954	WOS 10

with **John F. Watt?,** *as* JAMES ROBERTSON

Space Warning	Jan 1953	WOS 6

with **John F. Watt?,** *as* JOHN ROBERTSON

The Final Threat	Apr 1954	WOS 10
The Green Cloud	Feb 1951	WOS 1
The Purple Sun	Oct 1953	WOS 8
Satellite in Space	Jan 1954	WOS 9

with John F. Watt?, as NEIL J. SPA(U)LDING

Last Survivor	Feb 1954	WOF 12
Martian Outcast	May 1952	WOS 3

with John F. Watt?, as EDWARD STOKES

Spawn of the Void	Feb 1951	FSS 4

H. H. BOYESON (UK)

No Priority	Aut 1951	NW 11

RAY (Douglas) BRADBURY, 1920- (USA)

Asleep in Armageddon	May 1953	AUT 33

Reprint from *Planet Stories* (Win 1948)

Welcome, Brothers!	Jan 1953	AUT 29

Reprint of "Mars is Heaven" from *Planet Stories* (Fal 1948)

T. BRISSENDEN (UK)

The Inner Sphere	Dec 1955	VSS 18
Operation Orbit	Dec 1954	VSS 8

JOHN BRODY (UK)

The Dawn Breaks Red	Sum 1950	NW 7
World in Shadow	Jun 1949	NW 4

as JOHN BODY

Strange Incident	May 1954	SFF 3

L. T. BRONSON—see: E. C. Tubb

LIONEL BROOKS (UK)

A Date with Past	Dec 1954	AUT 52

R. BROTHWELL (UK)

Agent of Earth	Apr 1952	WOF 5
The Isolationists	Jan 1952	WOS 2
Power Politics	Jan 1953	FSS 9
Space Trader	Feb 1951	FSS 4

BURGESS BROWN—see: Eric Burgess

REGINALD BROWN (UK)

The Black Menace of Zenolius	Aug 1954	SFF 6

Forced Landing on Elvarista	Mar 1954	SFF 1

IAN BRUCE—see: Kenneth Boyea and John Watt

JOHN (Kilian Houston) BRUNNER, 1934- (UK)

Death Do Us Part	Nov 1955	SF 16
Host Age	Jan 1956	NW 43
The Man Who Played the Blues	Feb 1956	SF 17
Nuisance Value	Feb 1956	AUT 66
Puzzle for Spacemen	Dec 1955	NW 42
The Talisman	Sep 1955	SF 15
Thing Friday	Feb 1956	NW 44
The Uneasy Head	Nov 1955	NW 41
Visitors' Book	Apr 1955	NW 34

as K. HOUSTON BRUNNER

Brainpower	Spr 1953	NEB 2
Fiery Pillar	Aug 1955	NW 38
Tomorrow Is Another Day	Mar 1954	AUT 43

as TREVOR STAINES

Proof Negative	Feb 1956	SF 17

as KEITH WOODCOTT

The Biggest Game	Feb 1956	SF 17
No Future in It	Sep 1955	SF 15

K. HOUSTON BRUNNER—see: John Brunner

(Henry) KENNETH BULMER, 1921- (UK)

All Glory Forgotten	Jun 1954	NW 24
Asylum	Apr 1955	NW 34
Bitter the Path	Aug 1954	NW 26
The Black Spot	Feb 1955	NW 32
Come to Prestonwell	Nov 1955	AUT 63
The Day of the Monster	Jul 1955	AUT 59
First Down	Apr 1954	AUT 44
It Takes Two	Oct 1954	AUT 50
Know Thy Neighbor	Sep 1955	AUT 61
The Old Firm	Feb 1956	AUT 66
Ordeal	Mar 1955	AUT 55
Plaything	Nov 1955	NW 41
Psi No More	Jun 1955	SF 14
Some Other Time	May 1954	AUT 45
Sunset	Nov 1955	NEB 14
Total Recall	Aug 1955	NW 38

as PETER GREEN

Firecracker Fool	Aug 1955	AUT 59
To Shake the Stars	Jul 1954	AUT 47

as CHESMAN SCOTT

Galactic Impersonation	Feb 1955	VSS 10
The Second Pyramid	Jun 1955	VSS 13
The Void Looks Down	Jul 1954	VSS 5

as H. PHILIP STRATFORD

Time Travel Business	Dec 1955	AUT 64

with John Newman, as KENNETH JOHNS

Audrey	Sep 1955	AUT 61 (nf)
Future Indefinite	Feb 1956	NW 44 (nf)
Our Invisible Shield 1	Jul 1955	AUT 59 (nf)
Our Invisible Shield 2	Aug 1955	AUT 60 (nf)
Project Air	Feb 1956	AUT 66 (nf)
Research Nuclear Reactors	Dec 1955	AUT 64 (nf)
Tools of Tomorrow	Oct 1955	AUT 62 (nf)

ERIC (Alexander) BURGESS, 1912- (UK)

as BURGESS BROWN

Fire	Jun 1954	NW 24

JOHN F(rederick) BURKE, 1922- (UK)

as JONATHAN BURKE

The Adjusters	Apr 1955	SF 13
An Apple for the Teacher	Apr 1955	NEB 12
Asteroid Crusoe	Sep 1954	AUT 49
Cancel Tomorrow	Jun 1953	AUT 34
The Censors	Jan 1954	AUT 41
Chessboard	Jan 1953	NW 19
Desirable Residence	Jun 1955	AUT 58
Detective Story	Mar 1954	SF 7
The Envied	Nov 1954	AUT 51
Ever Been to Uranus?	Apr 1955	SF 13 (nf)
For You, the Possessed	Dec 1953	AUT 40
Free Treatment	Dec 1954	VSS 8
The Gamble	May 1954	NW 23
Golden Slumbers	Mar 1953	NW 20
Job Analysis	Dec 1955	AUT 64
Let There Be Rain	Aug 1955	AUT 60
Loneliest World	Aug 1953	AUT 36

Old Man of the Stars	Oct 1953	AUT 38
Once upon a Time	May 1954	SF 8
The Perfect Secretary	Sep 1954	NW 27
Personal Call	Apr 1955	AUT 56
Private Satellite (Part 1)	Sep 1955	AUT 61
Private Satellite (Part 2)	Oct 1955	AUT 62
Stand-In	Mar 1954	AUT 43
Time to Go Home	Spr 1953	SF 6

ARTHUR J. BURKS, 1898-1974 (USA)

Hydra	Sum 1951	NW 10

AUBREY BURL (UK)

Traveller's Tale	Jun 1955	AUT 58

ALAN BURNS, 1929- (UK)

Citizen's Rights	Sep 1955	AUT 61

W. W. BYFORD (UK)

Back to Forward	Oct 1954	AUT 50 (nf)
Cold Power	Feb 1955	AUT 54 (nf)
Divine Wind	Mar 1955	AUT 55 (nf)
The Gravity of the Situation	Nov 1954	AUT 51
Gravity Strings and Saucers	May 1955	AUT 57 (nf)
Invisible Daylight	Dec 1954	AUT 52 (nf)
Modern Metals: Beryllium	Aug 1955	AUT 60 (nf)
Modern Metals: Cobalt	Sep 1955	AUT 61 (nf)
Modern Metals: Selenium	Oct 1955	AUT 62 (nf)
Modern Metals: Uranium	Nov 1955	AUT 63 (nf)
Modern Metals: Zirconium	Dec 1955	AUT 64 (nf)
Scientists Are People	Oct 1955	AUT 62 (nf)
Space and Mr. Newton	Sep 1954	AUT 49 (nf)
Space Ship Shape	Jan 1955	AUT 53 (nf)

STUART J(ames) BYRNE, 1913- (USA)

Lady of Flame	Feb 1953	AUT 30

Reprint of "The Golden Guardsmen" from *Other Worlds* (Apr-Jul 1952)

DAVID CAMPBELL—see: Leonard G. Fish

H(erbert) J(ames) CAMPBELL, 1925- (UK)
SEE ALSO: JON J. DEEGAN and ROY SHELDON, house pseudonyms

Albert Einstein	Oct 1954	AUT 50 (nf)
All Men Kill	Sum 1953	NEB 3
Aristotle	Jul 1954	AUT 47 (nf)
The Battery	Dec 1954	AUT 52 (nf)

Chaos in Miniature	Feb 1952	AUT 18
Francis Bacon	Jun 1954	AUT 46 (nf)
Galileo Galilei	Sep 1954	AUT 49 (nf)
The Hydrogen Bomb	Jun 1954	AUT 46 (nf)
John Stuart Mill	Aug 1954	AUT 48 (nf)
London Circle	Aug 1954	AUT 48 (nf)
Mice—Or Machines	Jun 1952	AUT 22
Milestones of Science—The Clock	Mar 1955	AUT 55 (nf)
The Moon Is Heaven	Dec 1951	AUT 16
Mutations	Oct 1953	AUT 38 (nf)
Possible Life-Forms on Other Planets (1st of 3 parts)		
	Feb 1954	AUT 41 (nf)
Projectionist	Feb 1954	NEB 7
The Rule	Feb 1955	AUT 54 (nf)
Space Academy	Jan 1956	AUT 65 (nf)
	Reprint from *Boys Own* (Mar 1953)	
Things Are on the Move	Spr 1952	SF 4 (nf)
World in a Test Tube	Apr 1951	AUT 8

JULIAN CAREY—see: E. C. Tubb

ROGER CARNE—see: Sydney J. Bounds

(Edward John) "TED" CARNELL, 1912-1972 (UK)

1951 International Convention	Aut 1951	NW 11 (nf)

MORLEY CARPENTER—see: E. C. Tubb

DON CARRIWAY (UK)

The Man Who Said Xiipxertilly	Nov 1955	AUT 63

D. G. CARSON—see: David S. Gardner

TOM CARSON (UK)

Tabarni Document	Aug 1954	AUT 48

H. M. CARSTAIRS (UK)

Journey Without Return	Oct 1955	VSS 17

ARTHUR CARTER—see: Richard de Mille

BRANSON D. CARTER—see: T. W. Wade

HENRY CARTER (UK)

Creatures of the Blitz	Feb 1956	WW 2

JAMES E. CARVER (UK)

Making Rain to Order	Dec 1955	AUT 64 (nf)

A(rthur) BERTRAM CHANDLER, 1912-1984 (AUSTRALIA)

And All Disastrous Things	Spr 1951	NW 9
Coefficient X	Spr 1950	NW 6
Finishing Touch	Jul 1952	NW 16
Jetsam	Mar 1953	NW 20
Late	Apr 1955	SF 13
Next in Line	Spr 1952	SF 4
Pest	Jan 1952	NW 13
Position Line	Jun 1949	NW 4
The Serpent	Sep 1952	NW 17
Six of One	Jul 1954	SF 9
The Wrong Track	Feb 1955	SF 12
Zoological Specimen	May 1954	NW 23

as GEORGE WHITLEY

Castaway	Spr 1950	NW 6

MAX CHARTAIR—see: John Glasby

DOUGLAS F. CHATT (UK)

The Electronic Brain	Apr 1955	AUT 56 (nf)

JOHN CHRISTOPHER—see: Christopher Youd

MARGOT S. CLAIR (UK)

Fire Burn and Cauldron Bubble	Jun 1949	GT 1 (nf)

ARTHUR C(harles) CLARKE, 1917- (UK)

The Forgotten Enemy	Sep 1949	NW 5
Guardian Angel	Win 1950	NW 8
Reprint from *Famous Fantastic Mysteries* (Apr 1950)		
History Lesson	Win 1950	SF 2
Reprint from *Startling Stories* (May 1949)		
Is There Too Much?	Jan 1953	AUT 29 (nf)
The Sentinel	Apr 1954	NW 22
Reprint of "The Sentinel of Eternity" from *Ten Story Fantasy* (Spr 1951)		
The Shape of Ships to Come	Jun 1949	NW 4
Spacesuits Will Be Worn	Sum 1951	NW 10 (nf)
Time's Arrow	Sum 1950	SF 1

as CHARLES WILLIS

Silence, Please!	Win 1950	SF 2

L. J. CLARKE (UK)

Hide Out	Mar 1955	VSS 11
Slip-Up	Jan 1955	VSS 9

W. B. CLARKE (see Norman Lazenby)

W. E. CLARKSON (see Sydney J. Bounds)

PHILIP (Ellerby) CLEATOR, 1908- (UK)

The Cycle	Sum 1950	SF 1

W. P. COCKCROFT, 1913- (UK)

Last Man on Mars	Jul 1954	SF 9

DAVID H. COHEN (UK)

as HARRY COHN

And Worlds Live Too	Jul 1955	VSS 14
The Cytricon	Jun 1955	VSS 13 (nf)
Personalities in Fandom 6: Dennis Cowan	Jul 1955	VSS 14 (nf)
Personalities in Fandom 10: Don Allen	Dec 1955	VSS 18 (nf)
Personalities in Fandom 2: Ethel Lindsay	Feb 1955	VSS 10 (nf)
Personalities in Fandom 7: Forrest J Ackerman	Aug 1955	VSS 15 (nf)
Personalities in Fandom 8: Joan W. Carr	Sep 1955	VSS 16 (nf)
Personalities in Fandom 5: Mal Ashworth	Jun 1955	VSS 13 (nf)
Personalities in Fandom 9: Mike Wallace	Oct 1955	VSS 17 (nf)
Personalities in Fandom 11: Nigel Lindsay	Feb 1956	VSS 19 (nf)
Personalities in Fandom 3: Pete Campbell	Mar 1955	VSS 11 (nf)
Personalities in Fandom 4: Ron Bennett	Apr 1955	VSS 12 (nf)
Personalities in Fandom 1: Terry Jeeves	Jan 1955	VSS 9 (nf)

as NORTHERNER

Whither Fandom?	Jan 1955	VSS 9 (nf)

HARRY COHN—see: David H. Cohen

LES COLE (UK)

Unborn of Earth	Sep 1954	SF 10

MAXWELL M. COMMANDER (UK)

The Day It Rained Worms	Oct 1955	VSS 17
Maternal Nightmare	Apr 1955	VSS 12

RICK CONROY (UK)

Eve Hated Adam	Jul 1953	AUT 35
Manna from Heaven	Apr 1953	AUT 32
Martians in a Frozen World	Oct 1952	AUT 26

RANDALL CONWAY—see: John Glasby

DAVID C. COOKE (UK)

Package of Power	Jul 1954	SFF 5

Reprint from *Science Fiction Quarterly* (Sum 1940)

DOUGLAS BRIAN COOKSON, 1939- (UK)

Preview	Mar 1955	VSS 11

EDMUND COOPER, 1926-1982 (UK)

Jar of Latakia	Sep 1954	AUT 49

RAY COSMIC/RAY CORMIC—see: John Glasby

JOHN C. CRAIG (UK)

The Violet Glow	Sep 1954	SFF 7

JUSTIN CROOME (UK)

Woman Running	1955	WWD 1

LELSIE A(fred) CROUTCH, 1915-1969 (CANADA)

Salvage Job	Mar 1954	SFF 1

Reprint from *Future* (Dec 1941)

A. R. CUNNINGHAM (UK)

There's Many a Slip	Sep 1955	VSS 16

P. W. CUTLER (UK)

Reconnaisance	Dec 1954	NW 30
Take a Letter	May 1954	SF 8

NORMAN DALE—see: E. C. Tubb

THORNTON DALE (UK)

When Churchyards Yawn	Jun 1949	GT 1

LEO DANE (UK)

Visitant	Sep 1955	VSS 16

D. R. DAVIES (UK)

The Merchants	Jun 1954	AUT 46

LESLIE J. DAVIES (UK)

Invisible Barrier	Dec 1954	VSS 8
Showpiece	Oct 1955	AUT 62
The Tiger Man	Aug 1955	VSS 15

RICHARD DE MILLE, 1922- (USA)

The Phoenix Nest	Jan 1954	AUT 41

as ARTHUR CARTER

Family Secret	Jul 1954	SF 9
The Other Door	Apr 1955	NW 34

RONALD (Alfred Thomas) DEACON, 1921- (UK)

The Deadly City (w/Peter Baillie)	Nov 1954	VSS 7
The Fishers (w/Peter Baillie)	Mar 1955	VSS 11
Nova (w/Peter Baillie)	Jul 1955	VSS 14
Time, Please! (w/Peter Baillie)	Feb 1956	VSS 19

JON J. DEEGAN (House pseudonym)

Robert G. Sharp (noted as "RS" below) and *H. J. Campbell* both used this name, and Campbell had a strong editorial hand in all the stories.

Beyond the Barriers	Sep 1953	AUT 37	unk.
Old Growler and Orbis	May 1951	SFM 9	RS
Old Growler—Spaceship No. 2213	Feb 1951	AUT 4	RS
Planet of Power	Oct 1951	AUT 14	RS
Reconnoitre Krellig II	Jan 1951	AUT 2	RS
The Singing Spheres	Jul 1952	AUT 23	RS

WILLI DEINHARDT (Germany)

Galactic Interlude	Jan 1953	TOT 6
Laughing Gas	May 1953	TOT 7
Mad Heritage	May 1953	FSS 11

WILLIAM DE KOVEN (Pseudonym) (USA)

Bighead	Win 1950	NW 8

LESTER DEL REY, 1915-1993 (USA)
(Pseudonym of *Ramón Felipe San Juan Mario Silvio Enrico Smith Heathcourt-Brace Sierra y Alvarez-del Rey y de Los Uerdes*)

Alien	Aug 1955	NW 38
Reprint from *Star SF Stories 3*, Frederik Pohl, ed.		
Idealist	Jun 1954	NW 24
Reprint from *Star SF Stories 1*, Frederik Pohl, ed.		
A Pound of Cure	Sept 1954	NW 27
Reprint from *Star SF Stories 2*, Frederik Pohl, ed.		

PROFESSOR DELWOOD (Pseudonym) (UK)

The Expanding Universe	Oct 1954	AUT 50 (nf)
The Non-Expanding Universe	Nov 1954	AUT 51 (nf)

MARK DENHOLM—see: John Russell Fearn

G. GORDON DEWEY (USA)

The Tooth	Dec 1954	SF 11
Reprint from *The Magazine of Fantasy & Science Fiction* (Aug 1952)		

DOUGLAS DODD—see: John Russell Fearn

M. DOGGE (UK)

The Inner Worlds and My Uncle	Dec 1953	AUT 40

HAMILTON DONNE/HAMILTON DOWNE* (House pseudonym)
(used by *Norman Lazenby* and others; UK)

Fire-Ray Invaders	Jan 1951	TOT 2	unidentified
Martian Terror	Jun 1950	WOF 1	Norman Lazenby
One Million Years Ago	Aug 1950	FSS 2	Norman Lazenby
Space Pirates	Nov 1950	WOF 2	Norman Lazenby
*Terror from the Skies	Feb 1951	FSS 4	unidentified

DON J. DOUGHTY (UK)

Adoption	Spr 1950	NW 6

KATHLEEN DOWNE (UK)

Why Not a Woman?	May 1955	AUT 57 (nf)

RICKY DRAYTON—see: Michael Barnes

SHERIDAN DREW—see: John Russell Fearn

GEORGE DUNCAN—see: Sydney J. Bounds

GEORGE C. DUNCAN (UK)

The Dishwasher	Aug 1955	AUT 60
Hallucinogens	Nov 1954	AUT 51 (nf)
One Hour	Oct 1954	AUT 50
Planer Farms	Jul 1954	AUT 47 (nf)
Symbiosis	Apr 1955	AUT 56

CHARLES DYE, 1927-1955 (USA)

Prisoner in the Skull   From Dec 1954   NW 30 (three part serial)
          Reprint from U.S. hardcover ed. (Abelard, NY; 1952)

C. D. ELLIS (UK)

World of the Ancients	Nov 1951	WOF 4

JOHN ELLIS—see: Kenneth Boyea and John Watt

JAMES ELTON (UK)

Perilous Expedition	Nov 1951	WOF 4

MAX ELTON—see: John Russell Fearn

RON ELTON (UK)

Outside Looking In	Jun 1954	AUT 46

PAUL ENEVER (UK)

Ultimate Harvest	Aut 1953	NEB 4

RICHARD P. ENNIS (UK)

By Needle and Thread	Oct 1954	NEB 10
The Lonely Ones	Sep 1955	AUT 61

R. G. EVAND (UK)
(R. C. Evand on contents page)

What Happened to Clambake?	Nov 1954	SUS 3

E(dward) EVERETT EVANS, 1893-1958 (USA)

Fly by Night	Jan 1954	AUT 41
Insomnia Cure	Sep 1954	AUT 49
Never Been Kissed	Mar 1953	AUT 31
Was Not Spoken	Aut 1952	SF 5

GERALD EVANS, 1910- (UK)

"Re-Creation"   Dec 1951   FSS 5

JOHN EVANS (UK)

Dangerous Moon   Sep 1950   TOT 1

PAUL T. EVERS (UK)

Music of the Spheres   Jan 1955   VSS 9

KONSTANTIN FABER (UK)

The Man Who Loved Cats   1955   WWD 1

DERRY FALCON (UK)

Gordon's Town   Nov 1954   SUS 3

JOHN FALKNER—see: E. F. Gale

BRON FANE—see: R. Lionel Fanthorpe

R(obert) LIONEL FANTHORPE, 1935- (UK)

...And Very Few Get Out   Jul 1954   SN 2
The Clipper Ships of Space   May 1953   FSS 11

as BRON FANE

Conquest   Jun 1954   WOF 14

as JOHN RAYMOND

The Incredulist   Jul 1954   SN 2
              Credited to LIONEL ROBERTS on cover

as LIONEL ROBERTS

Discovery   Jul 1952   FSS 7
The Incredulist   Jul 1954   SN 2
       Credited to JOHN RAYMOND in contents, ROBERTS on cover
Last Command   Jun 1953   WOF 10
Marauders of the Void   Apr 1954   WOS 10
Martian Bonanza   Feb 1954   WOF 12
Raw Material   May 1953   FSS 11
Time Tangle   Oct 1953   FSS 13
Vengeance of Trelko   Apr 1952   WOF 5
Worlds Without End   Apr 1952   FSS 6

as TREBOR THORPE

Galactic Twin	Jun 1954	WOF 14
Princess in a Bubble	Jun 1953	WOF 10
Saucers from Space	Jan 1954	FSS 14

as PEL TORRO

The Green Hell of Venus	Apr 1954	FSS 15

SUSAN FARNHAM (UK)

Poltergeists over Portland	Jun 1949	GT 1 (nf)

F(rank) DUBREZ FAWCETT, 1891-1968 (UK)

The Law of the Nebulae	Feb 1954	VSS 2	
Tripe? But the Authors Know Their Onions	Sep 1954		VSS 6 (nf)

as SIMPSON STOKES

The Super Disintegrator	Jan 1954	VSS 1

JOHN (Francis) RUSSELL FEARN, 1908-1960 (UK)

Black-Out	Win 1950	SF 2
First of the Robots	Apr 1954	SFF 2

as Anonymous

It Came from Outer Space	May 1954	VSS 4
Them!	Jul 1954	VSS 5

as MORTON BOYCE

Nemesis	Jun 1955	VSS 13

Reprint of "The Last Hours" as by *John Russell Fearn* from *Amazing* (Aug 1942)

as MARK DENHOLM

Waters of Eternity	Nov 1953	WOU 1

as DOUGLAS DODD

Mars for Sale	Oct 1955	VSS 17

Reprint of "The Man Who Bought Mars" as by *Polton Cross* from *Fantastic Adventures* (Jun 1941)

as SHERIDAN DREW

Imperfect Crime	Sep 1955	VSS 16

Reprint of "The Mental Gangster" by *Thornton Ayre*, *Fantastic Adventures* (Aug. 1942)

as MAX ELTON

Chaos in Paradise   Feb 1956   VSS 19
    Reprint of "War of the Scientists" as by *John Russell Fearn* from *Amazing* (Apr 1940)
Hero Worship   Dec 1955   VSS 18
    Reprint of "He Conquered Venus" as by *John Russell Fearn* from *Astonishing* (Jun 1940)

as VOLSTED GRIDBAN, *house pseud.*

Alice, Where Art Thou?   May 1954   VSS 4
March of the Robots   Jan 1954   VSS 1
The Others   Apr 1954   VSS 3
A Saga of 2270 A.D.   Feb 1954   VSS 2

as GEOFFREY GRAYSON

They Made It Possible 1: Pioneers in Electricity   Sep 1954   VSS 6 (nf)

as MALCOLM HARTLEY

Out of the Past   Jan 1955   VSS 9
    Reprint of "Man Without a World" as by *Dom Passante* in *Future Fiction* (Mar 1940)

as MARVIN KAYNE

The Grey Avenger   Jul 1955   VSS 14
    Reprint of "Phantom from Space" as by *John Russell Fearn* from *Super Science Stories* (Mar 1940)

as HERBERT LLOYD

Murmuring Dust   Apr 1955   VSS 12
    Reprint of "Microbes from Space" as by *Thornton Ayre* from *Amazing* (Jun 1939)

as DOM PASSANTE

Across the Ages   Sep 1954   SFF 7
    Reprint from *Future* (Oct 1941)

as FRANCIS ROSE

Saturnian Odyssey   Nov 1954   VSS 9
    Expanded rewrite of "Outlaw of Saturn" as by *John Cotton* from *Science Fiction* (Mar 1939)

as FRANK ROSE

After Twenty Years	Feb 1955	VSS 10

Reprint of "The Voice Commands" as by *Dennis Clive* from *Science Fiction*
(Jun 1940)

as WARD ROSS

No Place on Earth	Dec 1954	VSS 8

Reprint of "World Reborn" as by *Thornton Ayre* from *Super Science Stories*
(Mar 1940)

AS VARGO STATTEN

Before Atlantis	Feb 1954	VSS 2
Beyond Zero	Jan 1954	VSS 1
The Conqueror's Voice	Nov 1954	VSS 7 (five part serial)

Reprint of "The Voice of the Conqueror" as by *J. R. Fearn* from *Star Weekly*
(10 Jul 1954)

Here and Now	From Jul 1955	VSS 14 (five part serial)

Reprint as by *J. R. Fearn* from *Star Weekly* (2 Apr 1955)

The Master Mind	Apr 1954	VSS 3
A Matter of Vibration	Apr 1955	VSS 12
Reverse Action	May 1954	VSS 4
Rim of Eternity	Jul 1954	VSS 5
Second Genesis	Feb 1956	VSS 19

Reprint of "Cosmic Juggernaut" as by *J. R. Fearn* from *Planet Stories* (Sum 1940)

Something from Mercury	Sep 1954	VSS 6
Three's a Crowd	Jun 1954	VSS 13

as JOHN WERNHEIM

The Copper Bullet	Jan 1954	VSS 1

G. M. FEIGEN (UK)

The Foundling Dummy	Oct 1955	AUT 62

BRUCE FENTON—see: Kenneth Boyea & John F. Watt

LEONARD G. FISH (UK)
SEE ALSO: *Anonymous Stories*

The Alien	Dec 1951	FSS 5
Hell Planet	Mar 1951	TOT 3

as DAVID CAMPBELL

Expedition Eternity	Mar 1951	TOT 3
The Problem Ship	Feb 1951	FSS 4

B. (i.e., William David) FLACKES (Ireland)

as CLEM MACARTNEY

Ten Years to Oblivion	Aug 1951	AUT 12

LESLIE FLOOD (UK)

Inquest—By Request	Nov 1952	NW 18 (nf)
A Merit For Fantasy	May 1952	NW 15 (nf)
The 1954 Fantasy Award	Sep 1954	NW 27 (nf)
The 1955 Fantasy Award	Sep 1955	NW 39 (nf)

FREDERICK FODEN (UK)

Stanhope's Moon	Apr 1950	FSS 1

BRINDLEY FORD (UK)

Relativity	Oct 1953	AUT 38
The Shining Ark	Sep 1953	AUT 37

KENNETH FOSTER (UK)

BEMS in the House	Sep 1955	VSS 16
A Cold in the Head	Feb 1955	VSS 10

PRESTON FOXE (UK)

Space-Lane Incident	Apr 1954	SFF 2

GREGORY FRANCIS—see: James Macgregor and Francis Parnell

CHARLES E(dward) FRITCH, 1927- (USA)

Anachronism	Oct 1954	NEB 10
Birthday Present	Sep 1955	SF 15

E. F. GALE (UK)

as JOHN FALKNER

A Brainy Affair	Oct 1953	AUT 38

DANIEL F(rancis) GALOUYE, 1920-1976 (USA)

Tonight the Sky Will Fall	Jul 1953	AUT 35

Reprint from *Imagination* (May 1952)

WANLESS GARDENER (UK)

Auto-Fiction Ltd.	Feb 1955	SF 12

DAVID S. GARDNER (UK)

Cold Storage	Feb 1954	NEB 7
Decision Deferred	Apr 1955	NEB 12
Liverpool Science Fiction Society	Sep 1954	AUT 49 (nf)
Mr. Udell	Sum 1953	NEB 3
Staying Guests	Jul 1954	NW 25

as D. G. CARSON

| When Johnny Comes Home | Jul 1954 | SUS 1 |

KENNETH (William) GATLAND, 1924- (UK)

| The Guided Bomb | May 1955 | AUT 57 |

RALPH GAYLEN (UK)

| Only Death Brings Piece | From Feb 1955 | VSS 10 (six part serial) |

WALTER (Herbert) GILLINGS, 1912-1979 (UK)

as HERBERT HUGHES

| Jinn in the Test Tube | Sum 1950 | SF 1 |

as VALENTINE PARKER

| The Dawn of Space Travel | Win 1950 | SF 2 (nf) |

as THOMAS SHERIDAN

| The Battle of the Canals | Sum 1950 | SF 1 (nf) |
| Bogy in the Sky | Win 1950 | SF 2 (nf) |

JOHN (Stephen) GLASBY, 1928- (UK)

as MAX CHARTAIR

Chronolei	Jan 1954	WOS 9
The Cloak of Darkness	May 1954	SN 1
The Devil at My Elbow	Oct 1954	OTW 1
Edge of Darkness	Jun 1954	WOF 14
Frog	Jul 1954	SN 2
Haunt of the Vampire	Sep 1954	SN 3
A Little Devil Dancing	Win 1954/5	OTW 2
Lurani	Jan 1955	SN 5
Mask of Asmodeus	May 1955	SN 7
Paradise Planet	Apr 1954	WOF 13
Point of No Return	Jan 1953	TOT 6
The Road to Anywhere	Jun 1954	TOT 11
The Saviour	Apr 1954	TOT 10

Star's End	Oct 1953	WOS 8
The Ugly Ones	Aut 1955	SN 8
Without a Shadow of a Doubt	Mar 1955	SN 6
The Zegrembi Bracelet	Nov 1954	SN 4

as RANDALL CONWAY

The Aphesian Riddle	Apr 1954	FSS 15
The City	May 1953	TOT 7
The Gods of Fear	May 1954	SN 1
The Hungry Gods	May 1955	SN 7
The Hungry House	Mar 1955	SN 6
Hunter's Moon	Jul 1954	SN 2
The Man Who Lost Thursday	Aut 1955	SN 8
The Seventh Image	Oct 1954	OTW 1
They Fly by Night	Nov 1954	SN 4
Time to Die	Win 1954/5	OTW 2
Time Trouble	Apr 1954	WOF 13
The Whisper of the Wind	Jan 1955	SN 5
Will O' the Wisp	Sep 1954	SN 3

as RAY COSMIC/*RAY CORMIC

Allomorph	Oct 1953	WOS 8
The Chair	Nov 1954	SN 4
The Dark Ones	Jan 1955	SN 5
Ghost Moon	Sep 1952	WOF 7
The Golden Scarab	Aut 1955	SN 8
Loreli	Mar 1955	SN 6
Lycanthrope	May 1954	SN 1
A Matter of Concealment	Oct 1953	TOT 9
The Nightmare Road	Oct 1954	OTW 1
Shadow Over Endor	May 1955	SN 7
*Something from the Sea	Sep 1954	SN 3
The Stairway	Win 1954/5	OTW 2
Void Warp	Jul 1953	WOS 7
World of Tomorrow	Apr 1954	FSS 15

as MICHAEL HAMILTON

Angel of the Bottomless Pit	Oct 1954	OTW 1
Computer Insane	Jun 1954	TOT 11
Coven of Thirteen	Win 1954/5	OTW 2
The Crystal Fear	May 1955	SN 7
The Laughter of Space	Jan 1954	WOS 9
The Other Seance	Sep 1954	SN 3
A Place of Meeting	Aut 1955	SN 8
Somewhere in the Moonlight	Jan 1955	SN 5
Time Pit	Apr 1953	FSS 10
Vengeance of Set	May 1954	SN 1
Voice of the Drum	Mar 1955	SN 6
Zerzuran Plague	Sep 1953	WOF 11

as J. J. HANSBY

Genius	Sep 1955	VSS 16
The Illusion Makers	Jul 1954	VSS 5
"Ugly Duckling"	Apr 1954	VSS 3
A World Named Creation	Jan 1955	VSS 9

as A. J. MERAK

Beyond the Rim	Jun 1954	WOF 14
Bifurcation	May 1953	TOT 7
The Byarkil Eaters	Apr 1954	WOF 13
The Crystal Skull	Sep 1954	SN 3
The Devil's Canvas	May 1954	SN 1
The Golden Hibiscus	Jan 1953	WOS 6
House of Unreason	Nov 1954	SN 4
Mischa	Jan 1954	WOS 9
Moon King	Oct 1953	WOS 8
Moonbeast	May 1955	SN 7
Moondust	Oct 1952	FSS 8
My Name Is Satan	Jan 1955	SN 5
A Place of Madness	Oct 1954	OTW 1
Planet of Desire	Jun 1954	TOT 11
The Reincarnate	Aut 1955	SN 8
The Storm Movers	Sep 1953	WOF 11
Stowaway	Apr 1954	TOT 10
Such Worlds Are Dangerous	Apr 1954	FSS 15
The Supernaturalist	Mar 1955	SN 6
Things of the Dark	Jul 1954	SN 2
Ultimate Species	Jun 1953	AUT 34
The Unseen	Win 1954/5	OTW 2
Veiled Planet	May 1953	FSS 11

A(lan) A(nthony) GLYNN, 1929- (UK)

Demon Dimension	Aug 1953	FSS 12
Fear World	Jan 1953	TOT 6
Mission to the Red Moon	Oct 1952	FSS 8
Objective Pluto	Aug 1953	TOT 8
Perseus	Jul 1952	FSS 7
Planetoid of Peril	May 1953	FSS 11
Realm of Danger	Apr 1953	WOF 9
Sargasso of Space	Jul 1952	TOT 4
Tables Turned	Jun 1953	WOF 10
Unrecorded Incident	Oct 1953	WOS 8
The Weird Lovers	Nov 1954	SN 4

as ANTHONY MARTIN

Backtrack	Sep 1953	WOF 11
Dungeon of Time	Aug 1953	TOT 8

R. H. GODFREY—see: E. C. Tubb

H(orace) L(eonard) GOLD, 1914- (USA)

Man of Parts   Jun 1955   NW 36
Reprint from *The Old Die Rich* (1955)

MAURICE GOLDSMITH (UK)

Eclipse   Apr 1954   NW 22 (nf)

JOY K. GOODWIN (UK)

The Bomb and the Blizzard   Aug 1955   AUT 60 (nf)
Photography of the Future   Dec 1954   AUT 52 (nf)
Xerography   Mar 1955   AUT 55 (nf)

MILLARD VERNE GORDON—see: Donald A. Wollheim

S. GORDON (UK)

Dark Universe   Nov 1954   VSS 7
Stranger in Time   Jul 1954   AUT 47

DALE GRAHAM, 1938- (UK)

as D. A. LeGraeme

Adaptibility   Aug 1952   WOF 6
The Expanding Bacillus   Jun 1953   WOF 10
Lambda Point   Jul 1953   WOS 7
The Lighter   May 1952   WOS 3
Safari on Venus   Jan 1953   TOT 6
Time Warp   Apr 1954   WOF 13

ROGER PHILLIPS GRAHAM, 1909-1965 (USA)

as ROG PHILLIPS

A Man Named Mars   Jun 1953   AUT 34
Reprint from *Other Worlds* as by A. R. STEBER (Oct 1950)

WALTER GRAHAM (UK)

How We Find Our Way Around   Apr 1955   AUT 55 (nf)

GEOFFREY GRAYSON—see: John Russell Fearn

PETER GREEN—see: H. Kenneth Bulmer

CHARLES GREY/GRAY—see: E. C. Tubb

VOLSTED GRIDBAN—see: John Russell Fearn

E. A. GROSSER (USA)

Out of Nowhere	Oct 1954	SFF 8

Reprint from *Future* (Oct 1941)

J(ohn) W(illiam) GROVES, 1910- (UK)

Robots Never Weep	Win 1950	NW 8

MARTIN GULLIVER—see: Norman Lazenby

ALAN GUTHRIE—see: E. C. Tubb

Dr. H. (Pseudonym) (UK)

Permanent Magnets	Jan 1956	AUT 65 (nf)

J. HARVEY HAGGARD, 1913- (USA)

Messenger to Infinity	Jun 1954	SFF 4

Reprint from *Science Fiction Quarterly* (Win 1942)

MICHAEL HAMILTON—see: John Glasby

THELMA D. HAMM (Mrs. E. Everett Evans), 1905?-1994 (USA)

Servant Problem	Aug 1954	AUT 48

PAUL HAMMOND—see: Sydney J. Bounds

J. J. HANSBY—see: John Glasby

JIM (i.e., James Judson) HARMON, 1933- (USA)

The Well-Dressed Spaceman	Apr 1955	AUT 56 (nf)

CHARLES L(eonard) HARNESS, 1915- (USA)

The Rose	Mar 1953	AUT 31

CHUCK HARRIS (UK)

Omega	Apr 1954	VSS 3

JOHN (Wyndham Parkes Lucas) BEYNON HARRIS, 1903-1969 (UK)

as JOHN BEYNON

No Place Like Earth	Spr 1951	NW 9
Not So Simple	Feb 1953	AUT 30 (nf)

Time to Rest	Sep 1949	NW 5

Reprint from *Arkham Sampler* (Win 1949)

as JOHN WYNDHAM

Chronoclasm	Sep 1954	SF 10

Reprint from *Star SF Stories 1*, Frederik Pohl, ed. (1953)

Compassion Circuit	May 1955	NW 35

Reprint from *Fantastic Universe* (Dec 1954)

Opposite Numbers	Apr 1954	NW 22
The Pattern of Science Fiction	Mar 1954	SF 7 (nf)
Pawley's Peepholes	Win 1951	SF 3

Reprint of "Operation Peep" from *Suspense* (Sum 1951)

MICHAEL HARRISON, 1907-1991 (UK)

Getaway	Dec 1955	NW 42

MALCOLM HARTLEY—see: John Russell Fearn

PETER HAWKINS, 1924- (UK)

Circus	Aut 1952	SF 5
The Exterminators	Mar 1953	NW 20
Haven	Jul 1954	SF 9
Hideaway	May 1952	NW 15
Life Cycle	Spr 1951	NW 9
Outworlder	Spr 1952	SF 4
Ship from the Stars	Jul 1954	NW 25

GEORGE (i.e., Oswyn Robert Tregonwell) HAY, 1922- (UK)

Man, Woman—and Android	Jun 1951	AUT 10

PETER J. HAZELL (UK)

The Blackdown Miracle	Nov 1954	AUT 51

LESLIE V. HEALD (UK)

The Monument	Jan 1952	WOS 2
Out of the Past	Apr 1952	FSS 6

ROBERT A(nson) HEINLEIN, 1907-1988 (USA)

The Green Hills of Earth	Jan 1956	NEB 15

Reprint from *Saturday Evening Post* (Feb 1947)

Ordeal in Space	Aug 1954	NEB 9

Reprint from *Town and Country* (May 1948)

Rebellion on the Moon	Apr 1955	NEB 12

Reprint of "The Long Watch" from *American Legion Magazine* (May 1948)

N. K. HEMMINGS (AUSTRALIA)

Loser Take All	Win 1951	SF 3

ALBERT HERNHUTER (USA)

Only Human	May 1953	AUT 33

MICHAEL HERVEY, 1914- (UK)

Enigma	Sum 1953	NEB 3

W. B. HICKEY—see: Herbert Livingstone

PHILIP E(mpson) HIGH, 1914- (UK)

The Statics	Sep 1955	AUT 61

ALFRED HIND, 1923?- (UK)

Hollister and Me	Apr 1954	VSS 3
Homo Twice Over	Sep 1955	AUT 61
Out of the Blue	Sep 1952	WOF 7 as *A. Hind*
Rogue Ship	Apr 1953	WOF 9

as THOMAS ROCHDALE

Reaction	Mar 1951	TOT 3

WALTER D. HINDE (UK)

Temporal Fission	Feb 1956	VSS 19

TREVOR HOLLOWAY (UK)

Packing by Science	Dec 1955	AUT 64 (nf)
Scientific Photography	Jan 1956	AUT 65 (nf)

GEORGE HOLT—see: E. C. Tubb

D. RICHARD HUGHES (UK)

Breathing Space	Jan 1954	VSS 1

HERBERT HUGHES—see: Walter Gillings

GEOFFREY HUMPHRYS (UK)

The Marriage Prompters	Oct 1954	NEB 10

ALAN HUNTER, 1923- (UK)

The Piper	Sep 1953	AUT 37

JOHN (Charles) HYNAM, 1915-1974 (UK)

as JOHN KIPPAX

Again	Jan 1956	AUT 65
Dimple	Dec 1954	SF 11
Down to Earth	May 1955	AUT 57
Hounded Down	Nov 1955	SF 16
Mossendew's Martian	Apr 1955	SF 13
Mother of Invention	Dec 1955	AUT 64
Special Delivery	Jun 1955	SF 14
Trojan Hearse (w/Dan Morgan)	Dec 1954	NW 30

DAVID IRISH (UK)

Birthday Star	Jan 1956	NEB 15

C. V. JACKSON (UK)

Is There an Inventor in the House?	Aug 1954	AUT 48 (nf)
Medical Progress by 2000 A.D.	May 1954	AUT 45 (nf)

J. AUSTIN JACKSON—see: Norman Lazenby

E. R. JAMES (UK)

Advent of the Entities	Sum 1950	SF 1
Asteroid City	Mar 1952	NW 14
Blaze of Glory	Apr 1954	NEB 8
Emergency Working	Sep 1952	NW 17
Highwayman Green	Jun 1955	NW 36
Man on the Ceiling	Jul 1954	NW 25
The Minus Men	Aug 1954	NW 26
The Moving Hills	Win 1951	SF 3
Not As We Are	Aut 1952	SF 5
The Rebels	Jun 1949	NW 4
Report on Adam	Apr 1955	NEB 12
Ride the Twilight Rail	Jun 1953	NW 21
Robots Never Weep	Aut 1952	NEB 1
Rockfall	Nov 1954	NW 29
Smoothies Are Wanted	Apr 1955	SF 13
Space Capsule	May 1954	NW 23
Where No Man Walks	Nov 1952	NW 18
World Destroyer	Jul 1955	NW 37

with F. G. Rayer

The Lava Seas Tunnel	Mar 1954	AUT 43

MACK JAMES—see: **Kenneth Boyea and John Watt**

RICHARD JAMES (UK)

Man Wanted	Feb 1956	WWD 2

STEPHEN JAMES (UK)

The Purple Flower	Feb 1951	WOS 1

D. F. JAMESON (UK)

Jovian Flypaper	Sep 1952	WOS 4

ANDY JENKS (UK)

The God from the Machine	Feb 1956	WWD 2

KENNETH JOHNS—see: **H. Kenneth Bulmer and John Newman**

L. S. JOHNSON—see: **T. W. Wade**

W. BOLLINGBROKE JOHNSON—see: **Morris Bishop**

MACK JONES—see: **Kenneth Boyea and John Watt**

RICHARD (Arthur Martin) JORDAN, 1913- (UK)

Cuckoo	Dec 1953	AUT 40
My Name Is Ozymandias	Aug 1953	AUT 36
Present from Mars	Jan 1955	AUT 53
Rondo in Time	Nov 1955	AUT 63
Sheamus	Jun 1955	SF 14
Zone of Youth	Sep 1954	SF 10

MILTON KALETSKY (USA)

Space-Ship Derby	May 1954	SFF 3

Reprint from *Science Fiction Quarterly* (Sum 1940)

WILLIAM S. KALS (CANADA)

Top Secret	Feb 1954	AUT 42

MARVIN KAYNE—see: **John Russell Fearn**

GORDON KENT—see: **E. C. Tubb**

FRANK G. KERR (UK)

Electronics—To Come	Jan 1952	NW 13 (nf)

R. C. KERWOOD (UK)

Machine-Men of Avalon	Sep 1952	WOS 4

A. P. KIFT (UK)

Go to the Ants	Dec 1953	AUT 40

JOHN KIPPAX—see: John Hynam

LILLIAN KIRBY (UK)

Jonathan Elder's Letter	1955	WWD 1

FRANK C. KNELLER—see: Kenneth Boyea and John Watt

C(yril) M. KORNBLUTH, 1923-1958 (USA)

Dominoes	Oct 1954	NW 28

Reprint from *Star SF Stories 1*, Frederik Pohl, ed.

Gomez	Feb 1955	NW 32

Reprint from *The Explorers*, by C. M. Kornbluth (1954)

The Mindworm	Nov 1955	SF 16

Reprint from *Worlds Beyond* (Dec 1950)

The Remorseful	Nov 1954	NW 29

Reprint from *Star SF Stories 2*, Frederik Pohl, ed.

Take Off	From Apr 1954	NW 22 (three part serial)

Reprint from *Take Off* (Doubleday, NY: 1952)

WALTER KUBILIUS, 1918-1993 (USA)

When the Earth Shook	Oct 1954	SFF 8

Reprint from *Future* (Oct 1942)

DUNCAN LAMONT (UK)

The Editor Regrets	Nov 1955	SF 16
Magic Touch	Jan 1956	NW 43

ERIC LAMONT (Pseudonym?)
(same unknown author as *R. J. Norton*; UK)

The Star Ship	Jan 1951	TOT 2

S. M. LANE (UK)

Won't Power	Oct 1954	AUT 50

JOHN LAW (UK)

They Come from Outer Space	May 1955	AUT 57 (nf)

TRIONA LAW (UK)

Are You Colour-Conscious?	Oct 1955	AUT 62 (nf)
Desirable Residence 1995, Part I	Nov 1955	AUT 63 (nf)
Desirable Residence 1995, Part II	Dec 1955	AUT 64 (nf)

RICHARD LAWRENCE—see: L. E. Bartle

JACK LAWSON (UK)

Space Patrol	Dec 1951	FSS 5

NORMAN (Austen) LAZENBY, 1914- (UK)
SEE ALSO: House pseudonym HAMILTON DONNE

The Cireesians	Jun 1949	NW 4
Gods of Helle	Jun 1950	WOF 1
The Mechans of Muah	Dec 1950	FSS 3
Moons of Fear	Jan 1951	WOF 3
Murder Is Hell	Jun 1949	GT 1
Nightmare Planet	Apr 1950	FSS 1
Plasma Men Bring Death	Aug 1950	FSS 2

as W. B. CLARKE

Stratoship X9	Jan 1951	WOF 3

as MARTIN GULLIVER

The Worm of Venus	Apr 1950	FSS 1

as J. AUSTIN JACKSON

Conquerors of the Moon	Jun 1950	WOF 1
World of Fear	Apr 1950	FSS 1

as BASIL SITTY

The Last Ten Men on Earth	Sep 1950	TOT 1

(Eu)GENE LEES (CANADA)

Stranger from Space	Mar 1954	SF 7

D. A. LeGRAEME—see: Dale Graham

LOUISE LEIPIAR (USA)

as L. MAJOR REYNOLDS

Holes, Incorporated	May 1953	AUT 33

Reprint from *If* (Sep 1952)

| It Will Grow on You | Dec 1953 | NEB 6 |

JOHN LEONARDS (UK)

| The Kiss of Death | Feb 1956 | WWD 2 |

RAYMOND LEROYD—see: T. W. Wade

JACK LEWIS (USA)

| Spaceborn | Oct 1955 | AUT 62 |

ARTHUR (Gordon) LEY, 1911-1968 (UK)

as ARTHUR SELLINGS

| The Haunting | Oct 1953 | AUT 38 |

F. LINDSLEY (UK)

| The Star Virus | Apr 1954 | AUT 44 |

HERBERT LIVINGSTONE, 1916- (USA)

as W. B. HICKEY

| Hilda | Jun 1955 | SF 14 |

Reprint as by H. B. HICKEY from *The Magazine of Fantasy & Science Fiction* (Sep 1942)

| Process | Feb 1954 | AUT 42 |

HERBERT LLOYD—see: John Russell Fearn

ROBERT DONALD LOCKE (USA)

| Final Curtain | Oct 1954 | NEB 10 |

R. G. LOMAX (UK)

| The Menace of the Discoids | May 1952 | WOS 3 |

GEORGE LONGDON—see: F. G. Rayer

Professor A(rchibald) M(ontgomery) LOW, 1888-1956 (UK)

The Adventure of Space	Jan 1956	AUT 65 (nf)
Crime, Punishment, and Morals in the Future	Aug 1955	AUT 60 (nf)
Food of the Future	Jul 1955	AUT 59 (nf)
Health and Medicine in the Future	May 1955	AUT 57 (nf)
Sport and Travel in the Future	Jun 1955	AUT 58 (nf)
Transport of Tomorrow	Apr 1955	AUT 56 (nf)

MARGARET LOWE (UK)

The Shimmering Tree	May 1954	SF 8

ROBERT A(ugustine) W(ard) "DOC" LOWNDES, 1916- (USA)

as RICHARD MORRISON

The Deliverers	Jul 1954	SFF 5

Reprint from *Science Fiction Quarterly* (Win 1942)

EDWARD W(illiam) LUDWIG, 1920-1990 (USA)

Occupation	Oct 1954	NW 28

Reprint from *The Magazine of Fantasy & Science Fiction* (May 1953)

CHRISTOPHER LYSTER (UK)

The Artifact	Jan 1956	NEB 15

CLEM MACARTNEY—see: B. Flackes

JAMES MURDOCH MACGREGOR, 1925- (UK)

The Broken Record	Sep 1952	NW 17

as J. T. MCINTOSH

Beggars All	Mar 1954	SF 7

Reprint from *The Magazine of Fantasy & Science Fiction* (Apr 1953)

The Big Hop	From May 1955	AUT 57 (two part serial)
Bluebird World	Jun 1955	NW 36
Divine Right	Feb 1954	NEB 7
The ESP Worlds	From Jul 1952	NW 16 (three part serial)
Five into Four	Sep 1954	SF 10
The Happier Eden	Dec 1953	NEB 6
The Lady and the Bull	From Nov 1955	AUT 63 (two part serial)
Live for Ever	Dec 1954	SF 11
Machine Made	Sum 1951	NW 10
Relay Race	Apr 1954	NW 22
The Solomon Plan	Feb 1956	NW 44
Something New Wanted	Jul 1954	SF 9
Stitch in Time	Aut 1952	SF 5
Then There Were Two	Win 1951	SF 3
The Volunteers	Spr 1953	SF 6
War's Great Organ	Sep 1953	NEB 2
The Way Home	Aug 1955	NW 38
When Aliens Meet	Win 1951	NW 12
The World That Changed	Mar 1952	NW 14

as H. J. MURDOCH

This Precious Stone	Jul 1954	SF 9

with Francis Parnell, as GREGORY FRANCIS

Ape	Sum 1951	NW 10
Hitch-Hikers	Dec 1954	NW 30 Parnell only
Question Mark	Win 1951	NW 12

STUART MACKENZIE (UK)

Fandom and the Future	Apr 1954	VSS 3 (nf)

KATHERINE (Anne) MACLEAN, 1925- (USA)

with MICHAEL PORGES

The Prize	Feb 1955	AUT 54

CHARLES ERIC MAINE—see: David McIlwain

DONALD MALCOLM, 1930-1975 (UK)

with A. E. Roy, as ROY MALCOLM

A Tenth Planet	Jun 1955	NW 36 (nf)
Whose Moon?	Feb 1956	NW 44 (nf)

ROY MALCOLM—see: Donald Malcolm and A. E. Roy

B. DIXON MALLORY (UK)

Parthenogenesis	Feb 1956	AUT 66 (nf)

JOHN F. MANDERS—see: Laurence Sandfield

GEORGE PAUL MANN, 1927- (UK)

Third Hand	May 1954	AUT 45

JOHN T(ruman) MANTLEY, 1920- (CANADA)

Uncle Clem and Them Martians	Feb 1956	SF 17

KATHERINE MARCUSE (UK)

21st Century Mother	Jan 1954	AUT 41
Children Should Be Seen	Jan 1956	AUT 65
The Holiday	Mar 1955	AUT 55

ANTHONY MARTIN—see: A. A. Glynn

JOHN R. MARTIN—see: T. W. Wade

PHILLIP MARTYN—see: E. C. Tubb

JOHN (Keith Hollis) MASON (CANADA)

Sacrifice   Mar 1954   SFF 10
Reprint from *Future* (Feb 1942)

RAY MASON—see: Kenneth Boyea and John Watt

HOWARD LEE McCAREY (UK)

Double Act   Jun 1955   SF 14

DAVID McILWAIN, 1921-1981 (UK)

as CHARLES ERIC MAINE

The Boogie Matrix	Jan 1954	AUT 41
Highway 1	Nov 1953	AUT 39
Repulsion Factor	Sep 1953	AUT 37
The Trouble with Mars	Jul 1955	AUT 59
Troubleshooter	Feb 1954	NEB 7
The Yupe	Dec 1954	NEB 11

J. T. McINTOSH—see: James Macgregor

D. R./J. MENCER/MENCET—see: Kenneth Boyea and John Watt

A. J. MERAK—see: John Glasby

(Josephine) JUDITH MERRIL, 1923- (USA)

Connection Completed   Feb 1956   SF 17
Reprint from *Universe SF* (Nov 1954)
Survival Ship   May 1955   NW 25
Reprint from *Worlds Beyond* (Jan 1951)

JOHN MICHEL, 1917-1969? (USA)

as HUGH RAYMOND

Glory Road   Jun 1954   SFF 4
Reprint from *Science Fiction Quarterly* (Fal 1942)

JEROME S. MILL (UK)

Hour of Zero   Sep 1955   .   AUT 61

RICHARD MILNE—see: Richard Milne Sharples

MERYL ST. JOHN MONTAGUE—see: Laurence Sandfield

W. MOORE (UK)

Pool of Infinity	Sep 1949	NW 5

D. A. MORGAN (UK)

One Good Turn	Nov 1954	VSS 7

DAN MORGAN, 1925- (UK)

Alcoholic Ambassador	Aug 1954	NEB 9
Alien Analysis	Jan 1952	NW 13
Amateur Talent	Dec 1953	AUT 40
Cleansing Fires	Dec 1954	AUT 52
Forgive Them	Sep 1954	AUT 49
Home Is Tomorrow	Jul 1953	AUT 35
Jerry Built	Jun 1954	NW 24
Kwakiutl	May 1955	AUT 57
The Lesser Breed	Feb 1955	AUT 54
Life Agency	Sep 1955	NW 39
Psychic Twin	Jun 1954	AUT 46
Trojan Hearse (w/John Kippax)	Dec 1954	NW 30

ALEX MORRISON (UK)

Star Mania	Dec 1955	AUT 64

RICHARD MORRISON—see: Robert A. W. Lowndes

MAURICE MOYAL (UK)

Plant Breeders	Jan 1956	AUT 65 (nf)

H. J. MURDOCH—see: James Macgregor

CYRIL MYRESCOUGH (UK)

A World in Exile	Dec 1954	NEB 11

GAVIN NEAL (UK)

Logical Deduction	Mar 1955	NW 33
Reluctant Hero	Jun 1955	SF 14
Short Circuit	Jan 1955	NW 31

KRIS (Ottman) NEVILLE, 1925-1980 (USA)

Old Man Henderson	Jun 1953	AUT 34

Reprint from *The Magazine of Fantasy & Science Fiction* (Jun 1951)

Passing the Torch	Jun 1953	AUT 34 (nf)

JOHN NEWMAN, d. 1992 (UK)

Automation	May 1954	NW 23 (nf)
Between the Stars	Feb 1956	NW 44 (nf)
Celestial Debris	Oct 1955	NW 40 (nf)
Energy	Dec 1954	NW 30 (nf)
Food of the Future	Apr 1955	NW 34 (nf)
Invisible Astronomy	May 1955	NW 35 (nf)
The Mighty Midgets	Jan 1956	NW 43 (nf)
P's and Q's	Sep 1955	NW 39 (nf)
Radiac	Jun 1954	NW 24 (nf)
Radio-Isotopes	Jul 1955	NW 37 (nf)
Semi-Conductors	Jul 1954	NW 25 (nf)
Silicones	Jan 1953	NW 19 (nf)
Solar Interference	Dec 1955	NW 42 (nf)
Spaceship Diet	Nov 1955	NW 41 (nf)
Ultrasonics	Feb 1955	NW 32 (nf)
Universe Times Two	Nov 1955	NEB 14

with H. Kenneth Bulmer, as KENNETH JOHNS

Audrey	Sep 1955	AUT 61 (nf)
Future Indefinite	Feb 1956	NW 44 (nf)
Our Invisible Shield 1	Jul 1955	AUT 59 (nf)
Our Invisible Shield 2	Aug 1955	AUT 60 (nf)
Project Air	Feb 1956	AUT 66 (nf)
Research Nuclear Reactors	Dec 1955	AUT 64 (nf)
Tools of Tomorrow	Oct 1955	AUT 62 (nf)

"NORTHERNER"—see: David H. Cohen

R. J. NORTON (Pseudonym?)
(same unknown author as *Eric Lamont*; UK)

Soldiers of Space	Jan 1951	TOT 2

CHARLES (Leroy) NUTT—see: Charles Beaumont

JAMES O'CONNELLY (UK)

Vengeance of the Snake	1955	WWD 1

PAT O'HARA (UK)

Robots	Jun 1954	AUT 46 (nf)

(Symmes) CHAD(wick) OLIVER, 1928-1993 (USA)

Any More at Home Like You?	Sep 1955	NW 39

Reprint from *Star SF Stories 3*, Frederik Pohl, ed. (1954)

T. OWENS (UK)

The Atom Bomb	Mar 1953	NW 20 (nf)

ARTHUR WATERHOUSE (Painter), d. 1968 (UK)

as ARTHUR WATERHOUSE

Adrift	Mar 1955	VSS 11
Invisible Impact	Feb 1954	VSS 2

NORMAN (Charles) PALLANT, 1910-1972 (UK)

Martian Mandate	Win 1950	SF 2

HAMILTON PARK (UK)

On Information Received	1955	WWD 1

VALENTINE PARKER—see: Walter Gillings

FRANK (Herbert Charles) PARNELL, 1916- (UK)

with L. E. Bartle, as FRANCIS RICHARDSON

The Trojan Way	Mar 1954	SF 7

with James Macgregor, as GREGORY FRANCIS

Ape	Sum 1951	NW 10
Hitch-Hikers	Dec 1954	NW 30 Parnell only
Question Mark	Win 1951	NW 12

DOM PASSANTE—see: John Russell Fearn

ALISTER B(lair) JOHNS PATERSON (UK)

as ARMSTRONG ALEXANDER

The Pendulum of Power	Jan 1954	VSS 1

ROD PATTERSON—see: Kenneth Boyea and John Watt

RON PAUL (UK)

Blue Rose	Apr 1955	AUT 56

EDWARD PEAL (UK)

The Thing in the Air	Jul 1954	VSS 5

BARRY PEARSON (UK)

The Great Zimilcoff	Feb 1956	WWD 2

MARTIN PEARSON—see: Donald A. Wollheim

LESLIE PERRI—see: Doris Wilson

PETER PHILLIPS, 1920- (UK)

Plagiarist	Sum 1950	NW 7
Unknown Quantity	Sep 1949	NW 5

ROG PHILLIPS—see: Roger Graham

EDGAR ALLAN POE, 1809-1849 (USA)

The Fall of the House of Usher	Feb 1956	WWD 2
	Reprint from 1839	

JOHN POOLE (UK)

Station Neptune	Dec 1951	FSS 5

MICHAEL PORGES (USA)

with KATHERINE MACLEAN

The Prize	Feb 1955	AUT 54

KENNETH POTTER (UK)

Wind Along the Waste	Apr 1954	NEB 8

W. H. POWERS (UK)

The Facts About Hypnotism	Nov 1955	AUT 63 (nf)
Hypnotism	Apr 1955	AUT 56 (nf)

ROBERT PRESSLIE (UK)

The Creep	From Jan 1956	AUT 65 (two part serial)
A Star Called Tommy	Oct 1955	AUT 62
Trespassers Will Be Prosecuted	Jun 1955	AUT 58

WALTER R. PRESTON (USA)

Lunar Sanctuary	Aug 1954	SFF 6
	Reprint from *Science Fiction Quarterly* (Win 1942)	

LEONARD PRUYN, 1898-1973 (USA)

In Time of Sorrow	Feb 1954	AUT 42

B. G. PUTTICK (UK)

The Expanding Universe	Jun 1954	AUT 46 (nf)

FRANK QUATTROCCHI (USA)

Addict	Apr 1954	AUT 44
Kid's Game	Jan 1954	AUT 41
Sword from the Stars	Jul 1953	AUT 35

JACK RAMSTROM (UK)

How They Landed	May 1953	AUT 33

HENRY RAWLE (UK)

Dr. Gabrielle's Chair	Apr 1954	SFF 2

F(rancis) G(eorge) RAYER, 1921-1981 (UK)

Adaptability	Spr 1950	NW 6
The Ark	Sum 1950	SF 1
Co-Efficiency Zero	Dec 1954	SF 11
Come Away Home	Sep 1954	NW 27
The Coming of the Darakua	Jan 1952	AUT 17
Dark Summer	Sep 1954	SF 10
Deus Ex Machina	Win 1950	NW 8
Earth Our New Eden	Apr 1952	AUT 20
Ephemeral This City	Mar 1955	NW 33
Firstling	Dec 1953	NEB 6
The Jakandi Moduli	Dec 1955	NW 42
Kill Me This Man	Jan 1955	NW 31
Man's Questing Ended	Jul 1952	NW 16
Necessity	Sep 1949	NW 5
The Peacemaker	Sep 1952	NW 17
Pipe Away Stranger	Jul 1954	NW 25
Plimsoll Line	Spr 1952	SF 4
Power Factor	Jun 1953	NW 21
Prison Trap	Sum 1951	NW 10
Quest	Sum 1950	NW 7
Seek Earthmen No More	Mar 1954	SF 7
Space Prize	May 1954	SF 8
Stormhead	Oct 1955	NW 40
This Night No More	Sep 1955	NEB 13
Thou Pasture Us	Spr 1953	NEB 2
Time Was	Win 1951	NW 12
Trader's Planet	Spr 1953	SF 6
The Undying Enemy	Win 1951	SF 3

| The Voices Beyond | Nov 1955 | NW 41 |
| We Cast No Shadow | Dec 1952 | AUT 28 |

as G. R. LONGDON

The Falsifiers	Feb 1956	NW 44
No Heritage	Win 1951	NW 12
Of Those Who Came	Nov 1952	NW 18
The Temporal Rift	Jul 1952	NW 16

with E. R. James

| The Lava Seas Tunnel | Mar 1954 | AUT 43 |

HUGH RAYMOND—see: John Michel

JOHN RAYMOND—see: R. Lionel Fanthorpe

WILFRED READER (UK)

| The Essential Chemist | Apr 1955 | AUT 56 (nf) |

CLIFFORD C(ecil) REED, 1911- (SOUTH AFRICA)

| Jean—Gene—Jeanne | Nov 1954 | AUT 51 |

JOHN RENOLDS (UK)

| Black Pirate | Jan 1951 | TOT 2 |

L. MAJOR REYNOLDS—see: Louise Leipiar

R(obert) M. RHODES (USA)

| Dangerous Power | Feb 1953 | AUT 30 |
| The Toy | Apr 1953 | AUT 32 |

KANE RICE (UK)

| He Wanted a Gun | Nov 1954 | SUS 3 |

FRANCIS RICHARDSON—see: L. E. Bartle and Francis Parnell

HARRY RICHMOND (UK)

| The Master Mind | Sep 1954 | SUS 2 |

PETER J. RIDLEY, 1928- (UK)

...And It Shall Be Opened	Aut 1953	NEB 4
The Ass's Ears	Aut 1952	NEB 1
Rake's Progress	Feb 1951	WOS 1

EVERET RIGBY (UK)

Treachery from Venus	Jan 1951	WOF 3

PETER E. RIGBY (UK)

Parting	Jan 1955	AUT 53

ANTHONY RIGHTON (UK)

The Charlady Who Travelled Faster Than Light	Feb 1956	WWD 2

ARTHUR F. ROBERTS (UK)

Digital Computer	Win 1951	NW 12 (nf)

LIONEL ROBERTS—see: R. Lionel Fanthorpe

JAMES ROBERTSON—see: Kenneth Boyea and John Watt

JOHN ROBERTSON—see: Kenneth Boyea and John Watt

MACLEOD ROBERTSON (UK)

Megalocosmos	Oct 1953	AUT 38

VINCENT ROBERTSON—see: T. W. Wade

THOMAS ROCHDALE—see: Alfred Hind

ROSS L(ouis) ROCKLIN, 1913-1988 (USA)

as ROSS ROCKLYNNE

Alphabet Scoop	Sep 1953	NEB 5

ROSS ROCKLYNNE—see: Ross L. Rocklin

LEE RONDELLE (UK)

Cosmic Mirror	AUT 1951	NW 11

WILLIAM L. ROPER (USA)

Nuclear Explosions and the Weather	Sep 1955	AUT 61 (nf)

FRANCIS ROSE—see: John Russell Fearn

FRANK ROSE—see: John Russell Fearn

JAMES ROSS—see: Sydney J. Bounds

WARD ROSS—see: **John Russell Fearn**

RICHARD ROWLAND (UK)

Ferrymam	May 1955	NW 35
Where's the Matter	Dec 1954	SF 11

A(rchibald) E(dmiston) ROY, 1924- (UK)

The Way to the Planets 1: Halfway Camps	Jun 1955	AUT 58 (nf)
The Way to the Planets 2:	Jul 1955	AUT 59 (nf)
The Way to the Planets 3: The Satellite Vehicles	Aug 1955	AUT 60 (nf)
The Way to the Planets 4: The Space Station	Sep 1955	AUT 61 (nf)
The Way to the Planets 5: Laboratory in Space 1	Oct 1955	AUT 62 (nf)
The Way to the Planets 6: Laboratory in Space 2	Nov 1955	AUT 63 (nf)
The Way to the Planets 7: Space Medicine	Dec 1955	AUT 64 (nf)
The Way to the Planets 8: Objective—The Moon	Jan 1956	AUT 65 (nf)
The Way to the Planets 9: Our Nearest Neighbour	Feb 1956	AUT 66 (nf)

with Donald Malcolm, as ROY MALCOLM

A Tenth Planet	Jun 1955	NW 36 (nf)
Whose Moon?	Feb 1956	NW 44 (nf)

ERIC FRANK RUSSELL, 1905-1978 (UK)

Astronomy	Jul 1955	NW 37 (nf)
Boomerang	Dec 1954	NEB 11
Down, Rover, Down	Nov 1955	NEB 14
Fly Away Peter	Apr 1954	NEB 8
I Hear You Calling	Dec 1954	SF 11
Sustained Pressure	Dec 1953	NEB 6
This One's on Me	Aut 1953	NEB 4

as NIALL WILDE/NIGEL WILDE

Heart's Desire	Nov 1955	SF 16

Niall in contents, *Nigel* on story

DEAN RYAN (UK)

Buried in Space	Nov 1952	WOS 5
Cosmic Conception	Apr 1953	FSS 10
Tomorrow Is Also a Day	Jun 1953	WOF 10

Professor JAMES J. RYAN (USA)

The Ryan Flight Recorder	Sep 1955	AUT 61 (nf)

LAURENCE SANDFIELD, 1921- (UK)

All Change	Mar 1953	NW 20

Emergency	Jun 1953	WOF 10
Interplay	Aug 1954	NW 26
Mightier Weapon	Aug 1952	WOF 6

as JOHN F. MANDERS

Colonist	Aug 1952	WOF 6

as MERYL ST. JOHN MONTAGUE

Mission Venus	Jul 1953	WOS 7

CHESMAN SCOTT—see: H. Kenneth Bulmer

CLIFFORD SEARLE (UK)

The Point of No Return	Oct 1955	VSS 17

DAN F. SEESON (UK)

A New Comet	Dec 1955	VSS 18 (nf)
Solar System 1: The Sun	Feb 1955	VSS 10 (nf)
Solar System 2: The Moon	Mar 1955	VSS 11 (nf)
Solar System 3: Mercury	Apr 1955	VSS 12 (nf)
Solar System 4: Venus	Jun 1955	VSS 13 (nf)
Solar System 5: The Earth	Jul 1955	VSS 14 (nf)
Solar System 6: Mars	Aug 1955	VSS 15 (nf)
Solar System 7: The Minor Planets	Sep 1955	VSS 16 (nf)
Solar System 8: Jupiter	Oct 1955	VSS 17 (nf)
Solar System 9: Saturn	Dec 1955	VSS 18 (nf)
Solar System 10: Uranus	Feb 1956	VSS 19 (nf)

ARTHUR SELLINGS—see: Arthur Ley

RICHARD MILNE (Sharples) (UK)

as RICHARD MILNE

Horror from the Swamps	Jun 1949	GT 1

BOB SHAW, 1931- (UK)

Aspect	Aug 1954	NEB 9
Departure	Oct 1955	AUT 62
The Journey Alone	Apr 1955	NEB 12
Sounds in the Dawn	Jan 1956	NEB 15
The Trespassers	Dec 1954	NEB 11

LEN SHAW (UK)

The Bridge	Jul 1954	AUT 47
Forever Today	Apr 1954	AUT 44

Holiday Task	Jul 1955	AUT 59
The Phoenix Treatment	Jan 1956	AUT 65
The Silver Box	Mar 1955	AUT 55
Syllabus	Feb 1956	SF 17
Wedding Bells for Sylvia	Nov 1955	AUT 63

W. SHAW (UK)

The Manipulators	Oct 1952	FSS 8
Quietus	Sep 1952	WOF 7

ROBERT SHECKLEY, 1928- (USA)

The Last Weapon	Aug 1954	NW 26

Reprint from *Star SF Stories 1*, Frederik Pohl, ed. (1953)

The Odour of Thought	Jul 1954	NW 25

Reprint from *Star SF Stories 2*, Frederik Pohl, ed., (1953)

Paradise II	Jul 1955	NW 37

Reprint from *Times To Come*, August Derleth, ed. (1954)

ROY SHELDON (House pseudonym)
SHINY SPEAR series written by *H. J. Campbell** (UK)

*Beam of Terror	Sep 1951	AUT 13 H. J. Campbell
*Energy Alive	Apr 1951	AUT 7 H. J. Campbell
Gold Men of Aureus	Feb 1951	AUT 3 unidentified
*Phantom Moon	Mar 1951	AUT 6 H. J. Campbell
*The Plastic Peril	Sep 1952	AUT 25 H. J. Campbell
Space Warp	Mar 1952	AUT 19 unidentified
*Star of Death	Nov 1952	AUT 27 H. J. Campbell

ANTHONY SHEPPARD (UK)

The Old School Tie	Jan 1955	AUT 53

THOMAS SHERIDAN—see: Walter Gillings

ROBERT SILVERBERG, 1935- (USA)

The Gorgon	Feb 1954	NEB 7

BASIL SITTY—see: Norman Lazenby

KEN(neth Frederick) SLATER, 1917- (UK)

Who's Who in Fandom	Jan 1954	VSS 1 (nf)

JOHN SLOAN—see: T. W. Wade

JOSEPH SLOTKIN (USA)

The Mailman	Dec 1954	SF 11

To Touch the Stars	Feb 1956	SF 17

ART SMITH (UK)

The Big Slowdown	Apr 1954	TOT 10

K. E. SMITH (UK)

The Kid	Oct 1954	AUT 50

LAWRENCE SMITH—see: Sydney J. Bounds

NEIL J. SPA(U)LDING—see: Kenneth Boyea and John Watt

JOY SPOCZYNSKA (POLAND)

Three Against Carbon 14	Dec 1955	VSS 18

TREVOR STAINES—see: John Brunner

JAMES STANFIELD—see: T. W. Wade

LEE STANTON (UK)

Mushroom Men from Mars	Jan 1951	AUT 1
Report from Mandazo	Nov 1951	AUT 15
Seven to the Moon	Mar 1951	AUT 5

VARGO STATTEN—see: John Russell Fearn

MANNING STERN—see: T. W. Wade

DAL(las) (George) STIVENS, 1911- (UK)

Free Will	Feb 1955	SF 12

EDWARD STOKES—see: Kenneth Boyea and John Watt

SIMPSON STOKES—see: F. Dubrez Fawcett

M. G. STONE (UK)

Beast Men of Mars	Feb 1951	FSS 4

ERIC STORM—see: E. C. Tubb

H. PHILIP STRATFORD—see: H. Kenneth Bulmer

RICK STRAUSS (UK)

Without Love	Jan 1955	AUT 53

JEROME STRICKLAND—see: Lan Wright

KELVIN STRIKE (UK)

The Best Laid Scheme	Dec 1953	AUT 40

PETER SUMMERS (UK)

Brain and Body	Sep 1954	AUT 49 (nf)
Brain and Mind	Oct 1954	AUT 50 (nf)
Free Will	Jan 1956	AUT 65 (nf)
Get Integrated	Feb 1955	AUT 54 (nf)
Plants Against Disease	Aug 1955	AUT 60 (nf)
Space Travel and the Law	Jun 1954	AUT 46 (nf)
Stand on Our Feet	Apr 1955	AUT 56 (nf)

H. C. SUTER (UK)

Lightning Stroke Counter	Jan 1956	AUT 65 (nf)

DWIGHT V(reeland) SWAIN, 1915-1992 (USA)

Cry Chaos!	Apr 1953	AUT 32

Reprint from *Imagination* (Sept 1951)

JOHN SYLVASSEY—see: T. W. Wade

GEORGE B. TAIT, 1910- (UK)

Down in Our Village in Somerset	Aug 1955	AUT 60

as ALAN BARCLAY

The Dragon	Feb 1955	SF 12
Enemy in Their Midst	Aut 1952	SF 5
The Firebird	Aug 1954	NW 26
The Hard Way	Jun 1953	NW 21
The Hot Potato	Jan 1956	NW 43
The Lever and the Fulcrum	Apr 1954	AUT 44
Louey	Feb 1956	SF 17
Only an Echo	Apr 1954	NW 22
The Real McCoy	Apr 1955	NW 34
Rock 83	Oct 1955	NW 40
The Single Ship	Sep 1955	NW 39
Walk into My Parlor	May 1954	NW 23
Welcome, Stranger!	Aut 1951	NW 11

LEE TAYLOR (UK)

The Amateur's Microscope	Jul 1954	VSS 5 (nf)
Astronomical Telescopes	May 1954	VSS 4 (nf)

JOHN TAYNE (UK)

Aliens on Earth	Mar 1955	AUT 55 (nf)
All About Comets	May 1954	AUT 45 (nf)
All About Evolution	Aug 1954	AUT 48 (nf)
The Scientist's Life 1: The Botanist	Jun 1955	AUT 58 (nf)
The Scientist's Life 2: The Chemist	Jul 1955	AUT 59 (nf)
The Scientist's Life 3: The Physiologist	Aug 1955	AUT 60 (nf)
The Scientist's Life 4: The Physicist	Sep 1955	AUT 61 (nf)
There's Trouble in the Future!	Jul 1954	AUT 47 (nf)

WILLIAM F(rederick) TEMPLE, 1914-1989 (UK)

Destiny Is My Enemy	Sep 1953	NEB 5
Double Trouble	Win 1951	SF 3
Errand of Mercy	Mar 1954	AUT 43
Eternity	Feb 1955	SF 12
Immortal's Playthings	Jan 1953	AUT 29
Limbo	Sum 1953	NEB 3
Man in a Maze	Feb 1955	AUT 54
Mansion of a Love	Sep 1955	NEB 13
Martian's Fancy	Sum 1950	NW 7
Mind Within Mind	May 1953	AUT 33

Reprint of "The Brain Beast" from *Super Science* (Jul 1949)

Pawn in Revolt	Aut 1953	NEB 5
Pilot's Hands	Feb 1954	NEB 7
Scientist and Censor	Mar 1953	AUT 31 (nf)
Uncle Buno	Nov 1955	SF 16

R. THOMPSON (UK)

Sauce for the Goose	Aug 1955	AUT 60

TONY C. THORNE (UK)

Inside Information	Dec 1953	NEB 6
Timely Encounter	Sep 1954	VSS 6

TREBOR THORPE—see: R. Lionel Fanthorpe

PEL TORRO—see: R. Lionel Fanthorpe

JOHN TOUCAN—see: William Bird

HARVEY TRENT (UK)

Frogman's Frenzy	Sep 1954	SUS 2

MARK TRENT (UK)

Customer's Risk	Aug 1955	VSS 15
Question Answered	Nov 1955	NEB 14

KENN TREVOR (UK)

Marionette Murder	Sep 1954	SUS 2

E(dwin) C(harles) TUBB, 1919- (UK)

Agent	Jun 1955	SF 14
Alien Dust	Jan 1953	NW 19
Alien Impact	May 1952	AUT 21
Asteroids	Feb 1956	AUT 66
Bitter Sweet	Sep 1954	SF 10
Closing Time	Oct 1954	NEB 10
Confessional	Spr 1953	SF 6
Conversation Piece	Oct 1953	AUT 38
Dark Solution	Spr 1953	NEB 2
Death Deferred	May 1954	AUT 45
Decision	Aug 1955	AUT 60
Emancipation	Feb 1954	NEB 7
The Enemy Within Us	Dec 1954	SF 11
Entrance Exam	Win 1951	NW 12
Episode	Apr 1954	NEB 8
Ethical Assassin	Jun 1955	AUT 58
Follow My Leader	Jun 1955	SF 14 (nf)
Forbidden Fruit	From May 1954	VSS 4 (three part serial)
Freight	Sum 1953	NEB 3
Greek Gift	Aut 1951	NW 11
Grounded	Win 1951	SF 3
Hidden Treasure of Kalin	Oct 1954	AUT 50
Home Is the Hero	May 1952	NW 15
Homecoming	Oct 1954	NW 28

Reprint from *Universe SF* (May 1954)

The Inevitable Conflict	From Jan 1954	VSS 1 (three part serial)
Into Thy Hands	Nov 1954	NW 29
Investment	Jan 1956	NEB 15
The Last Day of Summer	Feb 1955	SF 12
Lawyer at Large	Dec 1955	NW 42
Little Girl Lost	Oct 1955	NW 40
Logic	Sep 1954	AUT 49
Men Only	Jul 1952	NW 16
Mistake on Mars	Jan 1956	AUT 65
Murder Most Innocent	Mar 1955	AUT 55
No Short Cuts	Sum 1951	NW 10
Nonentity	Feb 1955	AUT 54
Occupational Hazard	Jul 1954	SF 9
One Every Minute	Sep 1955	AUT 61
Operation Mars	Dec 1954	NEB 11
Perac	Jul 1955	NW 37
The Pilot	Aut 1953	NEB 5
Pistol Point	Jun 1953	NW 21
Planetbound	Sep 1955	NEB 13
Poor Henry	Apr 1955	SF 13
The Predators	Sep 1955	SF 15

Project One	Aug 1954	NEB 9
Quis Custodiet	Nov 1955	NEB 14
The Robbers	Dec 1954	NW 30
Rockets Aren't Human	Mar 1953	NW 20
School for Beginners	Feb 1955	NW 32
See No Evil...	Aug 1955	NW 38
The Shell Game	Nov 1955	AUT 63
Star Haven	Dec 1954	AUT 52
Star Ship	From Apr 1955	NW 34 (three part serial)
Subtle Victory	Nov 1953	AUT 39
Tea Party	Dec 1953	NEB 6
That Zamboni	Oct 1955	AUT 62
Third Party	Mar 1952	NW 14
Tomorrow	May 1954	SF 8
The Troublemaker	Sep 1953	NEB 5
Unfortunate Purchase	Mar 1954	SF 7
Venus for Never	Dec 1955	AUT 64
The Wager	Nov 1955	SF 16
Without Bugles	Jan 1952	NW 13

as ALICE BEECHAM

Lover, Where Art Thou?	Mar 1955	AUT 55

as ANTHONY BLAKE

When He Died	Feb 1956	AUT 66

as L. T. BRONSON

First Effort	Sep 1952	WOF 7

as JULIAN CAREY

Blow the Man Down	Oct 1955	AUT 62
Repair Job	May 1955	AUT 57

as MORLEY CARPENTER

Test Piece	Feb 1954	VSS 2

as NORMAN DALE

The Veterans	Mar 1955	NW 33

as R. H. GODFREY

No Place for Tears	Apr 1955	AUT 56

as CHARLES GREY/*CHARLES GRAY

Helping Hand	Nov 1952	WOS 5

Honour Bright	Aug 1953	FSS 12
Intrigue on Io	Sep 1952	TOT 5
Museum Piece	Apr 1954	FSS 15
*Precedent	May 1952	NW 15
There's No Tomorrow	Sep 1952	WOF 7
*Unwanted Heritage	Nov 1952	NW 18
Visiting Celebrity	Jan 1954	FSS 14

as ALAN GUTHRIE

Dear Ghost	Sep 1955	SF 15
No Space for Me	Jul 1955	NW 37
The Pensioners	Jan 1956	NW 43
Samson	May 1955	NW 35

as GEORGE HOLT

The Answer	Feb 1956	VSS 19
Brutus	Apr 1955	AUT 56
Emergency Exit	Sep 1954	VSS 6
Kalgan the Golden	Aug 1955	VSS 15
Lost Property	Dec 1955	VSS 18
Oversight	Mar 1955	VSS 11
Skin Deep	Dec 1954	VSS 8

as GORDON KENT

Heroes Don't Cry	Jan 1953	NW 19

as PHILLIP MARTYN

Forgetfulness	Apr 1955	NW 34

as ERIC STORM

Lone Wolf	Aug 1953	AUT 36

as KEN WAINWRIGHT

Sleeve of Care	Feb 1956	AUT 66

as FRANK WEIGHT

Prime Essential	Dec 1955	NW 64

as DOUGLAS WEST

The Dogs of Hannoie	Sep 1955	SF 15

as ERIC WILDING

Death-Wish	Feb 1955	AUT 54

Unwanted Eden	Nov 1955	AUT 63

as FRANK WINNARD

First Impression	Feb 1956	AUT 66

(Arthur) WILSON TUCKER, 1914- (USA)

The Job Is Ended	Sep 1955	SF 15

Reprint from *Science Fiction Sub-Treasury* by Wilson Tucker (1954)

My Brother's Wife	Jun 1955	SF 14

Reprint from *The Magazine of Fantasy & Science Fiction* (Feb 1951)

Science into Fantasy	May 1954	SF 8
The Time Masters	From Sep 1955	NW 39 (three part serial)

Reprint from novel (Rinehart, U.S., 1953)

Wild Talent	From Aug 1954	NW 26 (three part serial)

Reprint from novel (Rinehart, U.S., 1954)

HELEN M. URBAN (UK)

Heart Ache	Jan 1956	AUT 65
Pass the Salt	Apr 1955	SF 13

ERLE VAN LODEN—see: Lisle Willis

A(lfred) E(lton) VAN VOGT, 1912- (USA)

Enchanted Village	Mar 1952	NW 14

Reprint from *Other Worlds* (Jul 1950)

Haunted Atoms	Apr 1955	AUT 32

Reprint from *Ten Story Fantasy* (Spr 1951)

Letter from the Stars	Aut 1952	NEB 1

Reprint from "Dear Pen Pal" from *Arkham Sampler* (Win 1949)

RICHARD VARNE (UK)

In a Misty Light	Apr 1955	SF 13
Regulations	Oct 1954	NW 28

(Mari)LYN VENABLE (USA)

Parry's Paradox	May 1955	AUT 57

T(homas) W. WADE (UK)

Assignment on Venus	Sep 1952	WOS 4
Globe of Dread	Oct 1953	TOT 9
The Impending Heritage	Apr 1952	WOF 5
The Incredible Scourge	Sep 1952	TOT 5
The Indigenous Revolt	Oct 1952	FSS 13
Integral Menace	Jan 1954	WOS 9
The Irreparable Sunset	Dec 1951	FSS 5

Journey to the Dawn	Dec 1952	WOF 8
Lilliput Minor	Nov 1953	WOU 1

Credited to MANNING STERN in contents

The Minacious Termites	Jan 1952	WOS 2
Minerals from Mars	Oct 1952	FSS 8
Mistakes Do Happen	Nov 1952	WOS 5
The Peril from the Moon	Feb 1951	WOS 1
Pioneer for Saturn	Jan 1953	FSS 9
Sirius Rampant	Apr 1952	FSS 6
There Is No Future	Feb 1954	WOF 12

as BRANSON D. CARTER

Anno Mundi	Sep 1952	WOS 4

as L. S. JOHNSON

Struggle for Callisto	Jan 1952	WOS 2

as RAYMOND LeROYD

The Aquatic Piracy	Apr 1952	WOF 5

as JOHN R. MARTIN

Last Throw from Ganymede	Oct 1952	FSS 8

as VINCENT ROBERTSON

The Crystalline World	Sep 1952	TOT 5
The Moment in Time	Oct 1953	TOT 9

as JOHN SLOAN

The Elder Race	Jan 1951	WOF 3

as JAMES STANFIELD

The Encompassed Globe	Mar 1951	TOT 3

as MANNING STERN

Lilliput Minor	Nov 1953	WOU 1

Credited to *T. W. Wade* in contents, STERN on cover

as JOHN SYLVASSEY

Spawn of the Void	Nov 1953	WOU 1

KEN WAINWRIGHT—see: E. C. Tubb

CEDRIC WALKER (UK)

Manhunt	Spr 1951	NW 9
The Scapegoats	Aut 1951	NW 11

ALISTAIR WALLACE (UK)

The Jewelled Dagger	Feb 1956	WWD 2

CLIFFORD WALLACE—see: Sydney J. Bounds

J(ames) M(organ) WALSH, 1897-1952 (AUSTRALIA)

The Belt	Sum 1950	SF 1
The Last Fifty Years and the Next	Aut 1952	SF 5

B(arney?) WARD (UK)
SEE ALSO: *Anonymous Stories*

Pirates of the Black Moon	Jul 1952	FSS 7
Weird Planet	Dec 1952	WOF 8

EDWARD WARD (UK)

Aftermath	Jan 1951	TOT 2

E. LORING WARE (UK)

We're Not Optimistic Enough	Aug 1955	AUT 60 (nf)

HARRY (Backer) WARNER Jr., 1922- (USA)

Recoil	Aug 1954	AUT 48
Ujutjo	Dec 1954	NEB 11

ARTHUR WATERHOUSE—see: Arthur W. Painter

JOHN F. WATT (SCOTLAND)

Kenneth Boyea was a cartoonist who worked with Scottish writer John F. Watt, a prolific contributor to the Spencer magazines. See his entry for Watt's collaborations with Boyea.

CLARKSON WAVERLY (UK)

Death Has No Boundaries	Jun 1949	GT 1

FRANK WEIGHT—see: E. C. Tubb

VERONICA WELWOOD (AUSTRALIA)

Last Journey	Aut 1954	AUT 48

JOHN WERNHEIM—see: John Russell Fearn

DOUGLAS WEST—see: E. C. Tubb

JAMES WHITE, 1928- (Northern Ireland)

Assisted Passage	Jan 1953	NW 19
Boarding Party	Jul 1955	NW 37
The Conspirators	Jun 1954	NW 24
Crossfire	Jun 1953	NW 21
Curtain Call	Aug 1954	NEB 9
Dynasty of One	Sep 1955	SF 15
In Loving Memory	Jan 1956	NEB 15
Outrider	May 1955	NW 35
Pushover Planet	Nov 1955	NEB 14
Question of Cruelty	Feb 1956	NW 44
Red Alert	Jan 1956	NW 43
The Star Walk	Mar 1955	NW 33
Starvation Orbit	Jul 1954	NW 25
Suicide Mission	Sep 1954	NW 27

GEORGE WHITLEY—see: A. Bertram Chandler

DAVID WILCOX (UK)

Transition	Nov 1953	AUT 39

NIALL WILDE—see: Eric Frank Russell

ERIC WILDING—see: E. C. Tubb

EWEN WILLIAMS (UK)

Night Call	Nov 1954	SUS 1

ANTHONY G. WILLIAMSON (UK)

The Day of All Else	Jul 1954	AUT 47
Duet for Two	Jan 1956	AUT 65
A Hitch in Time	Aug 1955	AUT 60
Just One Way Home	Dec 1955	AUT 64

IAN WILLIAMSON (UK)

Chemical Plant	Win 1950	NW 8

GEORGE (Anthony Armstrong) WILLIS, 1897-1976 (UK)

as ANTHONY ARMSTRONG

Homeward Bound	Sep 1954	VSS 6
Illusion	May 1954	VSS 4

CHARLES WILLIS—see: Arthur C. Clarke

LISLE WILLIS, 1919- (UK)

as ERLE VAN LODEN

Demons of Daavol	Nov 1952	WOS 5
Interplanetary Zoo	May 1953	TOT 7
Outpost on Orbit 097	Apr 1953	FSS 10
Synthesis of Knowledge	May 1952	WOS 3

WALTER A. WILLIS, 1919- (UK)

Chicago—Biggest Ever!	Jan 1953	NW 19
Who's Who in Fandom	Apr 1954	VSS 3

DORIS WILSON (USA)

as LESLIE PERRI

Space Episode	May 1954	SFF 3

Reprint from *Future* (Dec 1941)

FRANK WILSON (UK)

Has It All Happened Before?	May 1955	AUT 57 (nf)
How to Make a B.E.M.	Jan 1955	AUT 53 (nf)
Logic Is Fun 1	May 1954	AUT 45 (nf)
Logic Is Fun 2	Jun 1954	AUT 46 (nf)
Logic Is Fun 3	Jul 1954	AUT 47 (nf)
Logic Is Fun 4	Aug 1954	AUT 48 (nf)
Man's Face in the Future	Oct 1955	AUT 61 (nf)
The Ways of Science 1	Sep 1954	AUT 49 (nf)
The Ways of Science 2	Oct 1954	AUT 50 (nf)
The Ways of Science 3	Nov 1954	AUT 51 (nf)

RICHARD WILSON, 1920-1987 (USA)

Mary Hell's	Mar 1954	AUT 43
Robot's Gambit	Jul 1954	AUT 47
Science Fiction Story	Sep 1954	AUT 49
Wide-Open Ship	Jul 1954	SFF 5

R. C. WINGFIELD (UK)

The Mutilants	Jul 1954	AUT 47

FRANK WINNARD—see: E. C. Tubb

GRAHAM WINSLOW (UK)

Dimensional Destiny	May 1954	AUT 45
The Room	Jan 1956	AUT 65

STEWART WINSOR (UK)

Weapons for Yesterday	Nov 1952	NW 18

DONALD A(llen) WOLLHEIM, 1914-1990 (USA)

as MILLARD VERNE GORDON

Bomb	Jul 1954	SFF 5

Reprint from *Science Fiction Quarterly* (Win 1942)

as MARTIN PEARSON

Cosmos Eye	Oct 1954	SFF 8

Reprint from *Science Fiction Quarterly* (Spr 1941)

Destiny World	May 1954	SFF 3

Reprint from *Future* (Dec 1941)

Planet Passage	Mar 1954	SFF 1

Reprint from *Future* (Oct 1942)

Pogo Planet	Oct 1954	SFF 8

Reprint from *Future* (Oct 1941)

KEITH WOODCOTT—see: John Brunner

M(artin) C(harlton) WOODHOUSE, 1932- (UK)

The Higher Mathematics	Jun 1954	AUT 58

(Lionel Percy) "LAN" WRIGHT, 1923- (UK)

The Con Game	Oct 1955	NW 40
The Conquerors	May 1954	SF 8
Counterpoint	Sep 1955	NEB 13
Cul De Sac	Aug 1954	NEB 9
The Ethical Question	Jul 1954	NW 25
Fair Exchange	Jan 1955	NW 31
"Heritage"	Apr 1952	FSS 6

LAW WRIGHT on title page

The Human Element	Jun 1953	NW 21
Insurance Policy	Spr 1953	SF 6
...Is No Robbery	Mar 1953	NW 20

The Long Trek	Oct 1953	FSS 13
The Messengers	Nov 1954	NW 29
No Moon Tonight	Oct 1953	TOT 9
Operation Exodus	Jan 1952	NW 13
Project—Peace!	Sep 1952	NW 17
Strangers in the Town	Sep 1954	NW 27
"We're Human Too"	Apr 1953	WOF 9

as JEROME STRICKLAND

"The Legacy"	Apr 1952	FSS 6

JOHN WYNDHAM—see: John Beynon Harris

CHRISTOPHER SAMUEL YOUD, 1913- (UK)

Monster	Sum 1950	SF 1

as JOHN CHRISTOPHER

Aristotle	Feb 1954	AUT 42
Reprint from *Science Fiction Quarterly* (Feb 1953)		
Balance	Spr 1951	NW 9
Bleamish	Nov 1953	AUT 39
Breaking Point	May 1952	NW 15
Conspiracy	Jan 1955	AUT 53
Death Sentence	Mar 1954	SF 7
Reprint from *Imagination* (Jun 1953) as by WILLIAM VINE		
Escape Route	Jun 1954	NW 24
Manna	Mar 1955	NW 33
Mr. Kwotshook	Spr 1953	SF 6
Reprint from *Avon Science Fiction and Fantasy Reader* (Jan 1953)		
Museum Piece	Apr 1954	NW 22
Planet of Change	Aug 1953	AUT 36
The Prophet	Mar 1953	NW 20
Resurrection	Spr 1952	SF 4
Talent	Dec 1954	NEB 11
The Tree	Aut 1951	NW 11
Reprint of "Tree of Wrath" from *Worlds Beyond* (Jan 1951)		

ANONYMOUS STORIES
SEE ALSO: *John Russell Fearn*

The Forgotten Days	Sep 1950	TOT 1	by Leonard G. Fish?
Space Adventurer	Dec 1952	WOF 8	by B. Ward?
Treasure in Space	Dec 1950	FSS 3	by Leonard G. Fish?
The Visitors	Nov 1950	WOF 2	by Leonard G. Fish?

BOOK TITLE INDEX

References are to item numbers in the first two sections of this book. Authors' surnames are given in parentheses.

219

SHORT STORY TITLE INDEX

References are to page numbers in the fourth section of this book. Authors' surnames are given in parentheses.

ABOUT THE AUTHORS

PHILIP HARBOTTLE was born at Wallsend on Tyneside, England on October 2, 1941. Interested in SF and fantasy as long as he can remember, he believes he caught the virus at the age of three, when his mother took him to a Disney cartoon featuring "Willie the Whale." Two years later, during a short spell in the hospital, he had a pile of American Newspaper Comic Supplements, where he found *Superman*. During the late '40s and early '50s, his youthful imagination was further nurtured by other comic strip characters like *Captain Marvel*, *Garth*, and *Dan Dare*. In 1954, he found SF books in GRIDBAN's (Fearn) *A Thing of the Past*, followed by Tubb's *The Resurrected Man*. Following his self-publication of studies on Fearn and Tubb, he was offered editorship of a new Australian/British SF magazine, *Vision of Tomorrow* (the same year in which he was married). Since then, he has been a literary agent and consultant on many SF reference books and anthologies. Currently working as an administrator in Local Government, he is the literary executor of the Fearn estate, and is researching Fearn's biography. In 1992, he was asked by the *Daily Mirror* to write scripts for the long-running *Garth* SF cartoon strip. His only daughter was featured as a character in E. C. Tubb's DUMAREST novel, *Angado*.

STEPHEN HOLLAND was born at Broomfield, Essex, England on April 13, 1962 (a Friday!), and was educated at King Edward VI Grammar School, Chelmsford. He has been an avid reader for as long as he can remember, jumping right to Agatha Christie, James Hadley Chase, and John Creasey. He quickly built up a library of popular fiction ranging from boys' adventure stories and comics to '50s paperbacks, particularly SF and crime. In addition to numerous articles on comics published in Britain, Holland, and Germany, he has written articles on paperbacks for Britain and America. He has written "The Trials of Hank Janson" (a study of the British gangster-fiction writer), fantasy and SF comic strips for D. C. Thomson, and is working on various fiction and nonfiction projects. Currently, he is editor of the magazine *Comics World*.

Look for the companion volume to this book: *Vultures of the Void: A History of British Science Fiction Publishing, 1946-1956*, published by The Borgo Press in 1992.